Landscapes at Risk?

The Future for Areas of Outstanding Natural Beauty

**Edward Holdaway
and
Gerald Smart**

London and New York

First published 2001 by Spon Press
11 New Fetter Lane, London EC4P 4EE

Simultaneously published in the USA and Canada by Spon Press
29 West 35th Street, New York, NY 10001

Spon Press is an imprint of the Taylor & Francis Group

Typeset in New Baskerville and Optima by EverGreen Graphics, Craigweil on Sea, West Sussex
Printed and bound in Great Britain by Bell & Bain Ltd, Glasgow, Scotland

British Library Cataloguing in Publication Data
A catalogue record for this book is available from the British Library

Library of Congress Cataloging in Publication Data
Holdaway, Edward
    Landscapes at risk?: the future for areas of outstanding natural beauty / Edward
  Holdaway and Gerald Smart.
       p. cm
    Includes bibliographical references (p.).
    1. Landscape protection – Government policy – England. 2. Landscape
  protection – Government policy – Wales. I. Smart, Gerald. II. Title.

QH77. E5 H66 2000
333.7'2'0942—dc21   00–030862

ISBN 0–419–24630–4

Contents

List of colour plates and maps	viii
Foreword	ix
Acknowledgements	x
Illustration acknowledgements	xii
Abbreviations	xiv
Introduction: the challenges for protected landscapes	1
The need for this book	2
The challenge of 'living landscapes'	3
The challenge of international influences	3
The challenge of the wider approach to countryside policy in the UK	5
The challenge of long-term trends	6
The scope of the book	6
Part One Setting The Scene	9
1 The family of protected landscapes in the UK	11
The post-war reports	11
The *National Parks and Access to the Countryside Act*, 1949	13
The 1960s and beyond: the debate widens	16
Scotland	18
Northern Ireland	19
Other types of protected landscapes	20
The family of protected landscapes as part of a wider community of protected areas	22
Commentary: only part of the story	23
2 The geography and importance of Areas of Outstanding Natural Beauty	25
The geography of the AONB family	25
The importance of AONBs – more than just scenery	38
Commentary: a treasury of nationally important natural and cultural resources of great economic value	45

3 **What has been happening to AONBs?**   47
Changes in their fabric   47
Loss of tranquillity   49
Rural communities   50
Perceptions of pressures on the landscape   52
Some long-term trends likely to affect AONBs   56
Commentary: adverse change and growing
pressures but the total picture is missing   59

Part Two   Recurrent Themes   63

4 **The development of national policy for AONBs**   65
The 1980 AONB review   65
The 1989/90 AONB review   67
The 1990s: a further look at financial and
administrative needs   69
1998: the resulting Advice to Government from the
Countryside Commission and the Countryside
Council for Wales   72
The Renton Bill 1999   76
The response of government   78
Scotland   79
Parks for Life and the European Landscape Convention   81
Commentary: recurrent themes   84

5 **The evolution of AONB management**   89
Administration: the framework of partnership   89
Staffing: the core of partnership   93
Organisation of AONB Management   95
Management Plans: the means by which partnership
can operate   98
Finance and new sources of funding   104
The roles of the partners: public, private and
voluntary sectors   105
Awareness and understanding   107
Commentary: a patchwork quilt   111

Part Three   Wider Countryside Issues   113

6 **Land management**   115
Agriculture   115
Forestry and woodlands   120
The wider environment   124
Wildlife conservation   127
Recreation and tourism   136

	Traffic and transport	143
	Commentary: the multi-resource role of management in AONBs	147
7	**Rural development, planning and sustainability**	**150**
	Rural development policies	150
	Designation and rural development	156
	Local action for the rural economy in AONBs	158
	Planning guidance	159
	Strategic and local plans	162
	Control of development in AONBs	164
	Sustainable development	169
	Commentary: a dilemma	171

Part Four   The Future – Landscapes No Longer At Risk?   **175**

8	**AONBs: fit for the challenge?**	**177**
	Challenges to protected landscapes	177
	Key requirements to meet these challenges	178
	A review of the protected landscape system in England and Wales	180
	National Parks and AONBs	181
	A review of AONBs	183
	A review of the Advice Papers and the Renton Bill	185
	Commentary: the need for a new agenda	187

9	**A new agenda for AONBs**	**189**
	A statutory framework	190
	Action points for successful implementation	192
	The wider context	198
	A radical twist to the agenda	199
	A message for the family of protected landscapes	201
	Postscript	202

Appendices		**204**
	1. Designated Areas of Outstanding Natural Beauty	204
	2. Case studies	206
	3. IUCN categories of protected areas and guidelines for protected area management – Category V Protected Landscapes	232
	4. Some notes on further reading	235

| **Index** | | **238** |

Colour plates and maps

Colour illustrations appear between pages 58 and 59, 106 and 107, 154 and 155, and 194 and 195.

Series illustrating examples of:

Protected landscapes in the UK – Plates 1 to 5 and 19
The geographical characteristics of AONBs – Plates 6 to 16

Examples of special considerations in AONBs:

The rural economy and agriculture – Plates 17, 18 and 20
Wildlife – Plates 21 to 23
Historic and cultural features – Plates 24 to 26
Vernacular architecture – Plates 27 to 29
Open landscapes – Plates 31 and 32

Examples of trends affecting AONBs:

Agricultural developments – Plates 33 to 36
Loss of tranquillity and presure for development –
    Plates 30 and 37 to 40
Growth of recreation and tourism – Plates 41 to 45
Long-term changes in climate, lifestyles and major land uses –
    Plates 46 to 48

Examples of policy and management needs in AONBs:

Promotion of awareness – Plate 50
Land ownership and land management – Plates 51 to 54
Links with the wider environment – Plate 55
Links with the historic environment – Plate 56
Links with biodiversity – Plate 57
Managing recreation and traffic – Plates 58 to 61
Fostering the local economy – Plates 62 to 64

Foreword

It is not surprising that England and Wales should have a system designed to protect beautiful landscapes. From the rugged Cornish coast to the downlands of the South and East, to the wilder beauty of the northern uplands and the Welsh mountains, a rich scenic variety is one of the defining characteristics of these countries.

Designating the best of these landscapes as either Areas of Outstanding Natural Beauty or National Parks has given them vital protection from development. But the AONBs still represent unfinished business and unfulfilled potential. Over the years they have struggled with severely limited resources, a direct consequence of no one having a legal responsibility for their well-being. That requires a management approach which uses robust long-term strategies to stem and then reverse the erosion of these landscapes by agricultural intensification or change, traffic growth and a creeping loss of local character. It also requires a strategic approach to the very large numbers of visitors to AONBs. That recreational demand needs to contribute positively to the success of these areas rather than adding another pressure to them.

Many local authorities make laudable efforts to manage these areas with the help of government agencies like the former Countryside Commission and now the Countryside Agency and the Countryside Council for Wales. Unfortunately those efforts fall well short of what is needed and the position of AONBs is in stark contrast to that of the National Parks. The Parks have become increasingly well provided for over the years, with National Park Authorities in place and performing excellently in managing their recreational use and conservation.

However AONBs are now receiving fresh attention. As evidenced by this new work Landscapes at Risk, consideration of how these areas should be viewed and provided for in the future is being guided by an appreciation of AONBs as living landscapes that need to be managed in ways that reflect their individual circumstances and needs. With the right arrangements AONBs have the potential to embrace and exemplify the sustainability agenda of the twenty-first century. But first of all local authorities and their partners need to be given the management powers and resources for the job.

I am grateful to the authors of this work. They have brought together in a truly comprehensive way and for the first time, the history, strengths and weaknesses of the AONB designation. As such their work provides a fascinating, important and accessible reference for policy makers, professional advisors and all those interested in the sustainable management of a vibrant, living countryside. But equally important, it sets out a thoughtful discussion on the purpose, operation and future of the designation. This culminates with the authors' new agenda for AONBs, which I am sure will inform a wider debate on the future of our protected landscapes.

EWEN CAMERON
Chairman, Countryside Agency
Cheltenham

Acknowledgements

We could not have written this book without the help of many people with an interest in protected landscapes. Busy as they all are, they have willingly spared a lot of time for discussion with us and have provided us with a veritable library of information about Areas of Outstanding Natural Beauty. Their expert knowledge of policy and management issues affecting these areas has contributed much to our own analysis of problems and our assessment of future needs, and their enthusiasm has been inspiring. We are deeply grateful to them. We would also like to express our special thanks to:

The Countryside Agency for a generous financial grant towards production of the book, for the Foreword contributed by its Chairman, Ewen Cameron, for the supply of data covering England, for the maps and for the use of its photo library as the main source of our illustrations; Agency staff at Cheltenham and in the regions who have been most supportive, especially Terry Robinson (Head of Local Identity), Andy Gale and Ray Woolmore (recently retired), and Liane Bradbrook and Paul Thomas in the photographic library.

The Department for the Environment, Transport and the Regions for access to the Countryside Information System and to Andy Stott and Alison Dorling from the Bristol office for explaining its intricacies and providing the information in a usable form, and for commenting on its use in Chapter 2.

The Countryside Council for Wales, for advice and information given by Rob Owen, and the supply of information for the maps; English Nature – Richard Leafe – for information on Natural Areas and the supply of SSSI data for the maps; English Heritage – John Fairclough – for perspectives and information on the cultural heritage and supply of data for the maps; Farming and Rural Conservation Agency – David Whelon (Bristol) – for information on Countryside Stewardship; Scottish Natural Heritage – John Mackay and Simon Brooks – for information and understanding of developments in Scotland; and Ross Millar (Environment and Heritage Service) and Tony Gates (Mourne Heritage Trust) for information and their explanations of the system in Northern Ireland.

Councillors, AONB Officers and others in our case study areas: Cllr Chris Robinson and David Dixon in the Blackdown Hills; Cllr Cherry Aston and Steve Rodrick in the Chilterns, and Michael Bush (Chairman of the Chiltern Society); in the Cotswolds Nick Hayward from Cotswold District Council and Robin Colley from Gloucestershire County Council; Don McKay in the Forest of Bowland; Merrick Denton-Thompson from Hampshire County Council; Richard Clarke and Gerry Sherwin in the High Weald; Sarah Jackson in the Mendip Hills; Tim Vene in Norfolk Coast; Alison Turnock in Purbeck Heritage Area, Dorset AONB; Martin Beaton and Phil Beldon in Sussex Downs; Dr Ruth Williams, formerly Wye Valley AONB Officer; also Rob Fairbank for information on transport management and on major land ownership in the Surrey Hills.

AONB Officers and others during our visits to AONBs: Tony Smith (Durham County Council), Peter Sansom (Northumberland County Council) and Phil Gray (East Cumbria Countryside Project) and Graham Coggins (North Pennines Heritage Trust) in the North Pennines; Brian Irving on the Solway Coast; Ian Henderson in Arnside and Silverdale; Paul Burgess in Nidderdale; Jonathan Mullard in Gower; Howard Sutcliffe in the Clwydian Range; John Wykes in Dorset; Robin Toogood in South Devon; Simon Hooton in Suffolk Coast and Heaths; Phil Couchman of Chichester Harbour; and Ian Boyd on the Isle of Wight.

The National Trust, from whom we received fascinating details of its work in AONBs, in particular about recreational policy, through Jo Burgon (Coast and Countryside Adviser); The Landscape Institute, for the very thoughtful and experienced opinions given by Paul Tiplady; Richard Bull of the Mendip Society; and David Coleman (Countryside Agency) and Dr Margaret Anderson (Wye College) for their perceptive comments on draft chapters.

Southampton University Cartographic Unit staff, Tim Aspden and Linda Hall, who have set a very high standard in the preparation of maps for the text.

And our Publishers, Spon Press, whose Senior Commissioning Editor, Caroline Mallinder, and Assistant Editor, Rebecca Casey, have given patient editorial advice and encouragement from start to finish; and Michael Packard and Cecil Smith for detailed editing and typesetting.

Finally and by no means least our wives for their tolerance and help over the two years of the project.

EH and GS
Abergwaun and Keyhaven
July 2000

Illustration acknowledgements

The authors and publishers would like to thank the following individual photographers and organisations, and the Countryside Agency in particular, for permission to reproduce their photographs:

Blackdown Hills Rural Partnership	64c
The Chiltern Society	55a & b
Clwydian Range AONB JAC	6b
Cotswolds AONB Partnership	14b
Countryside Agency	2(map),5(map),15(map)
	16b, 46b, 52b, 58b
Countryside Agency/Ian Allen	58a
Countryside Agency/Trevor Burrows	11a
Countryside Agency/David Burton	22c, 28a, 42a, 43b
Countryside Agency/CCW & DETR	21(map)
Countryside Agency/COI	31
Countryside Agency/CPRE	30(map)
Countryside Agency/DETR	17(map)
Countryside Agency/Phillip Dunn	37a, 38b
Countryside Agency/Patrick Eden	10b, 39a, 48a
Countryside Agency/English Heritage	24(map)
Countryside Agency/D. Hadley	26c
Countryside Agency/Jim Hallett	9a, 14a, 35a, 40a
Countryside Agency/Peter Hamilton	20
Countryside Agency/Jeremy Haslam	3a
Countryside Agency/Tony Hopkins	12a, 25a
Countryside Agency/Colin Horsman	23a
Countryside Agency/Kirsten Hughes	26a
Countryside Agency/Martin Jones	37b, 57a
Countryside Agency/MAFF	19(map)
Countryside Agency/John Morrison	8b
Countryside Agency/Michael Murray	10a
Countryside Agency/Martin Page	34, 44b
Countryside Agency/Graham Parish	29, 64a
Countryside Agency/Derry Robinson	8a
Countryside Agency/Nick Smith	62a & b
Countryside Agency/Barry Stacey	22b, 23c, 45a, 57b, 60b
Countryside Agency/Matthew Stevens	13a
Countryside Agency/Robert Thrift	64b

Abbreviations

AONB	Area of Outstanding Natural Beauty
ASSI	Area of Special Scientific Interest
BAP	Biodiversity Action Plan
CA	Countryside Agency
CADW	The Welsh equivalent of English Heritage
CAP	Common Agricultural Policy
CC	Countryside Commission
CCW	Countryside Council for Wales
CIS	Countryside Information System
CS	Countryside Stewardship
DETR	Department of the Environment, Transport and the Regions
DoE	Department of the Environment
EA	Environment Agency
EH	English Heritage
EN	English Nature
ERDF	European Regional Development Fund
ESA	Environmentally Sensitive Area
FC	Forestry Commission
FRCA	Farming and Rural Conservation Agency
FWAG	Farming and Wildlife Advisory Group
GIS	Geographic Information System
HMSO	Her Majesty's Stationery Office
IUCN	International Union for the Conservation of Nature
JAC	Joint Advisory Committee
LBAP	Local Biodiversity Action Plan
LEAP	Local Environment Agency Plan
LFA	Less Favoured Area
LGMB	Local Government Management Board
LTP	Local Transport Plan
MAFF	Ministry of Agriculture, Fisheries and Food
NA	Natural Area
NNR	National Nature Reserve
PPG	Planning Policy Guidance
RDA	Rural Development Area
RDC	Rural Development Commission
RPG	Regional Planning Guidance
RSPB	Royal Society for the Protection of Birds
cSAC	(candidate) Special Area of Conservation
SAM	Scheduled Ancient Monument
SNH	Scottish Natural Heritage
SPA	Special Protection Area
SSSI	Site of Special Scientific Interest
STAR	Strategic Traffic Action in Rural Areas
TEC	Training and Enterprise Council
TPP	Transport Policy and Programme

Introduction: The challenges for protected landscapes

Do the titles National Park, Area of Outstanding Natural Beauty, National Scenic Area, Heritage Coast, conjure up visions of magnificent places: Snowdonia, the South Downs, Loch Lomond, Flamborough Head, for example? Perhaps, but do they suggest that these wonderful landscapes have very different attributes and ways of meeting people's needs? Not so to everybody. Hardly 'terms of art', they are part of the official vocabulary of countryside planning, implying a selective approach to the conservation and enjoyment of a rich landscape heritage, distinctions that are not widely understood. They can be likened to members of a great family of protected landscapes, each of which has the family traits but displays individual characteristics and potential. This book focuses on one of them, the Areas of Outstanding Natural Beauty, which contain some of the most attractive landscapes in Britain. It is about their place in the family, their qualities, the challenges that they face, the steps being taken to look after them in the public interest, and how these steps might be guided in the future, in the interest of protected landscapes generally.

Areas of Outstanding Natural Beauty include spacious downs and wolds steeped in early history, bird-rich estuaries and marshes, colourful heaths, deep woodland and valleys, dramatic cliffs, sandy bays and sheltered creeks, and wild uplands. 'AONBs', to use the shortened form of their time-honoured but clumsy title, are widely distributed in England, Wales and Northern Ireland. Along with the National Parks of England and Wales and the National Scenic Areas of Scotland, their landscapes are recognised as being of the very highest quality, requiring special protection under British town and country planning legislation. They also fall within a world-wide category of Protected Areas, known as Protected Landscapes, devised by the International Union for Conservation of Nature and Natural Resources (IUCN).[1] These relate to areas of land or sea, which require special measures for protection and management on account of the national or international significance of their scenic, wildlife and heritage values. While the means may vary from country to country, the aims and scope of protection are readily justified by the great educational, cultural, recreational and spiritual benefits.

The need for this book

We have chosen to focus on AONBs in England and Wales for a number of reasons. Not least, it is over fifty years since the legislation that brought them into being was passed and, compared with National Parks, very little has been written about them. Furthermore their future is under scrutiny by government. While the timing may well be appropriate, there is a more compelling reason for looking at them in some depth. At the turn of the new century the world in which the protected landscapes in the UK find themselves is very different from the one in which they were conceived, and it will continue to present new challenges for them.

Like all countryside in these densely populated islands, AONBs have been influenced by man for centuries. Even the wildest can show traces of past occupation, and the more liveable areas have been shaped through the ages by farming, forestry, village settlement and rural industries. The pace of change has accelerated in the last 250 years: enclosures, new agricultural methods, improved communications, and the drift of population away to industrial cities. It is only from the late eighteenth century onwards, however, that their cultural value has become widely recognised in literature and the arts, and during the twentieth century that many of them have become popular residential areas and have attracted large numbers of visitors for open-air recreation.

These areas are essentially 'living and working landscapes', and as such they have undergone radical change. Post-war farming practices have removed familiar pastoral features, dense afforestation has intruded into open moorland, and there have been huge reductions in traditional rural jobs which, in turn, have seriously affected local economies and community structures. Furthermore there has been considerable development, such as housing, industry, roads and other infrastructure, as well as growth in recreation and traffic pressures in most AONBs in the last 50 years.

Meanwhile, although the establishment of the English and Welsh National Parks and the subsequent improvement of their administration and funding have been undoubted successes, AONBs have been left behind, relegated to a far lower priority with no stated responsibility for their management. Indeed, though covering rather more land than National Parks, they have come to be regarded as 'Cinderellas' in the whole family of protected landscapes. As will be shown in later chapters, much of the constructive thinking about them in the post-war reports[2,3] that led to the 1949 *National Parks and Access to the Countryside Act* was whittled away in practice. More recently, too, there has been a notable shift of policy in the UK towards the needs of the whole countryside and an integrated approach to rural issues, in harmony with the world-wide movements towards sustainable development and the maintenance of biodiversity. In some respects this trend spells a further reduction in priority for protected land-scapes, but there is no doubt that they are highly relevant to the needs of society, and will remain so. The question that is at the heart of the book is whether the management arrangements of the largest group of protected landscapes, the AONBs, are sufficiently robust to respond in a positive fashion to current trends and future chal-lenges, including those outlined above.

The challenge of 'living landscapes'

Before embarking on this in-depth examination of AONBs, it is impor-tant to explore briefly just what those challenges really are. Even with-out national and international influences the basic approach to pro-tected landscapes in the UK is in itself a challenge. Rather than being set aside for landscape conservation and protected against human interference, the protected areas are multi-purpose; they are land-scapes with communities where people live and work, and which are enjoyed by countless numbers of people. While they are protected through the application of strict planning policies, they are not 'no-go' areas so far as development is concerned. Their protection also depends on influencing the management of the land, most of which is in private ownership, and the activities that take place within them. It is a major challenge to ensure that the means of conserving and enhancing these areas is organised and funded in a way that recog-nises their national and international importance, on the one hand, as well as the interests and roles of the many stakeholders and local communities involved.

The challenge of international influences

International influences are having an increasingly important part to play in rural affairs in the UK. The environmental impact of the Common Agricultural Policy, with its overall priority for production is well known. However, there is a much wider range of global and European influences that have implications for the long-term future of AONBs. Some of these are bound up in international conventions and treaties and others in less formal, but none the less important initiatives.

Perhaps one of the most far-reaching is the *Convention on Biological Diversity*,[4] one of several major initiatives from the 'Earth Summit' in Rio de Janeiro in 1992. Signatories agreed that each nation should develop a strategy for the conservation and sustainable use of biological diversity. The UK response is set out in *Biodiversity: the UK Action Plan*, published in 1994. This has achieved a very high standing in government priorities and does, of course, embrace the whole countryside rather than just the protected landscapes. Indeed there seems to be very little recognition of the role that protected landscapes such as AONBs can play in implementing the UK strategy.

While this Convention is essentially strategic in its approach, a number of others were much more specific. The most significant are the *Ramsar Convention*,[5] the *EC Birds Directive*[6] and the *EC Habitats Directive*.[7] They are aimed at the conservation of species and habitats rather than the wider landscape. For those AONBs with significant parts designated under these measures, there is a major challenge to protect internationally important sites, especially to ensure that their management is well related to a wider geographical context.

On a less formal basis, over the last century or more, there has been a world-wide movement towards the establishment of national systems of protected areas. Of particular importance is the programme developed by IUCN – *Parks for Life*[8] – following their World Congress on National Parks and Protected Areas held in Caracas in 1992. The key message from the congress was that although protected areas alone cannot achieve a nation's sustainability and biodiversity objectives, they can play a significant part. They should not be considered in isolation from broader social and economic policies. New partnerships are needed, involving local communities. Above all, the isolationist view of protected areas, seeing them capable of surviving as oases, should be dropped. Instead they should be regarded as 'jewels in the crown', where the jewels and their setting are mutually supportive.

One of the main recommendations of the European Parks for Life programme was for the Council of Europe to implement a convention on landscape protection. For this it is pursuing a *European Landscape Convention*,[9] due to start in 2000. Its aim is to obtain Europe-wide recognition of the importance of landscape as an integral part of life and a crucial element in progress towards sustainability. Although this should be a matter of principle when considering, for example, the Common Agricultural Policy, public works, transport, forestry and tourism, there does not seem to be any move to establish regulatory measures or financial support. It is nevertheless part of a world-wide movement to raise the profile of landscape issues and set standards to be aimed at by every nation. The challenge for the management of AONBs will be to ensure that they meet such standards and, from their long experience, to act as exemplars of how to protect 'living landscapes'.

The challenge
of the wider
approach to
countryside policy
in the UK

Traditionally, landscape and wildlife conservation has focused on special areas. This is changing, with the view being taken, quite correctly, that the countryside must be looked at as a whole. It has been manifest in several ways, particularly by the creation in England, in 1999, of the Countryside Agency, embracing landscape, recreation and socio-economic matters; the description of the whole English landscape in programmes of Countryside Character and Natural Areas, developed by the former Countryside Commission and English Nature; the recent unsuccessful calls for a Ministry to cover all rural affairs; and the publication for the first time (in 1995 and 1996) of Rural White Papers for England and Wales.[10, 11]

This holistic approach should in theory raise no special problems for protected landscapes such as AONBs. In practice, however, there has been a tendency for it either to ignore them, or to give them lower priority than before. Such apparent silence is worrying. The two White Papers did in fact go some way to provide the context for protected landscapes. They stressed that designated areas should no longer be viewed in isolation from the rest of the countryside, and that new ways should be sought to enrich the quality of the countryside generally without weakening the protection of designated areas. Nevertheless the holistic approach presents a challenge to those responsible for protected landscapes to recognise the need to promote their interests strongly and to create a framework within which the multi-purpose nature of these areas can flourish.

The effective protection of countryside is indeed one of the objectives set out in *A Better Quality of Life: A Strategy for Sustainable Development for the UK*.[12] Special landscape designations such as National Parks and AONBs are at the heart of the Government's approach. However, in placing them in this position the Government has emphasised that conservation of the natural heritage must be integrated with local economic and social development, thus making sure that sustainability principles are fully accounted for in these areas. Turning this seemingly neat theory into practice is a complex task, a challenge to those responsible for their planning and management; it is not a fixed state of harmony, so much as a process of change. There needs to be a very clear understanding of the role of these most important landscapes as part of the nation's environmental capital, and of their capacity for change.

The challenge of long-term trends

The challenges for protected landscapes do not come solely from policy and from administrative circumstances. There are much broader trends with which AONBs have to contend in the future. As is more fully described in Chapter 3, *Climatic change* could have a direct physical impact on landscape character, quality and biodiversity. *Changes in life-style*, too, will cause continued pressure for development in villages and the countryside, and have for long been increasing leisure demands. *Changes in major land uses*, such as agriculture and forestry, could also have far-reaching effects on protected landscapes, although their future, like all the long-term trends referred to, is uncertain to say the least, extending to their nature, overall effects and timing. Although these trends and the way in which they materialise are likely to affect the countryside generally, their impacts could be more pronounced in protected areas because of the high quality of their landscape, wildlife and cultural resources.

The challenge to AONBs is twofold. First, research into environmental futures will continue to have messages of the utmost importance for these areas, and their managers must maintain a constant watch on its implications. Second, sustainability, that is, ensuring that meeting social and economic needs does not irreversibly damage the environment, and flexibility will continue to grow in importance as criteria for all policy decisions. To this end, the need for up-to-date systematic knowledge of the natural and community resources of each area becomes all the more important.

The nature of the challenges described above may make stark reading to those who manage these areas. On the one hand, there is a marked emphasis on wildlife conservation driven by international and European commitments, with an ill-defined role for AONBs. As yet, however, there are no such drivers for landscape. Equally, with the increasing emphasis on an integrated approach to the countryside, AONBs are in danger of being sidelined in processes that take an holistic outlook. Pressures such as those outlined in the previous paragraph are increasingly affecting their character. AONBs are potentially at risk. Since they contain large tracts of living and working countryside of the highest quality, they should be put in a position where not only are they adequately protected and managed in terms of their landscape, but become leading examples of biodiversity and sustainability, in conjunction with local interests, for the national benefit.

The scope of the book

How then, in the light of these challenges, does one approach the detailed examination of AONBs?

The first part of the book sets the scene, with Chapter 1 describing the scope of protected landscapes in the UK and the link with the wider family of protected areas. Chapter 2 explores in greater detail the geography of AONBs and explains why they are so important nationally. Chapter 3 then looks at the changes that have taken place in the fabric of AONBs, the pressures that are perceived to be affecting them now and the longer-term trends that are likely to affect them.

The second part of the book, under the heading 'Recurrent themes', looks at the development of policies for AONBs in Chapter 4 and their management in Chapter 5, with a view to establishing an understanding of the many factors that have been at play in their evolution in the last 50 years.

The third part examines how the many issues that are currently affecting the whole countryside interact with the conservation of the fine landscapes that AONBs contain, and how those responsible for AONBs have begun to tackle them. Chapter 6 explores the varied land management issues posed by agriculture and forestry, wildlife recreation and tourism and traffic and transport, whilst Chapter 7 examines the vexed questions of rural development, planning and sustainability.

Having considered the way in which the AONB concept has evolved in some depth in the first three parts, the fourth and final part looks to the future. Chapter 8 considers whether AONBs are fit for the challenges of the new millennium, and the final Chapter 9 sets out the Agenda for AONBs and what needs to be done to achieve it, seeking to draw out some broad principles that will contribute to the continuing debate about the future of AONBs in the UK and abroad.

In Appendix 2 there is a series of case studies of particular AONBs that demonstrate many of the points made in the main text. The book is also illustrated by maps and extensive sections of colour photographs of AONBs throughout England and Wales, which include their geographical characteristics, examples of special considerations in AONBs, of trends affecting them and of their policy and management needs.

References

[1] See Appendix 3 for details of IUCN categories and definition of the term 'Protected Landscape'.

[2] Ministry of Town and Country Planning, *National Parks in England and Wales*, Report by John Dower, Cmd 6628, HMSO, London, 1945.

[3] Ministry of Town and Country Planning, *Report of the National Parks Committee* (England and Wales), Cmd 7121, HMSO, London, 1947.

[4] *Convention on Biological Diversity* was one of several major initiatives stemming from the 'Earth Summit' in Rio de Janeiro in 1992.

5 *Convention on Wetlands of International Importance especially as a Waterfowl Habitat*, Ramsar, 1971.

6 *Council Directive 79/409/EEC* on the conservation of wild birds.

7 *Council Directive 92/43/EEC* on the conservation of natural habitats and of wild fauna and flora.

8 IUCN, *Parks for Life: Report of the IVth World Congress on National Parks and Protected Areas, Caracas, 1992*, Gland, Switzerland, 1993 and IUCN, *Parks for Life: Action for Protected Areas in Europe*, Gland, Switzerland & Cambridge, UK, 1994.

9 Congress of Local and Regional Authorities of Europe, *Recommendation 40* (1998) on the draft European Landscape Convention.

10 Department of the Environment and Ministry of Agriculture, Fisheries and Food, *Rural England: A Nation Committed to a Living Countryside*, Cm 3016, HMSO, London, 1995.

11 Welsh Office, *A Working Countryside for Wales*, Cm 3180, HMSO, London, 1996.

12 Department for the Environment, Transport and the Regions, *A Better Quality of Life: A Strategy for Sustainable Development for the United Kingdom*, Cm 4345, HMSO, London, 1999.

Part One
Setting the Scene

The introduction briefly described the place of AONBs in the family of Britain's best landscapes and in the international categories of protected areas. Part One comprises three chapters which set the scene for the entire book: the genesis of protected landscape policy in the UK as a whole, the important resources of AONBs that require such protection, and the pressures exerted on them now and in the future.

The family of protected landscapes in the UK 1

This first chapter traces the evolution of the AONB concept through a sequence of official reports, legislation and subsequent designation of individual areas, a train of events that was dominated by the need for early action to establish National Parks. In England and Wales the process was primarily concerned with landscape protection, and the chapter completes the story by referring briefly to the parallel establishment of measures for wildlife conservation, and for landscape protection in Scotland and Northern Ireland.

The post-war reports

The move towards protection of the best countryside began to attract government attention in real earnest in the 1940s, continuing the work of the pre-war National Park Committee, chaired by Sir Christopher Addison,[1] that reported in 1931. At that time, the rash of urban growth on the one hand, and various attempts to promote legislation on access to upland and mountainous areas, on the other, had provoked a number of responses. One was Addison's proposal to protect the best countryside by means of national and regional 'Reserves', which were two types of designated area that can, with hindsight, be seen as implying, officially, that National Parks should not stand alone. War intervened, but even at the height of hostilities fears about the longer-term future of the countryside led to the appointment in 1942 of the Committee on Land Utilisation in Rural Areas, chaired by Lord Justice Scott.[2] Scott was more positive than Addison about the purpose of National Parks and made very optimistic assumptions about the role of farming in maintaining traditional landscapes. National Parks should be primarily for public access, rather than treated as 'reserves', and they were long overdue. From then on, National Parks became a priority for government and, so far as England and Wales were concerned, led to the publication in 1945 of John Dower's seminal report, *National Parks in England and Wales*.[3]

Dower, a civil servant in the former Ministry of Works and Planning who had been influential in the publicity campaigns of the Standing Committee on National Parks, proposed 10 such Parks. These were to contain 'relatively wild country' in which there could be wide public access for recreation, and he set out ideas for their administration, including the establishment of a powerful National Parks Commission. He went on to list 12 areas that should be safeguarded as possible future parks, and 33 'Other Amenity Areas', of critical importance for preservation and recreation. The latter two groups contain well-known countryside such as the South Downs and Cotswolds, and other attractive landscapes of national or, in some cases, regional importance. His brief being primarily concerned with National Parks, however, Dower saw them as a second priority and made no proposals for their establishment and administration.

The National Parks Committee (England and Wales), chaired by Sir Arthur Hobhouse,[4] took Dower's vision further. Reporting in 1947, Hobhouse accepted Dower's main concepts, including the two aims for National Parks (to protect their countryside and ways of life, and to give opportunities for outdoor recreation), and made proposals for twelve Parks (see the map in Plate 1). He recommended that they should be administered by local *ad hoc* executive bodies on behalf of the National Parks Commission and the local authorities, and funded by the Exchequer. He also proposed 52 'Conservation Areas' (see Plate 3): tracts of countryside with scenic quality comparable to that of the parks, the character of which should be preserved, but where potential for recreation was less. His Committee worked closely with the Wildlife Conservation Special Committee, chaired by Sir Julian Huxley,[5] whose strategic recommendations underlie much of the present system of protected areas for nature conservation. This liaison influenced the actual choice of Conservation Areas, produced a new emphasis on their scientific value, and gave recreation a relatively low priority except in areas near to population centres. Hobhouse recommended that local government, using planning powers, should be responsible for the administration of Conservation Areas through Advisory Committees. These would include members nominated by the proposed National Parks Commission, and should be consulted on planning proposals of importance to the area, bringing in the Minister of Town and Country Planning when there was a dispute. There should be Exchequer grants for Conservation Areas, at about one-third of the rate for National Parks. A high standard of planning decisions would be the main public responsibility; it was assumed, following Scott, that landowners and farmers would be in a position to maintain landscape quality through traditional day-to-day management.

Dower's Amenity Areas and Hobhouse's Conservation Areas foreshadowed most of the current list of English and Welsh AONBs. Indeed, the areas chosen for designation largely followed Hobhouse's

BOX 1.1

**AONB
designation
criteria,
1971/2**

These criteria, in order of importance, were:

1. Quality of landscape, natural beauty, unspoilt or special quality (e.g., remoteness), of national significance;
2. Extent in terms of both total area and continuity, a smaller area being more acceptable for extensions than for new designations;
3. Unusual character in the sense of having unique characteristics or being of a landscape type under-represented among existing designated areas and Heritage Coasts, e.g., lowland valley landscapes, sandstone ridges, islands, estuaries.

Source:
Countryside Commission, *Review of Proposed AONBs*, Paper 73/21, Cheltenham, 1973

selection, a few being added or excluded in the light of new information. Interestingly, it was only in 1971/2 (see Box 1.1) that the Countryside Commission (successor to the National Parks Commission) undertook a qualitative assessment of large numbers of potential AONBs. In this it applied a more systematic approach than in the past, when areas had been considered individually.[6] Some Hobhouse areas, including the Denbigh Moors in North Wales, parts of the Pennines, Charnwood Forest in Leicestershire, Clipsham in Lincolnshire, and Dungeness have not materialised. Charnwood Forest, for example, was divided by the M1 Motorway, and Denbigh Moors were thought to contain only limited tracts of high quality landscape.[7] Some, for a variety of reasons, have been recognised by other area titles such as Heritage Coast (Cardigan, Glamorgan and Flamborough Coasts), Environmentally Sensitive Areas (Breckland), or Forest Parks (Delamere in Cheshire, and the Forest of Dean). On the other hand, the current list of AONBs includes the South Downs, which had been proposed by Hobhouse for a National Park but, until recently, were ruled out as being too intensively farmed. The list also includes areas of first-rate countryside that did not figure in these reports at all but were put forward as a result of local consultation: Chichester Harbour, Dedham Vale, the Lincolnshire Wolds, Solway Coast, Tamar Valley, and much of the Weald.

**The *National
Parks and Access
to the Countryside
Act*, 1949**

On the whole, the proposals for Conservation Areas were uncontroversial, both in the Hobhouse Committee and in written evidence to it. The same could be said of provision for them in the *National Parks and Access to the Countryside Act* of 1949, where debate in the run-up

BOX 1.2

National Parks and Access to the Countryside Act, 1949

The Commission may, by order made as respects any areas in England and Wales not being a National Park, which appear to them to be of such outstanding natural beauty that it is desirable that the provisions of this Act relating to such areas should apply thereto, designate the area for the purposes of this Act as an area of outstanding natural beauty…

(extract from Section 87 (1))

to legislation and in Parliament itself had centred on the controversial issues to be solved in creating the National Parks Commission, and in administering the National Parks themselves. Should the Commission's role be executive, as proposed by Hobhouse, or advisory, and should the local responsibilities be exercised by the special bodies he had recommended, or primarily by the new local planning authorities, the County Councils?[8] As a result of pressure within Whitehall and through Parliament, the Commission was formed as an advisory body with grant-giving powers and a number of responsibilities, especially towards National Parks, including their designation. The management of the Parks, in terms of planning, conservation, provision for recreation and encouragement of economic development, was assigned to Joint Boards with executive powers and the ability to levy, or exceptionally to special County Council Committees. Each of the latter was to consist of a majority of local authority members, and of others nominated by the Commission. In the event, only two Boards were created but, as will be explained later, the alternative arrangements did not stand the test of time, and major changes have had to be made, and funding increased. The lessons learned may have implications for other protected areas.

The overwhelming priority given to National Parks in the legislative process was probably the main reason why Hobhouse's Conservation Areas emerged from Parliament in a rather emasculated form (see Box 1.2). Somewhere along the line[9] the title was changed to Area of Outstanding Natural Beauty, this being seen as the sole criterion for designation, emphasising landscape importance rather than the wider combination of aesthetic and scientific value implied by the expression Conservation Area. Exchequer grants were to be available for a range of environmental and access improvements, but other main recommendations, such as the requirement to set up Advisory Committees, were omitted, and there was no specific duty for the Commission to initiate AONB designation, nor, at the time, any criteria for their selection. These limitations have been attributed to several factors: the difficult economic situation and the heavy work-load in Parliament of post-war legislation; the basic assumptions made by

Scott that farming would maintain traditional landscapes; the priority given to National Parks; the feeling that normal planning controls were adequate to prevent major development and the gradual loss of architectural character, and that recreation was not a venture to be promoted actively in AONBs. Thus local government should be allowed to get on with the job, using the new planning powers.[10]

With hindsight it can be seen that this paring down of Hobhouse's concept contributed to the lack of effective response to the pressures on AONBs briefly mentioned earlier. Critically, it was not seen that conservation of landscape and other natural resources in AONBs would require positive management in addition to planning control, and that a co-ordinated approach was essential to achieve it, involving public agencies, landowners and the voluntary sector, as well as the local planning authorities. A clear lead should have been given on organisation for this, but it was not done.

This 'early history' is only part of the story, however. Later chapters will show that many factors in the subsequent train of events had an influence on the inability of AONBs to withstand adverse changes, despite the enthusiasm of local councillors and staff in some areas. The actual timing of designation, without which strongly protective policies were difficult to apply in the national interest, was one of these. Urgent efforts were made to establish the National Parks. Despite some controversy over administrative arrangements, ten (Brecon Beacons, Dartmoor, Exmoor, Lake District, Northumberland, North York Moors, Peak District, Pembrokeshire Coast, Snowdonia, and Yorkshire Dales) were set up by 1957, within eight years of the Act (see Box 1.3). The Broads Authority was established under special

---

National Parks are designated under the *National Parks and Access to the Countryside Act* 1949 on account of their natural beauty, the opportunities they offer for outdoor recreation and their proximity to centres of population. Their aims, as amended by the *Environment Act*, 1995, are to conserve their beauty, wildlife and cultural heritage, to promote their understanding and enjoyment by the public, and to foster the well-being of their local communities. There are eleven National Parks and equivalent areas, ranging in size from 300 sq km (The Broads, designated under special legislation) to over 2000 sq km (Lake District), mainly in upland areas of England and Wales. They cover about 10% of the two countries. Each park is administered by a National Park Authority, consisting of members appointed by local authorities in the area and by central government, with powers for management and town and country planning in the park. Central government provides 75% and the local authorities 25% of a Park's approved expenditure.

BOX 1.3

National Parks in England and Wales

BOX 1.4

Areas of Outstanding Natural Beauty in England and Wales

Areas of Outstanding Natural Beauty in England and Wales are designated under the 1949 Act, solely on account of their natural beauty, with the aim of conserving and enhancing it. In size, AONBs range from 16 sq km (Isles of Scilly) to over 2000 sq km (Cotswolds), and although several of them cover important upland areas, most are located more on farmland, predominantly in the southern half of England, and in coastal areas, than is the case with National Parks. AONBs cover about 13.5% of England and Wales. Most AONBs have non-statutory advisory committees, led by local authorities but including representatives of interested organisations, to co-ordinate their conservation. They are financed by local authorities and to a limited extent by government agencies.

legislation many years later. This urgency may have caused AONBs to be thought of as second best to the high profile of National Parks, although they are officially recognised as being equal to the National Parks in terms of landscape quality and the planning protection that they ought to be given – a misconception – that has taken a long time to rectify. Indeed the first AONB designation, Gower, only took place in 1956, and progress towards the present English and Welsh total of 41 was made for a long time at the rate of two or three a year (see Box 1.4). A related factor has been the comparatively low level and uncertainty of funding and, as a result, AONBs have become the 'poor relations' to National Parks in the family of protected landscapes. Plate 2 illustrates the location of National Parks and AONBs.

The 1960s and beyond: the debate widens

Another factor was the surge of interest during the 1960s in the role of the wider countryside. Hitherto National Parks and AONBs in England and Wales had commanded most of the National Park Commission's attention. The wider countryside had not generally been thought to require positive attention beyond special protection from development in green belts, on good agricultural land, and in sites of scientific importance. Rural areas nevertheless were beginning to experience a different kind of pressure that could seriously threaten key resources. This was the huge increase in countryside recreation. Alerted by environmental groups, the Government responded in the 1966 White Paper 'Leisure in the Countryside'. It also set up a review of the English and Welsh coastline, at the time when the National Trust's 'Enterprise Neptune' had already begun to buy threatened sites. A new era began, in which legislation in the *Countryside Act*, 1968, replaced the National Parks Commission with a more widely cast Countryside Commission (hereafter abbreviated to CC), and did much to encourage provision for recreation in rural areas generally. The new measures – country parks, picnic areas and other access improvements – were soon taken up by forward-looking local authorities and landowners. Strangely AONBs were not directly affected by the Act, but these, and the additional finance made available for the management of 'Heritage Coasts' within them, offered them some relief. Equally, the broadening approach meant that the Commission's slender resources would be further stretched, and that local authorities might divert their own priorities more to the 'ordinary' countryside.

In the 1970s, however, events took a further new turn. Reports such as those of the 'Countryside in 1970' conferences[11] and the Countryside Review Committee (an inter-departmental group of government officials),[12] showed unease about lack of co-ordination in rural policy, including the relationship between agriculture and the environment. Even the very existence of single-purpose designations such as AONBs was questioned. Interestingly, the Countryside Review Committee proposed a two-tier system, in which there would be no distinction between National Parks and AONBs. A small top tier would be selected from each for rigorous conservation, and a second tier made up of the remainder of each, with important landscape and recreational value. Perhaps these ideas were too radical, at the time, to be taken further by politicians.

At the same time, more immediate concerns were being expressed about shortcomings in the National Park system and about its future administration within the new local government structure, for which preparations began in 1972. The 1974 Review of National Park Policies, chaired by Lord Sandford,[13] and the subsequent government response, established an important principle that when the two purposes of National Parks are in conflict, the first (conservation) must prevail. Simultaneously, government funding for the Parks was substantially increased, and each Park was required to have a single Board or Committee and its own officer, and to prepare a management plan. Further new impetus was given by the creation in 1989 of the National Parks Review Panel, chaired by Professor Ron Edwards, whose report in 1991[14] resulted in further modernisation of the administrative arrangements for National Parks under the *Environment Act*, 1995. This provided revised purposes for National Parks to embrace wildlife and cultural matters; and for new free-standing Boards to protect and manage each Park, including a new duty, in pursuing the primary purpose of designation, to seek to foster the economic and social well-being of local communities.

It is likely that the whole sequence of events from the 1960s, especially the widely welcomed new arrangements for National Parks contributed to the growing concern of CC about policy for AONBs. This concern soon became shared by the Countryside Council for Wales (CCW) which was set up in 1990 to take over the responsibilities of CC and the former Nature Conservancy Council in that country. As will be shown in later chapters, both CC and CCW have now conducted what amounts to a major review of AONBs and proposals for their future are now being considered at government level. Meanwhile, a new countryside organisation, the Countryside Agency (CA), has been formed by merging CC with the former Rural Development Commission. CA has given these proposals its full support.

One further development of importance relating to the wider countryside was the joint work by CC and English Nature on the landscape character and wildlife resource of English rural areas as a whole. This resulted in the publication by English Nature and CC in 1996 of the 'Character of England',[15] a map and descriptive summary which identifies broad areas with distinctive landscape and wildlife features, as a guide to sustainable change. The aim has been to increase understanding of scenic and ecological qualities, rather than act as an additional layer of countryside designation (the implications of this for designated areas are considered later). A few planning authorities had already been using much the same approach on a county or district scale as a basis for rural policies.

Scotland

Although this book is primarily concerned with the AONBs of England and Wales, reference needs to be made to protected areas in Scotland and Northern Ireland, since experience of their status and conservation arrangements has relevance to the future of AONBs and other protected areas. As with England and Wales the establishment of protected landscapes in Scotland's superb countryside also has a long and complicated history. In 1945, the Report on National Parks and the Conservation of Nature in Scotland (the Ramsay Committee, the Scottish equivalent of Hobhouse)[16] had recommended five areas for designation as National Parks. These included Loch Lomond and the Trossachs, Ben Nevis and Glencoe, and the Cairngorms, and were to become publicly owned. Ramsay's proposals were rejected on account of opposition from landowners and because of fears that they would prejudice efforts to revitalise the Highland economy. However, some vestige of national interest in these areas was retained by giving them added planning control in order to prevent unsuitable development.

Debate on the need for national parks continued, however. The Countryside Commission for Scotland, formed in 1967, published a report in 1974[17] recommending a park system which was designed to meet strategic objectives of countryside recreation and conservation in a way better suited to the form of government and land ownership in Scotland. This, having been accepted by government, needed to be followed up by the selection of areas with special landscape conservation requirements, and in 1978 the Commission completed a study which listed forty areas of outstanding scenic interest as part of the country's national heritage. These were widely distributed in the Highlands and Islands, and south to the Borders, Dumfries and Galloway, and the majority were not under severe recreational pressure. They included Ramsay's five priority and three reserve locations. All 40 were subsequently designated by the Secretary of State for Scotland, under the *Town and Country Planning (Scotland) Act, 1972*, as National Scenic Areas (NSAs), which gave them special planning protection but did not make any positive provision for conservation or recreation, nor for the co-ordination of management, nor for their administration. These vary in size from 9 sq km (St Kilda, a World Heritage Site) to nearly 1500 sq km (Wester Ross), and they cover about 12 per cent of the land and water area of Scotland. They are shown on the map in Plate 2.

It is clear that the controversies over Scotland's protected areas have resulted in a weak conservation regime. Scottish Natural Heritage, set up in 1992 to combine the roles of the Scottish Countryside Commission and the Nature Conservancy Council in Scotland, is now taking steps to strengthen it. These are contained in two advice papers on National Parks and NSAs submitted to government in 1999 following extensive consultation.[18] These envisage modest strengthening of the NSA designation, with an enhanced role and responsibilities for local authorities to manage them, and the establishment of National Parks, initially in Loch Lomond and the Trossachs and in the Cairngorms. Each National Park would have an independent National Park body, with a majority of local representation, to enhance the natural and cultural heritage and provide for their enjoyment, while meeting the social and economic development aspirations of local communities. It is not intended that they should take extensive powers from existing bodies, including the local planning authorities. As is shown in Chapter 4, these proposals have a bearing on the future range of responsibilities for management and the form of organisation in other protected landscapes.

Northern Ireland

There are no national parks, as such, in Northern Ireland; the concept aroused too much opposition. It has, however, been a comparatively straight forward move to designate protected landscapes in the

Province which, though including relatively wild and mountainous countryside with huge potential for recreation, are nevertheless called AONBs. Designation was originally intended to allow extra scrutiny of planning applications, as authorised by the former *Amenity and Lands (Northern Ireland) Act*, 1965. Five Areas were set up between 1965 and 1972 under this legislation. Since then the emphasis has changed from the single aim of protection to a wider purpose: conservation and enhancement of natural beauty, wildlife and historic objects, promoting enjoyment by the public, and providing access. They are more akin to English and Welsh National Parks, but without the administrative structure, than to AONBs. The encouragement of tourism is also an important motive. A further four Areas have now been designated under the *Nature Conservation and Amenity Lands (Northern Ireland) Order,* 1985. The total of nine, amounting to 20 per cent of the land of the Province, includes mountain, upland heath, dramatic coast, glens, loughs, sandy beaches and coves, and peaceful valleys. As well as superb scenic quality such as the Mourne Mountains, they have a rich wildlife, historic and geological interest, including the Giant's Causeway, a World Heritage Site. They are shown in Plate 2. The mechanisms for setting up administrative arrangements are very flexible. It is up to the Northern Ireland Environment Department to make proposals for each area. Consequently arrangements vary from formal to informal, though usually the Department and District Councils are the active partners.

These AONBs, with the possibility of two more in due course, are thought to provide the most appropriate ways to conserve the Province's finest landscape, protected landscape legislation in Northern Ireland being less comprehensive than in England and Wales. On the other hand the aims for their conservation, described above, make an interesting contrast with the more focused statutory requirements for English and Welsh AONBs. Perhaps there is a lesson to be learned here.

Other types of protected landscapes

National Parks, AONBs and National Scenic Areas, examples of which are illustrated in Plates 3 and 4, are the leading members of the family of protected landscapes of national importance in the UK. One other member needs to be considered – the Heritage Coast.

The need to protect the fine coastal heritage had become an important national issue by the 1960s, at a time when coastal recreation and development pressures were rapidly gaining momentum. The National Trust's very successful campaign 'Enterprise Neptune', starting in 1965, was instrumental in safeguarding by purchase and management some of the most famous headlands and popular stretches of open coast in England. The Trust now protects some 850 km of coastline. Simultaneously, the National Parks Commission, at the instigation of the Department of the Environment, undertook a comprehensive study of coastal conservation requirements in England and Wales. Reporting in 1970,[19] its successor the Countryside Commission (CC), proposed that 'the most scenically outstanding stretches of coast be defined and protected as Heritage Coast'. As most of them were likely to be in National Parks and AONBs formal designation was not considered necessary; definition should be a non-statutory process. This approach was formally recommended to local authorities by the Government in 1972 and, after pilot projects and offers of grant, was taken up with enthusiasm. The task of defining the actual areas was complete by 1992, and nearly 1500 km of Heritage Coast, more than one-third of the coastline of England and Wales, are now actively managed in the interest of landscape and wildlife, with provision for informal recreation.

The aims for Heritage Coasts include conservation of marine habitats and the control of pollution and litter. It will be seen from the Map in Plate 2 that all but eight of the 45 stretches of Heritage Coast are in AONBs or National Parks, mostly in AONBs. Their management has gradually been integrated with the wider process for each area, very much to the benefit of both, especially in the provision for recreation. Coastal conservation is still a very important issue in national and European environmental policy, and the experience gained in Heritage Coast work has much to offer the management of estuarine landscape and wildlife generally.

There is one other type of designation that needs to be introduced at this stage, because it tends to appear in lists of protected landscapes. Environmentally Sensitive Areas – ESAs, as they are known – are not protected areas as such; rather, they are mechanisms for funding agri-environment policies and are not formally part of the planning system. Established under the *Agriculture Act*, 1986, and coming within the terms of European Union agricultural policy, their purpose is to encourage the use of farming methods which will safeguard the characteristic landscape, wildlife and archaeological resources of each area. The criteria for selection of ESAs include both the national importance of the area's environment in its broadest sense, and the extent to which it is at risk due to farming practices. The scheme for ESAs was developed throughout the UK, the individual areas being selected by the Agriculture Departments in each country after consultation within government and with the statutory conservation bodies. In Wales ESAs have recently been supplanted by the country-wide agri-environment scheme Tir Gofal. In practice, in England, ESAs fall almost exclusively within National Parks and AONBs and areas where there is a concentration of SSSIs, and they are a very important means of funding agri-environment in the areas. The Ministry of Agriculture then supervises the local operation of the scheme.

The family of protected landscapes as part of a wider community of protected areas

National Parks, AONBs and National Scenic Areas were designated primarily on account of their national landscape importance, although, as described later, the close connection between landscape and wildlife habitats is such that these areas often contain a notable scientific and wildlife heritage. Sites of Special Scientific Interest – SSSIs as they are usually known – together with National Nature Reserves (NNRs), form the main geographical framework for wildlife conservation measures throughout Britain. Although derived initially from the same legislation as protected landscapes, that is, the *National Parks and Access to the Countryside Act*, 1949, they are selected solely on account of their ecological value. They largely focus on specific sites rather than extensive tracts of countryside as National Parks and AONBs do – an important point when one comes to look at the shortcomings of the system of protected landscapes. They contain our finest wildlife habitats, including many of the rarest plants and animals but, due to the inter-relationship between landscape and habitats mentioned above, they do significantly occur within areas of first-rate scenery. There are several thousand SSSIs and a similar form of designation in Northern Ireland (ASSIs). They are protected partly through the planning system and partly through the *Wildlife and Countryside Act*, 1981, in order to safeguard their scientific value. Schemes for their management have the same overall objective. Furthermore, the responsibility for their administration, whether by public ownership, management agreement or other means, rests with the wildlife conservation agencies; local government is not often directly involved. There is thus a clear 'family' difference, both in purpose and operation, between the designations that protect *habitats* and those that aim primarily to protect *landscapes*. The distinction is further emphasised by the fact that wildlife sites of particular inter-national value can come within the scope of European legislation addressing conservation and bio-diversity issues. There is no such formal link in the case of protected landscapes.

Collectively, these measures all aim to safeguard natural resources. Other area-based designations also exist. One of the best known, the green belt, is really a means of preventing urban sprawl, rather than of safeguarding landscapes or habitats of a special quality. It is frequently said that the number and variety of designations and the inconsisten-cies in their treatment causes confusion in the minds of the public, and that AONBs, too often regarded as 'negative', are among the least understood. There may be some truth in this attitude; perhaps what appears as a plethora should really be seen as a community of protected areas, with a common interest in sustainability.

This chapter has endeavoured to set the scene for the whole book. It has looked at the provenance of AONBs, and the context of UK protected area policy within which they should be studied. It has shown how the realities of the legislative process whittled away sound proposals for their administration to cope with these pressures, and has noted the low priority that was consequently given to their establishment and management. As a result, they have long been regarded as poor relations to the National Park members of the family. It has also suggested that some lessons might be learned from experience with other forms of protected designations. This is far from the whole story, however. The next series of chapters show the importance AONBs in resource terms, describe in more detail the pressures they are under, and give an account of successive attempts by central government to improve their standing through policy reviews and other measures to secure their positive management.

References

[1] *Report of the National Park Committee*, Cmd 3851, HMSO, London, 1931.

[2] Ministry of Works and Planning, *Report of the Committee on Land Utilisation in Rural Areas*, Cmd 6378, HMSO, London, 1942.

[3] Ministry of Town and Country Planning, *National Parks in England and Wales*, Cmd 6628, HMSO, London, 1945.

[4] Ministry of Town and Country Planning, *Report of the National Parks Committee (England and Wales)*, Cmd 7121, HMSO, London, 1947.

[5] Ministry of Town and Country Planning, *Conservation of Nature in England and Wales, Report of the Wildlife Conservation Special Committee*, Cmd 7122, HMSO, London, 1947.

[6] Countryside Commission, *Review of Proposed Areas of Outstanding Natural Beauty*, Paper 73/21, Cheltenham, 1973.

[7] A full account is given in the unpublished Designation History Series written for the Countryside Commission by Ray Woolmore, formerly Senior Planning Officer, in 1998/9.

[8] For a full account of the passage of the Act through Parliament, see Cherry, G.E., *Environmental Planning 1939 – 1969*, Volume 2, *National Parks and Recreation in the Countryside*, HMSO, London, 1975. Also Blunden, J.A. and Curry, N., *A People's Charter*, Chapter 4, HMSO, London, 1990.

9   Anderson, M.A., Areas of Outstanding Natural Beauty and the 1949 National Parks Act, *Town Planning Review*, 1990, Vol. 61, pp. 311 – 339.

10   Ibid.

11   Nature Conservancy Council and Royal Society of Arts, *Countryside in 1970* Reports, London, 1970.

12   Department of the Environment, *Countryside Review Committee Discussion Papers, Topic No 4, Conservation and the Countryside Heritage*, HMSO, London, 1979.

13   Department of the Environment, *Report of the National Park Policies Review Committee*, HMSO, London, 1974.

14   Countryside Commission, *Fit for the Future, Report of the National Parks Review Panel*, CCP 334, Cheltenham, 1991.

15   Countryside Commission and English Nature, *The Character of England: Landscape, Wildlife and Natural Features*, CCX41, Cheltenham, 1996.

16   *Report of the Scottish National Parks Survey Committee*, Cmd 6631, HMSO, Edinburgh, 1947.

17   Countryside Commission for Scotland, *A Park System for Scotland*, Perth, 1974.

18   Scottish Natural Heritage, *National Parks for Scotland, Advice to Government*, Perth, 1999 and *National Scenic Areas, Advice to Government*, Perth, 1999.

19   Countryside Commission, *The Coastal Heritage*, HMSO, London, 1970.

The geography and importance of AONBs 2

In the first chapter the position of AONBs in the national family of protected landscapes was established. Continuing to set the scene, this chapter looks more closely at the geography of AONBs and at the reasons why they are regarded as such an important part of our national environmental heritage and why they need to be conserved.

The geography of the AONB family

The great variety of geographical features in the AONB family is one of its hallmarks. Notwithstanding the uniqueness of each AONB, it is possible to draw a general picture without doing disservice to individual ones. To understand fully the nature of each AONB a perusal of the series of landscape assessments published by the Countryside Commission is essential.

An examination of the map of AONBs in Plate 5 shows, as was mentioned in Chapter 1, a marked concentration in the lowlands of southern, eastern and south-western England: 26 of the 41 areas lie south-east of a line from the Severn to the Humber estuaries. In some respects this is not surprising because the National Parks, apart from the Norfolk and Suffolk Broads and the New Forest in Hampshire are regarded as upland phenomena, with their emphasis on the wide-open spaces for access. Nevertheless this is an important distinction when one considers popular perceptions of AONBs as 'lowland agricultural England', particularly so when this perceived difference between AONBs and National Parks is used as part of an argument to belittle the importance of AONBs. Somehow the fact that the majority of AONBs are seen as essentially farmed landscapes seems to count against them. However, it will be shown below that the label 'lowland agricultural England' is somewhat misplaced.

While the National Parks are very much 'upland' in character, it is important to remember that many of the areas designated AONB

Table 2.1 Classification of AONBs by main characteristics

	Upland	Lowland	Coastal
Moor or Heath	North Pennines Forest of Bowland Malvern Hills Nidderdale Clwydian Range Cornwall (Bodmin Moor) Shropshire Hills	Dorset Surrey Hills Cannock Chase Suffolk Coast & Heaths Shropshire Hills Sussex Downs High Weald East Devon Quantock Hills	Cornwall Isles of Scilly Gower Dorset
Woodland		Quantock Hills Arnside & Silverdale Chilterns, Wye Valley Tamar, Kent Downs Sussex Downs, High Weald Malvern Hills Howardian Hills Cannock Chase Cotswolds East Hampshire Shropshire Hills, Surrey Hills	
River Valley/ Estuaries/ Harbours		Wye Valley Dedham Vale Tamar Valley South Devon	Suffolk Coast & Heaths South Hampshire Solway Chichester Harbour Cornwall Isle of Wight Norfolk
Arable (chalk and limestone)		Chilterns, Cotswolds Cranborne Chase Dorset East Hampshire Kent Downs Lincolnshire Wolds North Wessex Downs Surrey Hills Sussex Downs	
Pastoral Mixed Farming		Blackdown Hills Shropshire Hills High Weald Dedham Vale Dorset, Mendips Cotswolds	
Hard/Cliff Coast			Isles of Scilly, Cornwall Gower, Dorset, Kent Downs, Lleyn E., S. & N. Devon Sussex Downs Anglesey, Isle of Wight
Soft/Low Coast			Northumberland, Norfolk South Hampshire Chichester Harbour Solway Coast Suffolk Coast & Heaths Anglesey, Gower Arnside & Silverdale

actually are hilly: for example, the chalk and limestone escarpments of the Chilterns, the Sussex Downs or the Cotswolds, the dramatic cliffs of the South West and the great variety of relief in the Shropshire Hills. Indeed some areas like the North Pennines and Nidderdale are truly upland. It is ironical that critics of the range of landscapes covered by AONB designation cite the preoccupation with hills, seemingly at the expense of flat landscapes, as a significant shortcoming. Perhaps they have a point when one considers that an area like the Somerset Levels and Moors seems to have slipped through the net. It is important to stress that there are significant tracts of lowland, especially on the coast, that have been designated, as Table 2.1 demonstrates. When relief is combined with the features described below one has something rather more than 'lowland agricultural England'.

Table 2.1 shows a very simple classification of the character of AONBs, backed by the illustrations in Plates 6 – 14. That quite a number of them appear in a variety of boxes in this book demonstrates the variety of scenery found within so many of them. Dorset is a classic in terms of its variety with lowland heaths, chalk and limestone hills, and dramatic cliffs. The Sussex Downs, the Surrey Hills and the Shropshire Hills, to name but a few, also have an extraordinary variety. In contrast some areas like the Suffolk Coast, South Devon, the Solway Coast and the North Pennines have very distinct characteristics.

This pattern is confirmed by analysis of the Countryside Character Map of England published by the Countryside Commission and English Nature.[1] The map in Plate 15 shows the character areas overlaid by the boundaries of AONBs. Examples are illustrated in Plate 16. Table 2.2 shows that only the Isles of Scilly AONB coincides exactly with a character area and that six are set within single-character, but larger areas. It also shows that a further 14 have 70 per cent or more of their area covered by a single characteristic feature. This suggests that there is quite a strong correlation between the two, with 21 out of 37 AONBs having 70 per cent or more of their area covered by just one character area. It also shows that there are just seven AONBs that have between five and eight character areas, none of which is heavily dominant.

LAND COVER

It is not easy to find figures of the land cover of each AONB. Only a few of their management plans have comprehensive assessments. However, it is possible to gain an insight into the overall picture through the Countryside Information System (CIS) developed by the DETR.[2] One of the data-sets CIS holds is the Land Cover Map of

Table 2.2   AONBs and Character Areas (CA)

1. AONBs with single CA

Identical area: Isles of Scilly

Part of larger CA: Chichester Harbour, Isle of Wight, South Hampshire, Solway Coast, South Devon, Suffolk Coast & Heaths

2. AONBs with one CA dominating

90% or more of AONB:	Arnside & Silverdale (94%), Cannock Chase (94%), High Weald (91%), North Pennines (91%)*	Blackdown Hills (95%), Chilterns (95%), Northumberland (97%),
80% – 90% of AONB:	Howardian Hills (80%), Lincolnshire Wolds (87%)	Cotswolds (87%),**
70% – 80% of AONB:	Dedham Vale (77%), Kent Downs (70%),	East Devon (73%), Mendip Hills (71%)

3. AONBs with two CAs dominating (not in list above)

90% or more of AONB:	Forest of Bowland (42 + 49 = 91%), North Devon (48 + 52 = 100%), Shropshire Hills (67 + 31 = 98%),	Nidderdale (61 + 34 = 95%), Quantock Hills (59 + 41 = 100%), Wye Valley (60 + 40 = 100%)
80% – 90% of AONB:	East Hampshire (54 + 27 = 81%), Sussex Downs (25 + 60 = 85%)	Surrey Hills (27 + 55 = 82%),

4. AONBs with the greatest number of CAs

8 CAs:	North Wessex Downs (1 covers 58% of AONB, 7 < 20% each),
	Dorset (0 > 50% of AONB)
7 CAs:	Cornwall (0 > 50% of AONB)
6 CAs:	Malvern Hills (1 covers 58% of AONB, 5 < 20% each)
5 CAs:	Cranborne Chase & West Wiltshire Downs (0 > 50% of AONB), Norfolk Coast (0 > 50% of AONB), Sussex Downs (1 covers 60% of AONB, 4 < 25%)

NB   * North Pennines has 6 CAs, of which 5 cover 9% of the AONB, i.e. the fringe
      ** Cotswolds has 7 CAs, of which 6 cover just 13% of the AONB

Source: DETR, *Countryside Information System*, derived from CC data on AONBs (1994) and joint CC and EN data on Character Areas (1996).

Table 2.3   Land Cover of AONBs in England

(% of each element in each AONB)

	Conifer woodland	Deciduous woodland	Total woodland	Tilled land	Managed grass
National average	**3.2**	**5.0**	**8.3**	**21.5**	**27.3**
Arnside & Silverdale	0.2	14.8	15.0	10.7	34.0
Blackdown Hills	2.1	11.4	13.5	11.0	61.9
Forest of Bowland	1.7	5.4	7.1	8.3	50.4
Cannock Chase	11.9	17.2	29.1	20.0	22.9
Chichester Harbour	0.5	5.8	6.2	27.0	18.0
Chilterns	0.9	13.7	14.7	32.6	37.3
Cornwall	0.4	8.0	8.4	6.2	44.8
Cotswolds	0.4	7.7	8.1	38.5	30.9
Cranborne Chase & W Wilts Downs	2.3	11.4	13.7	39.1	35.6
Dedham Vale	0.5	4.1	4.6	41.7	38.9
Dorset	2.5	8.0	10.5	18.5	52.4
East Devon	3.3	10.5	13.8	18.6	43.9
East Hampshire	1.5	10.1	11.6	33.5	37.5
High Weald	2.3	17.6	19.9	14.8	49.4
Howardian Hills	2.1	5.5	7.6	50.1	27.4
Isle of Wight	4.3	9.2	13.5	19.3	35.8
Isles of Scilly	n/a	n/a	n/a	n/a	n/a
Kent Downs	0.8	12.0	12.9	35.3	37.8
Lincolnshire Wolds	0.3	4.4	4.6	69.0	16.7
Malvern Hills	0.8	13.0	13.8	23.6	39.2
Mendip Hills	2.8	9.4	11.2	9.9	56.7
Nidderdale	0.9	5.6	6.5	11.4	30.7
Norfolk Coast	2.5	3.5	6.0	48.0	12.2
North Devon	1.0	7.4	8.3	9.7	44.8
North Pennines	1.1	1.9	3.0	6.2	24.2
North Wessex Downs	1.3	7.5	8.8	46.7	28.6
Northumberland Coast	0.2	0.3	0.6	36.2	19.3
Quantock Hills	3.3	12.6	15.9	22.3	32.4
Shropshire Hills	1.9	10.4	12.3	15.6	50.6
Solway Coast	0.1	0.5	0.6	4.7	45.9
South Devon	0.7	5.3	6.1	21.4	33.6
South Hampshire Coast	5.4	16.4	21.9	11.3	22.6
Suffolk Coast & Heaths	2.0	4.1	6.1	29.8	39.2
Surrey Hills	5.4	21.9	27.4	13.1	45.1
Sussex Downs	3.6	14.0	17.7	22.9	37.4
Tamar Valley	n/a	n/a	n/a	n/a	n/a
Wye Valley	4.6	18.7	23.3	21.6	34.1

Source: DETR, Countryside Information System, derived from ITE Land Cover Map, 1990.

Great Britain. This is a digital map of land cover in Great Britain from satellite data based upon a hierarchical classification of 25 major land-cover types. Table 2.3 is derived from this information for England. An examination of the table gives further clues as to the nature of the family of English AONBs. With regard to woodland, 20 AONBs have more than the average woodland cover (conifer and deciduous) for England of 8.3 per cent, and of these six have more than double. Furthermore, 27 AONBs have more than the average deciduous cover of 5.0 per cent, of which 16 have more than twice the average. While only six AONBs have above the average conifer cover of 3.2 per cent in relation to managed grassland, most AONBs are well above the average cover of 27.3 per cent, with 11 having more than 40 per cent, and only seven have below average figures. Fifteen AONBs have more than the average area of 22.5 per cent tilled land, of which eight are in the chalk areas. Four AONBs have more than double the average, the highest being the 69 per cent in the Lincolnshire Wolds. In Wales the proportion of tilled land in the four AONBs is just 5.5 per cent, with 36 per cent managed grass and 14 per cent woodland cover.[3]

Looking to other sources of information, figures for woodland, moor and heath and the coast provided by individual AONBs to the Funding Study[4] reinforce the broad picture set out above, though it is interesting to note the differences in the amounts for some areas from one source to another. This is an interesting reflection on the paucity of information about AONBs, which must be of concern in relation to the preparation of management plans and to the monitoring of change in the landscape.

WOODLAND

The proportion of woodland is very significant in a number of AONBs, being substantially above the national average for England, and it is one of the main features contributing to their quality: for example, Surrey Hills 45 per cent, Cannock Chase 40 per cent, Arnside & Silverdale and Wye Valley 30 per cent, Sussex Downs 25 per cent, High Weald 23 per cent, Chilterns 21 per cent, Kent Downs 19 per cent, Malvern Hills, Tamar Valley and Howardian Hills, each 15 per cent.

MOOR AND HEATH

Moors and heaths are very important in the AONBs in northern England and Wales contributing, for example, in Nidderdale 60 per cent, North Pennines 62 per cent, Forest of Bowland 25 per cent, Cannock Chase 18 per cent and Gower 30 per cent. Lowland heath is also very important in the Surrey Hills, the Suffolk Coast and Heaths, Dorset, Cornwall, East Devon, the Quantocks and the Shropshire Hills. The importance of moors and heaths stems not so much from their spatial extent as the feeling of wilderness that they bring to the lowlands, and the opportunities they offer for recreation. As will be seen later they are also of great importance for their wildlife.

THE COAST

It is also important to remember that nearly half of the 41 AONBs have a significant length of coastline and that almost all the defined Heritage Coasts of England and Wales are within them. Some like

Anglesey, Lleyn, Gower, the Isles of Scilly, Cornwall, North, South and East Devon, Dorset, the Isle of Wight, South Hampshire, Suffolk and Norfolk, Northumberland and the Solway Coast, are totally dominated by the coast itself and all the issues associated with coastal areas. There are relatively few AONBs that contain significant estuaries and harbours. Most notable are Chichester Harbour with 50 per cent of the area, Norfolk Coast 25 per cent of the area, Tamar Valley, the estuaries of South Cornwall and the Camel 20 per cent of the area, Gower, Poole Harbour in Dorset, the Suffolk Coast and the AONBs bordering the Solent, all of which have the additional management issues relating to the use of water for recreation or commerce.

There are a number of other elements of the geography of AONBs which are important in understanding them as landscapes in which people live, work and play, and which help to define the kind of administration and management that is required. These elements include their size, their relationship to local authority areas, their proximity to population, socio-economic designations and the number of inhabitants, their relationship to agricultural designations, common land and open land.

SIZE OF AONBs

No guidance has been given as to the appropriate size for an AONB, and there is no upper or lower limit. There is an extraordinary variation from the smallest, the Isles of Scilly comprising 16 sq km, to the largest, the Cotswolds of 2038 sq km. While these are extreme examples. Table 2.4 shows that there is quite an even spread of size.

The size, therefore, does not have any particular bearing on whether a particular area is important. However, it does affect the kind of management activity that is required and, among many other factors, will influence the nature and scale of management structures and the level of resources needed to look after the area. This is particularly the case when the larger areas tend to have many more local authorities involved.

AONBs AND LOCAL AUTHORITY AREAS

A particular characteristic of AONBs is that they are often found at the edge of administrative areas, straddling numerous local authority boundaries. This marginality may account for some of the lack of attention to management described later. However, the complex pattern of administration is an important matter in the management of AONBs, dictating to a considerable degree the kind of organisation that is needed. There is no doubt that this situation has made co-ordinated action harder to achieve. The number of local authorities

Table 2.4 Size Range of AONBs

Less than 100 sq km	7	Quantock Hills, Cannock Chase, Chichester Harbour, South Hampshire Coast, Dedham Vale, Arnside & Silverdale, Isles of Scilly
100 to 199 sq km	10	Gower, Lleyn, Northumberland Coast, Malvern Hills, North Devon, Isle of Wight, Solway Coast, Mendip Hills, Clwydian Range, Tamar Valley
200 to 399 sq km	7	South Devon, East Hampshire, East Devon, Anglesey, Wye Valley, Howardian Hills, Blackdown Hills
400 to 599 sq km	4	Surrey Hills, Norfolk Coast, Suffolk Coast & Heaths, Lincolnshire Wolds
600 to 799 sq km	1	Nidderdale
800 to 999 sq km	7	Shropshire Hills, Cornwall, Forest of Bowland, Chilterns, Sussex Downs, Kent Downs, Cranborne Chase & West Wiltshire Downs
1000 to 1499 sq km	2	Dorset, High Weald
> 1500 sq km	3	Cotswolds, North Wessex Downs, North Pennines

Source: *Directory of Areas of Outstanding Natural Beauty*, available only on the Countryside Agency Website, www.countryside.gov.uk.

involved with each AONB is shown in Table 2.5. All but four of the 41 AONBs in England and Wales have more than one involved, whilst 28 of the 41 have four or more.

PROXIMITY OF AONBS TO CENTRES OF POPULATION

As mentioned in Chapter 1, one of the factors in the designation of National Parks was proximity to major centres of population so that they could be used for open-air recreation. Some, like the Peak District and the Yorkshire Dales and the North York Moors, were close to the large conurbations of the north. Others were relatively remote, like Exmoor and the Pembrokeshire Coast. Although not a criterion for designation of AONBs, their proximity to major centres follows a similar pattern. Some, like the Chilterns, Surrey Hills, Kent Downs, Sussex Downs, Gower, Dorset, Mendips and Cotswolds, are close to major centres of population. Others like Anglesey, Lleyn, North Devon, Blackdown Hills, Solway Coast and Norfolk Coast are relatively remote areas. When the pressures both for recreation and housing in AONBs are discussed in the next chapter, this relationship becomes all important and is yet another factor in determining what management and what resources are needed. It is also an

Table 2.5   AONBs and Local Authorities

No. of local authorities	AONB	Type of Authority(s)
1.	Anglesey	1U
	Isle of Wight	1U
	Isles of Scilly	1U
	Lleyn	1U
2.	Clwydian Range	2U
	East Devon	1C, 1D
	Gower	2U
	South Hampshire Coast	1C, 1D
3.	East Hampshire	1C, 2D
	Howardian Hills	1C, 2D
	North Devon	1C, 2D
	Northumberland Coast	1C, 2D
	Solway Coast	1C, 2D
4.	Arnside and Silverdale	2C, 2D
	Chichester Harbour	2C, 2D
	Lincolnshire Wolds	1C, 2D, 1U
	Nidderdale	1C, 3D
	Quantock Hills	1C, 3D
	South Devon	1C, 1D, 2U
	Suffolk Coast and Heaths	1C, 3D
	Wye Valley	1C, 2D, 1U
5.	Cannock Chase	1C, 4D
	Dedham Vale	2C, 3D
	Malvern Hills	2C, 2D,1U
	Mendip Hills	1C, 2D, 2U
	Norfolk Coast	1C, 4D
	Shropshire Hills	1C, 3D, 1U
6.	Blackdown Hills	2C, 4D
	Surrey Hills	1C, 5D
7.	Cornwall	1C, 6D
	Dorset	2C, 5D
	Tamar Valley	2C, 4D, 1U
8.	Forest of Bowland	2C, 6D
9.	North Pennines	3C, 6D
11.	Cranborne Chase and West Wiltshire Downs	4C, 7D
	North Wessex Downs	3C, 6D, 2U
12.	Kent Downs	1C, 9D, 2U
	Sussex Downs	2C, 9D, 1U
15.	Chilterns	4C, 10 D, 1U
	High Weald	4C, 11D
18.	Cotswolds	5C, 10D,3U

C = County Council, D = District Council, U = Unitary Authority

Source: *Directory of Areas of Outstanding Natural Beauty*, available only on the Countryside Agency website, www.countryside.gov.uk

important matter in relation to any discussion of the purposes of AONBs compared with those for National Parks.

SOCIO-ECONOMIC DESIGNATIONS

The map in Plate 17 shows the distribution of Rural Development Areas (RDAs) and European Union (EU) Objective 5b areas in relation to AONBs. Of the 37 AONBs in England, 26 are wholly or in part covered by the RDA designation, an indication that the socio-economic health of the area is not sound. Furthermore, 11 of the 26 within RDAs are also within Objective 5b areas: again a measure of the socio-economic problems being experienced. Plate 18 shows the nature of some of the areas so designated. The significance of this will emerge during the remainder of the book, when the relationship between policies for AONBs and rural development is discussed. However, it is useful to record their geographical relationship with AONBs, not least as a reminder that AONBs contain communities with people living and working within them. Although there are no figures available for the total population of all AONBs, it can be a significant figure for individual areas as Table 2.6 shows.

Table 2.6 Population of AONBs

Cotswolds	120,000
Chilterns	100,000
Dorset	90,000
Sussex Downs	47,000
Shropshire Hills	37,500
South Devon	33,000
Suffolk Coast & Heaths	23,490
North Devon	17,000
Northumberland Coast	2,500
Forest of Bowland	10,000
Gower	10,000

Source: *Directory of Areas of Outstanding Natural Beauty*, available only on the Countryside Agency website, www.countryside.gov.uk

RELATIONSHIP WITH AGRICULTURAL DESIGNATIONS

There is a particularly close relationship between Environmentally Sensitive Areas (ESAs) and AONBs, for the simple reason that one of the criteria for designating ESAs is the existence of a nationally important landscape, the quality of which depends to a significant degree on environmentally friendly farming. An examination of the map in Plate 19, which shows ESAs and AONBs along with National Parks, reveals a very strong correlation between the designations. The only ESAs not related to a nationally important landscape are those where there is a particularly strong concentration of wildlife interest, for example, the Somerset Levels and Moors, Breckland, Essex Coast and the North Kent Marshes. Overall 12 out of the 37 AONBs in England contain all or part of an ESA. Table 2.7 shows the

Table 2.7 AONBs with Environmentally Sensitive Areas in England

	% of area		% of area
Blackdown Hills	90	East Hampshire	16
Cornwall	7	Norfolk Coast	4
Cotswolds	38	North Pennines	11
Cranborne Chase & West Wilts Downs	26	Shropshire Hills	61
Dedham Vale	71	Suffolk Coast & Heaths	40
Dorset	13	Sussex Downs	53

Source: DETR, *Countryside Information System*, derived from FRCA data, 1997.

AONBs with an ESA and the proportion of the area covered, and an example is shown in Plate 20. It is important to note that only four AONBs are ESA-covered by 50 per cent or more – Blackdown Hills, Dedham Vale, Shropshire Hills and Sussex Downs – a matter that will be considered in later chapters. In Wales all the AONBs except Gower were covered by ESA designation, until the introduction in 1999 of the all Wales agri-environment scheme Tir Gofal, which has replaced them.

The relationship with Less Favoured Areas is marked by the fact that all the upland AONBs identified in Table 2.1, except the Malvern Hills, with the addition of a small part of North Devon adjacent to Exmoor, have significant areas where the farming is carried on in physically difficult circumstances. This is an important matter given the relationship between the way in which farming operations influence the landscape and the impact of farming support measures on the way the land is managed. For example, support for livestock has led to serious overgrazing in some areas. Table 2.8 shows the extent of the relationship.

COMMON LAND

The extent of Common land is an important matter to consider as part of the geography of AONBs. In the context of the current debate about access to open country, common land is of course a prime

Table 2.8 AONBs with Less Favoured Areas in England

	% AONB
Forest of Bowland	57
Cornwall (Bodmin Moor)	13
Nidderdale	62
North Devon	2
North Pennines	96
Quantock Hills	14
Shropshire Hills	41

Source: DETR, *Countryside Information System*, derived from FRCA data, 1997.

resource, often providing valuable recreational opportunities and in some cases a genuine feeling of remoteness. This is a particularly important feature in parts of south-east England where there are significant tracts of common in the south-west Surrey heathland area of the Surrey Hills and the Ashdown Forest part of the High Weald. In addition much common land is of value for wildlife as it has tended not to be improved agriculturally. For example, much of the common land in Surrey and East Devon is associated with lowland heath and in the Cotswolds with limestone grassland. Table 2.9 indicates the extent of common land in AONBs in England using boundaries digitised from the common land registers. Fifteen of the 37 AONBs in England have proportionately more than the density of 2.7 per cent for England as a whole. This is not only in the uplands where the North Pennines with 27 per cent, Nidderdale 12.9 per cent, have very large amounts, but also in lowland areas such as the Quantock Hills 14.5 per cent, Surrey 9 per cent, Cannock Chase 14.5 per cent, Arnside and Silverdale 9 per cent, and Solway Coast 7 per cent. Although in many instances the amount of common land seems small in percentage terms, commons can be very important features, not only in the terms described above but also as part of the environment of villages – the village green. This is particularly so in the AONBs of south-east England.

OPEN LAND

Table 2.9 also shows the proportion of English AONBs that might be considered 'open land'. These figures were produced by DETR as part of the consultation exercise in the debate about access to the countryside.[5] They contain an amalgamation of data about common land, Land Cover map data of mountain, moor and heath and a combination of calcareous land, slope and managed grassland to try to represent the category of 'downland'. They were produced simply to indicate possible scale and distribution and do not represent actual areas to which any regulations might apply. However, the important

Table 2.9   Common land and open land in English AONBs

	Common land % of area	Open land % of area
Arnside & Silverdale	9.9	0.3
Blackdown Hills	1.0	0.5
Forest of Bowland	6.8	5.7
Cannock Chase	14.6	0.6
Chichester Harbour	4.7	0.3
Chilterns	1.9	5.1
Cornwall	5.2	4.1
Cotswolds	0.7	7.1
Cranborne Chase & West Wilts Downs	1.4	5.2
Dedham Vale	0.2	0.0
Dorset	0.3	5.2
East Devon	3.9	0.7
East Hampshire	0.6	2.1
High Weald	1.7	1.2
Howardian Hills	0	0
Isle of Wight	0	0.6
Isles of Scilly	n/a	n/a
Kent Downs	0.43	4.2
Lincolnshire Wolds	0	0.5
Malvern Hills	6.7	0.5
Mendip Hills	3.1	0.5
Nidderdale	12.9	6.3
Norfolk Coast	3.6	1.1
North Devon	1.7	0.3
North Pennines	27.9	25.3
North Wessex Downs	0.3	6.1
Northumberland Coast	0.2	0.1
Quantock Hills	14.6	0.6
Shropshire Hills	4.5	1.8
Solway Coast	7.3	0.9
South Devon	0	0.1
South Hampshire Coast	0	0.1
Suffolk Coast & Heaths	1.1	0.7
Surrey Hills	9.3	4.0
Sussex Downs	2.6	7.9
Tamar Valley	n/a	n/a
Wye Valley	0.9	0.3

Source: Common land: DETR, *Countryside Information System*, derived from FRCA data, 1998. Open land: DETR, *Countryside Information System*, derived from FRCA Common Land data (> 1 ha) in England & Wales 1998, combination of ITE land cover map data of mountain, moorland and heath (>30%) and a combination of calcareous land, >5% slope and >25% managed grassland to try to represent the category of 'downland'.

point for AONBs is that within them there is potential for open access in addition to that which already exists, with an obvious impact on the resources needed to manage recreation and conservation in areas that are often sensitive to disturbance. The significance of AONBs as 'open space' is well demonstrated in the discussion of tranquil areas in Chapter 3 and in the examples shown in Plates 21 and 22.

The importance of AONBs – more than just scenery

Having described various aspects of the geography of AONBs in the first half of this chapter, the second half explores the reasons why they are considered to be nationally important. A full understanding of these reasons is valuable both for its own sake, and in the context of the discussion later in the book of the policies that affect AONBs both now and in the future, the relevance of these areas in the future and the arrangements needed to look after them.

The basis for their designation is set out in Section 87 (1) of the 1949 Act (Chapter 1) and is really very simple, merely stating that AONBs must be of 'outstanding natural beauty'. No definition was given nor was there any guidance in terms of criteria to be used in deciding whether an area is 'outstanding'. However, the Section 114 (2) of the Act did indicate that the conservation of the natural beauty of an area includes the conservation of its flora, fauna and geological and physiographic features. Yet, unlike for National Parks, there was no reference to recreation.

It was for the National Parks Commission to decide what areas were outstanding and whether the provisions of the Act should apply to them. Inevitably this was seen by some as a highly subjective process, there being no scientific way of measuring scenic quality. The process relied upon the Reports of the 1940s and the opinion of the Commission after discussion with local authorities. There was very little discussion with the general public. This was never seriously challenged until the proposal to designate the North Pennines – the thirty-eighth area to be designated – which was the subject of a public inquiry in 1985.

In evidence to the North Pennines AONB Inquiry, the Director of the Countryside Commission emphasised the paucity of guidance on the matter.[6] However, he did point to one important source, the Report of the National Parks Committee in 1947 chaired by Sir Arthur Hobhouse. As indicated in Chapter 1 the report listed 52 Conservation Areas, which subsequently formed the basis of the family of AONBs. They were described as 'areas of high landscape quality, scientific interest and recreational value'. The evidence to the inquiry also sought to explain how these areas came to be chosen, showing how the Hobhouse report had relied on the work of John Dower in his report in 1945.[7] He had stressed that while his selection of areas was personal, it was in fairly close accord with 'the consensus of informed public opinion'. The following explanation was given in the Director's evidence as to how this consensus was arrived at:

landscape appreciation in mid-twentieth century Britain was greatly influenced by the work of the poets, authors, composers and artists (including early photographers) of the nineteenth and early twentieth centuries. In particular, its roots lie in the writings of Wordsworth and Ruskin and in the work of the nineteenth century landscape artists. But appreciation of the British landscape was not exclusive to an artistic elite. During the first half of this century an awareness of the beauties of the countryside grew through the mass circulation of magazines, books and posters that popularised these values. The heyday of railway and coach travel, and the popularity of rambling and cycling, brought brief experiences of these fine landscapes to millions, even to those who lived in cities. It was this combination of the awareness of the beauties of the landscape amongst an influential artistic minority, and the more wide-spread and popular appreciation of what the countryside had to offer to the largely urban population which formed the 'consensus' of which Dower spoke, and on which he and Hobhouse drew in making their selection of fine landscapes for designation.

At the Inquiry the Commission maintained that the opinions put forward by Dower and Hobhouse remained valid forty years later. In the event the process was upheld and the role of the Commission was confirmed by the Secretary of State. The letter conveying the Secretary of State's decision[8] makes the nature of the process very clear:

> the Secretary of State shares the Inspector's view that assessment of landscape quality necessarily involves a subjective assessment and that within the consensus of informed opinion allied with the trained eye, and common sense, the matter is one of aesthetic taste.
>
> … the matters which the Commission may or may not take into consideration in assessing an area are not circumscribed by the Act, and, in the Secretary of State's view, matters relating to the flora and fauna of an area, and its geological and physiographical features are capable of being relevant matters which the Commission may take into account when considering whether an area should be designated.

Two important outcomes of the North Pennine Inquiry were that for the first time steps were taken to explain why individual AONBs are nationally important and extensive informal public consultation was introduced before the formal stages of the designation process. The Commission has now produced landscape assessments setting out why each area is important for all but one of the AONBs in England. It remains to be seen whether Wales follows suit. The series of assessments has gone a considerable way to articulate why individual AONBs are of national importance. The example in Box 2.1 is taken from the assessment of the Dorset AONB;[9] the headings immediately give a feeling for the many values that are tied up in the one

BOX 2.1

The outstanding qualities of the Dorset AONB

Contrast and diversity – a microcosm of England's finest landscapes

The landscape of the Dorset AONB is not just a fine landscape; it is a collection of fine landscapes, each of which has its own special scenic qualities and sense of place. For, arguably, nowhere is such diversity found within a relatively small area. The Jurassic country of the Cotswolds, the chalk downland of Wiltshire, the greensand ridges of the Blackdown Hills and clay vales of the Midlands, all find local expression in the Dorset AONB but, here, they often occur on a smaller scale, closely juxtaposed to create striking sequences of beautiful countryside, which are unique in Britain.

The transitions between the component landscapes of this mosaic are often particularly attractive, with strong contrasts in some areas and gentle intermingling in others. The ridge tops of west Dorset and the chalk escarpments add an extra dimension to the Dorset AONB landscape by providing stark contrasts of relief that serve to increase and emphasise its diversity. These areas of higher ground also allow the observer panoramic views to appreciate the complex pattern and textures of the surrounding landscapes.

Nowhere is the contrast and diversity of this rich assemblage of landscapes more graphically illustrated than in the Isle of Purbeck. Here, many of the characteristic landscapes of the Dorset AONB are represented on a miniature scale to create scenery of spectacular beauty and contrasts, which mirrors that of the whole AONB.

Within this overall context, there are numerous individual landmarks, such as hilltop earthworks, monuments and tree clumps, that help to contribute an individuality and 'sense of place' to the landscapes of the localities where they occur.

A living textbook and historical record of rural England

This area also boasts an unrivalled expression of the interaction of geology, man's influence and natural processes in the landscape. In particular, Dorset's coastline is renowned for its spectacular scenery, its geological and ecological interest, and its unique coastal features, including Chesil Beach, Lulworth Cove and fossil forest, Durdle Door and Old Harry rocks, to name but a few. For these reasons it remains a popular destination for educational field trips seeking to illustrate and explain the processes of landscape evolution.

Despite a long history of mineral extraction, which has left its mark on the AONB, there has been little large-scale industrial development. Much of

area, for their complexity, and that there is a great deal more to them than just scenery.

Despite the clear statements of why these areas are so important and the Commission's published advice[10] on the breadth of meaning the landscape displays a strong sense of continuity with the past, which is expressed through features such as irregular, historic field patterns, archaeological sites and picturesque villages.

'Hardy Country'

Over the centuries, Dorset's landscapes have inspired poets, authors, scientists and artists, many of whom have left a rich legacy of cultural associations. Undoubtedly the best known of these is Thomas Hardy, whose wonderfully evocative descriptions bring an extra dimension and depth to the appreciation of the Dorset landscape. The many interrelationships between the imaginary world of Hardy's novels and the real landscapes are a constant source of mystery, speculation and inspiration for visitors and local residents.

Wildlife of national and international importance

The diversity of the Dorset AONB's landscape is reflected in a similar rich diversity of wildlife habitats. Many of these are of such national importance that they are designated as SSSIs. Often these represent fragmented remnants of wetland, of unimproved chalk, limestone and acidic grasslands and of the lowland heaths of north Purbeck. The crumbling rock faces and ledges of coastal cliffs and disused quarries with their special geological interest and associated flora and flora are also included as SSSIs.

The first voluntary marine nature reserve was established off the Purbeck coast. The Purbeck marine nature reserve was created by the voluntary agreement of owners and users to help preserve the important intertidal and subtidal wildlife interest for the future – the nature trail allows divers to appreciate better and enjoy it.

The area of Chesil Bank and the Fleet has been designated as a Special Protection Area (SPA) and a Ramsar site for its interesting birdlife and wetland ecology. Both SPA and Ramsar designations indicate that these habitats are of international significance for wildlife. In addition Poole Harbour is a proposed SPA and Ramsar site and the Dorset heathlands a potential SPA.

Semi-natural ancient woodlands, a scarce national resource, are also found throughout the AONB, especially on the steep slopes of escarpments and coombes. Elsewhere ancient hedgerows and hedgebanks represent another important historical record and habitat.

Source: Countryside Commission, *The Dorset Downs, Heaths and Coast Landscape*, CCP 424, Cheltenham, 1993.

of natural beauty that embraces scenery and its components of wildlife, history and culture, AONBs have always been and still are perceived to have mere scenic designations. This is due in no small measure to the fact that responsibility for nature conservation and scenic interests was split between two organisations, the Nature Conservancy Council and the National Parks Commission. The way in which those two organisations and their successors have exercised their responsibilities has served to perpetuate this somewhat artificial distinction. Furthermore, in practice, designation of AONBs has focused on their scenic qualities, rather than on their inherent wildlife or cultural importance. This is well illustrated by the current discussions of the use of the AONB designation to achieve national recognition for the Somerset Levels and Moors and for the Forest of Dean. Wildlife, archaeology and history respectively are the key interests in the area, rather than scenic qualities, with the debate revolving around whether or not the AONB designation is appropriate in the particular context. This issue was also discussed by the Edwards Committee on National Parks,[11] which concluded that the first purpose of National Parks relating to natural beauty should be modified to embrace wildlife, historic and cultural interests. The recommendation was adopted in the 1995 *Environment Act*, thus giving the National Parks the necessary broad base for their existence. Given that AONBs are of the same quality as National Parks, it would be logical to give them the same basic purpose.

A further reason for the perception lingering on is that there is no national picture of what it is that makes this family of areas so important. Such a picture would need to embrace the importance of AONBs for their wildlife resources, archaeological and historic features, their association with poetry art and music, their value as special places for recreation and relaxation and as generators of economic activity on account of their special qualities. These aspects of the importance of AONBs are considered briefly below. A national picture would also be invaluable in raising awareness among both the general public and policy makers and in promoting a more comprehensive and co-ordinated approach to their management.

WILDLIFE IMPORTANCE

Table 2.10 shows the extent of national and international wildlife designations within English AONBs and Plate 21 shows the distribution for England and Wales. Perhaps the most significant figure is the extent of Sites of Special Scientific Interest (SSSIs). Of the 37 AONBs in England 19, a little more than half, have more than the 6.6 per cent national proportion of SSSIs per square kilometre, and of those 13, a little more than a third, have more than double the national proportion. Some AONBs have a very high proportion of their area designated, particularly on the coast, for example. Arnside and Silverdale, Chichester Harbour, Norfolk Coast, Northumberland Coast, South Hampshire Coast and Solway Coast, and in the uplands

Table 2.10   Wildlife significance of English AONBs

AONB	Area sq km	NNR Area ha	NNR % of AONB	SSSI Area ha	SSSI % of AONB	cSAC Area ha	cSAC % of AONB	SPA Area ha	SPA % of AONB	Ramsar Area ha	Ramsar % of AONB
Proportion of England area	—	—	0.5	—	6.6	—	3.8	—	2.6	—	1.3
Arnside & Silverdale	85	115	1.4	3809	45	3276	38.5	3057	35.9	3042	35.8
Blackdown Hills	419	4	0.1	670	1.6	0	0	0	0	0	0
Forest of Bowland	905	0	0	16 516	18.2	0	0	16 000	17.7	0	0
Cannock Chase	100	0	0	1385	13.9	0	0	0	0	0	0
Chichester Harbour	90	0	0	3101	34.5	2778	30.9	72	0.8	72	0.8
Chilterns	1031	175	0.2	3527	3.16	515	0.5	0	0	0	0
Cornwall	1367	1572	1.1	12 945	1.5	8639	6.3	27	0.1	0	0
Cotswolds	2336	654	0.3	4415	8.7	1144	0.5	0	0	0	0
Cranborne Chase	1087	369	0.3	3434	5.9	445	0.4	0	0	0	0
Dedham Vale	126	0	0	187	1.5	0	0	50	0.4	50	0.4
Dorset	1308	575	0.4	11 366	8.7	6173	4.7	523	0.4	523	0.4
East Devon	326	303	0.9	1939	5.9	1737	5.3	0	0	0	0
East Hampshire	447	241	0.5	1211	2.7	487	1.1	210	0.5	0	0
High Weald	1631	0	0	5137	3.1	0	0	3196	1.9	0	0
Howardian Hills	255	28	0.1	160	0.6	0	0	0	0	0	0
Isle of Wight	300	264	0.8	2631	8.8	4320	14.4	0	0	0	0
Isles of Scilly	n/a	n/a	n/a	n/a	n/a	n/a	n/a	n/a	n/a	n/a	n/a
Kent Downs	1093	98	0.1	4667	4.3	349	0.3	0	0	0	0
Lincolnshire Wolds	640	0	0	96	0.1	0	0	0	0	0	0
Malvern Hills	139	0	0	1168	8.4	0	0	0	0	0	0
Mendip Hills	248	74	0.3	2713	10.9	553	2.2	572	2.3	0	0
Nidderdale	696	0	0	19 167	27.5	0	0	0	0	0	0
Norfolk Coast	542	6135	11.3	9886	18.2	9457	17.4	8758	16.1	8856	16.3
North Devon	245	0	0	3768	15.4	2675	10.9	0	0	0	0
North Pennines	2158	7229	3.3	79 716	36.9	46 979	21.7	3884	1.8	0	0
North Wessex Downs	1886	396	0.2	3394	1.8	264	0.1	0	0	0	0
Northumberland Coast	200	2092	10.5	4296	21.5	7584	37.9	2386	11.9	2322	11.6
Quantock Hills	128	0	0	2696	21.1	0	0	0	0	0	0
Shropshire Hills	953	447	0.5	4793	5.0	600	0.6	0	0	9	0.1
Solway Coast	192	209	1.1	7666	39.9	7589	39.5	6418	33.4	6418	33.4
South Devon	461	202	0.4	2231	4.8	751	1.6	0	0	0	0
South Hampshire Coast	112	295	2.6	3467	30.9	2800	25.0	1122	10.0	1122	10.0
Suffolk Coast & Heaths	526	920	1.7	9446	17.9	3061	5.8	7821	14.9	5475	10.4
Surrey Hills	561	319	0.6	4824	8.6	2507	4.4	2176	3.9	263	0.5
Sussex Downs	1142	308	0.3	6589	5.8	662	0.9	194	0.2	0	0
Tamar Valley	n/a	n/a	n/a	n/a	n/a	n/a	n/a	n/a	n/a	n/a	n/a
Wye Valley	260	67	0.3	1487	5.7	574	2.2	0	0	0	0

Source: DETR, *Countryside Information System*, derived from English Nature data, SSSIs (1997), NNRs (1997), cSACs (1997), SPAs (1998), Ramsar (1998).

– for example, the Forest of Bowland, Nidderdale and the North Pennines – see illustrations in Plates 22 and 23. The extent of National Nature Reserve, Special Areas of Conservation (SAC), Special Protection Area (SPA) and Ramsar designations is not so widespread. However, the table does reveal that there is a significant group of some 14 AONBs which seems to have a particular concentration of the national and international designations: Arnside and Silverdale, Forest of Bowland, Chichester Harbour, Cornwall, Dorset, Isle of Wight, Norfolk Coast, North Devon, Northumberland Coast, North Pennines, South Hampshire Coast, Solway Coast, Suffolk Coast and Heaths and the Surrey Hills. In the four Welsh AONBs, 13 per cent are designated SSSI, 2.4 per cent NNR, 3.3 per cent Ramsar and 12 per cent SAC.[12]

ARCHAEOLOGY AND HISTORY

Archaeological and historic features are crucial in defining the importance of AONB landscapes, as the Dorset example shows; indeed most of the landscape assessments make some mention of them. However, there is no national picture of whether there are any particular concentrations of their national interest in AONBs. An examination of a map of scheduled ancient monuments overlaid by AONB boundaries (Plate 24) suggests that there may well be a higher than average proportion in some areas. Discussions with English Heritage reveal that such conclusions should be treated with some caution as there tend to be more easily identifiable features in designated areas, which have greater areas of pasture and moorland.

In England there has been no attempt to define important historic landscape areas. In contrast in Wales, CADW and the Countryside Council for Wales have identified a number of nationally important historic landscapes. Interestingly AONBs feature strongly with such areas being identified in Gower, Lleyn, the Wye Valley and the Clwydian Range. There is no doubt that they are full of history but that is of course true of the whole countryside. However, the fact that one can cite so many places of national importance that are in AONBs is a measure of their significance: the archaeological interest of all Welsh AONBs, Cranborne Chase and the North Wessex Downs; the ancient field systems in West Penwith, Cornwall; the mining heritage of Cornwall, the Mendips and the North Pennines; the religious communities of Anglesey and Northumberland, Tintern Abbey in the Wye Valley and Fountains Abbey in Nidderdale; designed landscapes such as Studley Royal in Nidderdale, Stourhead in Cranborne Chase and Castle Howard in the Howardian Hills; the architectural interest of market towns and villages in the Cotswolds, stone built farms in the Forest of Bowland and the oast houses of Kent. Examples are illustrated in Plates 25 – 29.

POETRY, ART AND MUSIC

AONBs have a special association with poetry art and music: for example, the Wye Valley, so movingly described by Wordsworth, in Dorset, Hardy's Wessex; Dedham Vale, the 'Constable Country'; Cornwall with its school of painters at St Ives and Newlyn; the Shropshire Hills, an inspiration to Housman and Vaughan Williams; the Suffolk Coast and Heaths, which include 'the Borough', Crabbe's setting for that most English of operas, Britten's *Peter Grimes*.

PLACES FOR PEOPLE

AONBs also have a special place in the minds of people: local communities proud of their living and working environments; city dwellers relaxing in nearby countryside, the Surrey Hills, Chilterns or Cannock Chase; tourists exploring the coast of Cornwall, Devon and Dorset and areas like the Cotswolds, which are on the international tourist map; sailors in Chichester Harbour, Poole Harbour or the estuaries of the Suffolk Coast; and walkers along the network of national trails such as the Pennine Way, the South Downs Way and the South West Coast Path. Indeed 17 of the 41 AONBs are traversed by 11 of the 12 national trails in England and Wales. Furthermore the public has access to these areas over an extensive network of rights of way.

THE ECONOMIC VALUE OF AONBs

Enjoyment by the public leads to another reason why AONBs are of such importance: their contribution to the local and national economy. This is a point that will be discussed in later chapters. However, it is important to record at this point the scale of support to the local economy that visitors to conserved landscapes bring. Recent research by the National Trust in south-west England has shown that 78 per cent of all trips to the region (12.6 million trips annually) are motivated by conserved landscape. These trips are estimated to last 67 million bed-nights each year with a visitor spend of £2,354 million. A total of 54,000 full-time equivalent jobs are supported directly or indirectly by such trips.[13]

Commentary: AONBs – a treasury of nationally important natural and cultural resources of great economic value

This chapter portrays the immensely varied geographical features of the family of AONBs, as well as the wide variety of nationally important resources that they contain. There is no doubt that their wildlife, historical and recreational qualities, as well as their scenic qualities, need to be more fully recognised in the legislation that underpins the designation in the same way as for National Parks. This would provide a sound basis for projecting their collective national importance, among both the general public and those directly involved with their well-being. At the same time it is also crucial that the value of AONBs to the local and national economy, resulting from their inherent qualities, needs to be fully recognised.

References

1   Countryside Commission and English Nature, *The Character of England: Landscape, Wildlife and Natural Features*, CCX41, Cheltenham, 1996.

2   *Countryside Information System:* developed by DETR to provide computerised access for policy advisers, planners and researchers to spatial information about the British countryside and to hold the results of the Countryside Surveys. The designated area information for AONBs in England is based on the presence or absence of a designation in each km square. Accordingly the area is slightly overestimated by the existence of a 'buffer' of up to 1 km around the designated area's edge. Thus care should be exercised in the use of the figures for anything but general indication of scale and distribution. The information for Wales is based on the actual area of a designation within each km square, giving a total density value. So comparison between England and Wales should be treated with caution.

3   Ibid.

4   *Protected Areas Funding Study*, report by Environmental Resources Management for the Countryside Commission, London, 1998.

5   Department of the Environment, Transport and the Regions, *Access to the open countryside in England and Wales*, a consultation paper, London, 1998.

6   Countryside Commission, Evidence to the public inquiry into the designation of the North Pennines AONB, Cheltenham, 1987.

7   Ministry of Town and Country Planning, *National Parks in England and Wales*, Cmd 6628, HMSO, London, 1945.

8   Letter from the Department of the Environment to the Countryside Commission, 11 September 1986.

9   Countryside Commission, *The Dorset Downs, Heaths and Coast Landscape*, CCP 424, Cheltenham, 1993.

10   Countryside Commission, *Landscape Assessment Guidance*, CCP 423, Cheltenham, 1993.

11   Countryside Commission, *Fit for the Future: Report of the National Parks Review Panel*, CCP334, Cheltenham, 1991.

12   DETR, *Countryside Information System*, derived from English Nature and Countryside Council for Wales data, SSSIs (1997), NNRs (1997), cSACs Wales (1997),cSACs England (1998), SPAs England (1998) and Ramsar (1997).

13   National Trust, *Valuing our Environment*, a study of the economic impact of conserved landscapes and of the National Trust in the South West 1998 by Tourism Associates, London, 1999.

What has been happening to AONBs? 3

The previous chapter looked at some of the characteristics of AONBs and why they are nationally important. The final chapter of Part III of the book looks at the changes that have been taking place in their fabric and at the changing pressures that are being applied to them by a wide range of influences. Yet one thing is certain: they are dynamic areas that have not been set in 1940s stone.

Difficulties arise when one starts to consider the comparatively simple question of what has been happening to AONBs. When AONBs were designated no work was undertaken to establish what the state of the landscape actually was, and furthermore, no statement was prepared about the character of the landscape or why it was of national importance. While all areas, except North Wessex Downs, now have such landscape assessments, only in the late 1990s were such statements prepared as part of the designation process in the case of the Blackdown Hills, Nidderdale and Tamar Valley. The assessments provide an excellent analysis of the qualities of each AONB; however, they do not provide a systematic basis for measuring and monitoring change, but rely on scraps of information about particular features in the landscape and on qualitative judgements. Furthermore it seems that none of the AONB management plans prepared so far has tackled this issue as fully as it deserves.

Changes in their fabric

So how can one begin to get some measure of change in the fabric of AONBs? First, one can get a feel for what has been happening from national data on the loss of habitats as shown in Table 3.1. Although these figures relate to the countryside in general, one can be certain that there will have been some degree of change as AONBs have not been immune from the forces at work, particularly agriculture, as is shown in Plates 33 – 36. The picture can be built up further by the use of such data that are available from individual AONBs in their

Table 3.1   National figures of loss or condition of landscape features

- 95 % of lowland grassland and hay meadow in England disappeared or were improved between 1947 and 1983 [1]

- 80 % of chalk downland was lost between 1947 and 1983 – in the county of Dorset 25 % of downland was lost in the 1950s and 1960s reducing the 19th century figure of 28,000 ha to 3000 ha [2]

- 40 % of lowland heath has been improved for agriculture or afforested [3]

- between 1984 and 1993 there was a net loss of 158,000 km of hedgerow in England, one third of the total that existed in 1984 [4]

- of the 112,600 km of dry-stone walls in England in 1994 only 13 % were in good condition, with another 38 % still stockproof. None of the rest was stockproof and 29 % were derelict [4]

- of the 123 estuaries in England, Wales and Scotland surveyed in 1989 by the RSPB, 80 were considered to be under some degree of threat, with 30 in imminent danger of permanent damage [5]

- between 1946 and 1984 44 % of heather moorland was lost in the Berwyn Mountains in Wales [6]

- of the 13 major habitats in Wales, CCW estimates that at least 8 are still declining either in quantity, quality or both [6]

Sources:
1–3   Evans, D., *A History of Nature Conservation in Britain*, 2 ed., Routledge, London, 1997.
4   Countryside Agency, *State of the Countryside 1999*, CA3, Cheltenham, 1999.
5   RSPB, *Turning the Tide, a Future for Estuaries*, Sandy, 1990.
6   Countryside Council for Wales and Forestry Commission, *A Living Environment for Wales*, 1999.

Table 3.2   Examples of changes in the landscape from AONB management plans and landscape assessments

Blackdown Hills	Rough grazing declined by 17 % between 1983 and 1997
Chilterns	Chalk grassland declined by 35 % between 1961 and 1980, 70 % between 1940 and 1980 5000 ha of the 15,000 ha of woodland is either unmanaged or inadequately managed
Cotswolds	The area of limestone grassland has reduced from about 40 % of the area in 1935 to 2 % today 47 % of the ancient woodland has been replanted as intensive forestry, mainly in the 1950s and 1960s
Dedham Vale	80 % of hedgerow trees were lost to Dutch Elm disease
Dorset	70 % of chalk downland was lost between 1934 and 1972 86 % of heathland has been lost
East Hampshire	Grassland and rough grazing decreased by 20.7 % between 1970 and 1988
Forest of Bowland	25 % of the 2222 km of dry-stone wall is derelict
Kent Downs	10 % of the woodland area was lost between 1961 and 1990, 8 % to agriculture and 18 % to development
Lleyn	Between 1920 and 1980s 51 % of dry heath and 95 % of wet heath was destroyed, most of it converted to agriculture
Mendip Hills	Identified as a 'hot spot' for the decline in farmland bird species by the RSPB in its biodiversity study of south-west England
Suffolk Coast	8 % of the Sandlings (heathland) lost this century, only 1700 ha left
Sussex Downs	25 % of chalk downland lost between 1966 and 1980 to agricultural improvement and scrub invasion

management plans and landscape assessments. Table 3.2 gives examples of figures culled from these sources.

It is impossible to deduce from the figures how much change has been taking place in AONBs. They simply confirm that the landscape is not standing still and that change tends to be for the worse, that is, through the loss of key features such as downland, heathland and woodland. They also show that in certain instances it is the lack of management rather than agricultural intensification that is causing the change: the deterioration of stone walls in Bowland, unmanaged woods in the Chilterns and a lack of grazing of downland in the Sussex Downs. That protected landscapes are not immune from change is shown by the results of the survey carried out in the National Parks.[1] In the period 1978 to 1988 there was an 11 per cent loss of rough pasture, 11 per cent increase in coniferous forest, 13 per cent increase in cultivated land, and 5 per cent increase in developed land.

Loss of tranquillity

A significant change that is giving increasing concern is the loss of 'tranquillity' in the countryside, caused by visual or noise intrusion from development or traffic. In 1995 the Council for the Protection of Rural England (CPRE), with the help of the Countryside Commission, published a map of England identifying tranquil areas.[2] They are places considered to be unspoilt by urban influences. Plate 30 provides a broad-brush picture of England. It was prepared at a regional level, ignoring local effects. The criteria for the definition of these areas are set out in Box 3.1. The exercise was enhanced by the comparison between the situation in the early 1960s and the early 1990s, which showed a significant decrease in tranquillity.

A perusal of the map shows that in the 1990s there are few significant areas of tranquillity. CPRE identified only three areas where rural tranquillity is so extensive that it is still possible to walk for 50 km or so in more than one direction without encountering major disturbance: north Devon extending into Cornwall and Somerset, the Welsh Marches and the Pennines north of Skipton. Such continuous areas of tranquillity covered most of rural England in the 1960s. Other extensive areas are the Lake District, east Yorkshire, Lincolnshire and north Norfolk. The illustrations in Plates 31 and 32 show examples of AONBs where open space and tranquillity are at the heart of their character.

As can be seen from the illustrations in Plates 37 to 40, many AONBs have suffered a loss of tranquillity and are increasingly hemmed in by urban development, notably those in the South East (Chilterns, Surrey Hills, Kent Downs, High Weald, Sussex Downs and East Hampshire).

BOX 3.1

Generalised criteria for the definition of tranquil areas

A tranquil area lies

- 4 km from the largest power stations

- 3 km from the most highly trafficked roads such as the M1 and M6; from large towns (e.g. the size of Leicester and larger) and from major industrial areas

- 2 km from most other motorways and major trunk roads such as the M4 and A1 and from the edge of smaller towns

- 1 km from medium disturbance roads, i.e. roads which are difficult to cross in peak hours, and some mainline railways

- beyond military and civil airfield/airport noise lozenges as defined by published noise data, and beyond very extensive opencast mining

Within tranquil areas the following linear elements are shown as creating a lower level of disturbance 1km wide:

- low disturbance roads

- 400 KV and 275 KV power lines

- some well trafficked railways

Within tranquil areas various sites also fall into this lower category, including large mining or processing operations, groups of pylons or masts, settlements greater than 2,500 in population, some half abandoned airfields and most windpower developments.

Source: Council for the Protection of Rural England and Countryside Commission, *Tranquil Areas in England,* 1995.

In contrast many of those along the coast of the South West (North Devon and Cornwall AONBs) and East Anglia (Norfolk Coast) and in the northern hills (North Pennines and Bowland) have changed relatively little and retain a relatively high degree of tranquillity. Significant numbers of AONBs are affected by traffic corridors, notably Dorset, Cranborne Chase, North Wessex Downs and Cotswolds.

A detailed study has been undertaken in the Sussex Downs.[3] It concluded that while no part of the AONB is completely free from distant noise on a still day, there is a high degree of remoteness/tranquillity to be found in the western half of it. In the eastern half there is a much greater degree of fragmentation, but it is still possible to find valleys where there is minimal disturbance.

Rural communities

While change in the fabric of the landscape is clearly central to the future of AONBs, it is also important to consider the state of rural communities and the way they are changing too, as a reminder of the fact that they are living and working landscapes. In Chapter 2 it was shown that a significant proportion of AONBs are wholly or partly within areas designated as RDAs and are within EU Objective 5b areas, both of which are indicators that the socio-economic health of their communities is not in a good state. This is an important matter when considering the future of many AONBs, as the pressure for creating economic activity and improving services could well have a detrimental effect on the qualities of the landscape, unless handled in accordance with the principles of sustainable development.

The availability of services in rural communities gives a measure of the range of problems experienced by those living within them. Table 3.3 sets out some of the key findings of the 1997 Survey of

Table 3.3 Availability of services in rural parishes

42 %	had no shop
70 %	had no general store
43 %	had no post office
28 %	had no village hall/community centre
75 %	had no daily bus service
49 %	had no school
29 %	had no pub
83 %	had no GP in the parish

Source: Rural Development Commission, *Survey of Rural Services*, Salisbury, 1997.

Rural Services.[4] Whilst these figures are for rural areas generally, there is no doubt that the communities in AONBs are not immune from these problems, as shown by data from the Sussex Downs in Table 3.4. Indeed for some of the remoter AONBs the problems are very serious, a situation that is recognised by their designation as RDAs and benefit from support under the EU structural funds. It is vital for those looking after AONBs to consider not only the health of the landscape but also of their communities, since the future of both is inextricably linked.

One matter of particular importance, because of its increasing impact on the countryside, is traffic and transport. Traffic is growing faster on rural roads than elsewhere. Between 1981 and 1997 traffic increased in non-built up (rural) areas by 75 per cent compared with 23 per cent in built up (urban) areas. Furthermore people in rural areas rely more heavily upon the car as their means of transport, with 84 per cent of households having a car compared with 69 per cent nationally. Such dependence on the car is no doubt caused in part by the poor public transport facilities in rural areas, where 75 per cent

Table 3.4   Rural Service provision in the Sussex Downs AONB

Parishes WITHOUT the following services	SDCB Area % without	East Sussex % without	West Sussex % without	England % without
VILLAGE SERVICES				
Permanent Shop	46	15	29	39
Post Office	52	26	37	40
Pub	22	7	10	26
EDUCATION				
Primary School	63	35	38	51
COMMUNITY FACILITIES				
Village Hall/Community centre	25	9	19	29
HEALTH CARE				
GP (Resident or visiting)	71	46	48	84
TRANSPORT				
Bus service (6 days per week)	46	78	62	63

Source: Sussex Downs Conservation Board, *Rural Community Needs*, 1993.

of rural parishes in 1997 had no daily bus service, 65 per cent had no service 6 days a week and 93 per cent had no rail service. When one considers the availability of services in rural areas (see Table 3.3) one can begin to understand the dependence on the car. Equally problematic is the fact that a significant proportion of households has no access to cars.

Perceptions of pressures on the landscape

The various figures quoted earlier in this chapter have given an impression of the changes that have taken place to some of the key features of AONBs. In the absence of more comprehensive data one has to rely on the perceptions of those people who are involved in AONBs as to the change and the pressures being experienced. The remainder of the chapter is devoted to those perceptions.

Chapter 1 indicated that in 1949 the prevailing attitude to the protection of nationally important landscapes was via a thriving agricultural industry strongly controlled by government and through development controlled by local authorities. Perhaps this was not surprising when the intensification of farming was unforeseen, agriculture employed a significant proportion of the rural population, there were few pressures for housing and industry, commuting had not become such a feature of life, there were relatively few visitors and car ownership and use were not widespread. Also it is generally accepted that economic activity changed dramatically in these protected landscapes and AONBs have been, and continue to be, under significant pressures.

The most recent test of people's perceptions of today's pressures on AONBs was in the Countryside Commission's consultation paper 'Providing for the Future' in 1997,[5] the main purpose of which is described in Chapter 4. The document listed the pressures as:

- New patterns of agriculture and woodland management affecting landscapes;
- Greater development pressures from housing, mineral extraction, road building and improvements, wind power stations, tourism and recreation;
- Adverse changes to the special character and qualities of AONBs;
- Changing patterns of recreation and more visits than in some National Parks;
- Significant alterations in the local economy and society.

The analysis of the replies to the consultation[6] showed that 90 per cent either strongly agreed or agreed with the Commission's interpretation of today's pressures on AONBs, citing the following particular issues:

- Greater development, including housing development;
- New agricultural patterns;
- Changing recreation patterns;
- Increasing visitor numbers;
- Tourism generally as opposed to visitor numbers;
- Car use;
- Economic and social change;
- Loss of identity/uniqueness;
- New patterns of woodland management;
- Infrastructure development.

As a number of the respondents pointed out, these issues are not unique to AONBs but are the same as those facing the whole countryside. The essential difference is, of course, that AONBs are nationally recognised landscapes and need to be treated as such if they are to be conserved. It was also pointed out that each AONB is unique, and that pressures vary in both location and intensity. This is an important point which emphasises the need to have a full understanding of all the forces for change that are operating in the area of each AONB. However, it is equally important to have a comprehensive view of what is happening to all AONBs as an aid to policy formulation. That such an overview does not really exist, except in the general terms set out by the Commission, must be a matter of concern. The development of such an overview would almost certainly depend on each AONB having one of its own area.

The Protected Areas Funding Study,[7] the purpose and import of which is also described in Chapter 4, through a survey of AONB Units, identified similar pressures on AONBs as shown in Table 3.5.

It shows that *agri-pastoral change* is clearly seen as the greatest pressure, in particular:

- Intensification and loss of species rich grassland;
- The CAP context and competition between price support and agri-environment accompanying measures;
- Changing management practices such as undergrazing and scrub invasion;
- Loss of traditional features such as hedgerows, stone walls and traditional orchards.

Table 3.5 Development Pressures in English AONBs

Development pressure	No. of AONBs ranking highest pressure	No. of AONBs ranking second highest pressure
Agri-pastoral change	13	8
Development control and planning		
• Housing	3	3
• Minerals	0	1
• Energy development	0	1
Recreation and tourism	7	5
Traffic and transport	7	7
Coastal defence	1	1

Source: *Protected Areas Funding Study*, report for the Countryside Commission by Environmental Resources Management, London, 1998.

It also shows the *significance of recreation and tourism as a pressure*. Few AONBs have figures to show the number of visitors each year. However, the quantities from the 12 AONBs that were able to give data show very significant numbers that are comparable with some National Parks as indicated in Tables 3.6 and 3.7.

The list of AONBs in Table 3.6 does not include the latest figures for the Chilterns which has a staggering 52.0 million leisure visits per year, and Dorset, where just the small Purbeck part of the AONB has 4.0 million visitors each year (see case studies in Appendix 2), and others like the Cotswolds and the Surrey Hills, for which no figures

Table 3.6   Visitor numbers in AONBs

AONB	Visitor numbers per annum (million)	Visitor days per annum (million)
Cannock Chase	2.5	
Chilterns		8.0 – 10.0
Cornwall	2.5 – 3.0	
Malvern Hills	1.5	
Mendip Hills	2.0	
Norfolk Coast	1.3	
North Pennines	1.2 bednights	3.3
South Devon	3.5	
Suffolk Coast	5.0	
Sussex Downs		32.5
Isle of Wight	2.7	
Wye Valley	2.0	

Source: *Protected Areas Funding Study*, report for the Countryside Commission by Environmental Resources Management, London, 1998.

are available, but it is well known that visitor numbers are very high. Overall the Study estimated that in excess of 100 million visits are made each year to all AONBs. If the figures for the Sussex Downs and the Chilterns are to be believed, the total figure could be well in excess of 100 million.

Illustrations of the nature and scale of recreation in AONBs are given in Plates 41 to 45. As will be seen in Chapter 6, pressures from visitors are manifest in a number of ways: conflicts between conservation, local communities and visitor numbers at honey-pot sites, on coastlines and along footpaths, leading to erosion and congestion along roads and at car parks and an overall loss of character and

Table 3.7   Visitors numbers in National Parks in England

National Park	Day trips (million)	Holiday (million)	Total (million)
Broads	1.62	3.78	5.40
Dartmoor	1.75	2.05	3.80
Exmoor	1.05	0.35	1.40
Lake District	3.61	10.29	13.90
North York Moors	4.40	2.80	7.80
Northumberland	0.56	0.84	1.40
Peak District	8.06	4.34	12.40
Yorkshire Dales	2.82	5.48	8.30
TOTAL	24.00	30.00	54.00
New Forest	2.97	3.63	6.60

Source: 'All Parks Visitor Survey' 1994, quoted in *Protected Areas Funding Study*, op.cit.

tranquillity. Nationally, demands for active sports are growing, particularly from water sports, cliff climbing, flying, cycling, riding and golf, and caravanning and camping.

Discussions with AONB managers during research for this book confirmed the importance of recreation and tourism. Not only is it an issue that had to be tackled because visitors come whatever, but also because it is seen in quite a number of AONBs as a positive force for helping the local economy and the protection of the environment. However, when one considers that the statutory basis of AONBs, unlike National Parks, does not refer to recreation, one is bound to reflect on whether there is cause for modification of the statutes, because the role they are playing is so similar to that of National Parks. This is an issue that is considered later.

Development pressures were also seen as ever-present, related to housing: in particular latent pressures associated with housing allocations, creeping infill and demands for social housing; suburbanisation close to AONB boundaries especially around coastal conurbations; demands for second and holiday homes; barn conversions and poor design. Minerals and waste management and wind farms were also seen as significant threats.

Few AONBs were able to provide estimates of the number of planning applications. Those quoted in the Funding Study seem, not surprisingly, to reflect the size and land use of the AONB with

- Low numbers (less than 300 per annum) in Cannock Chase, Mendip Hills, Solway Coast, which are small AONBs;
- Medium numbers (300 – 1000) in East Hampshire and the Chilterns;
- High numbers (more than 1000) in the Sussex Downs and South Devon.

The Study concluded that some 30,000 planning applications a year might affect AONBs as a whole. These figures give some indication of pressure, but they do not help in terms of the impact of development on the landscapes of AONBs generally or specifically, for which there is little systematic evidence.

Some long-term trends likely to affect AONBs

One of the great challenges for AONBs is the recognition and understanding of long-term trends, and the preparation for and reaction to them. Experience, including the well-known turn of events since the Scott Committee made their assumptions about the role of farming in 1949, has shown that forecasts of this kind should be treated with the greatest caution. Nevertheless, the following long-term trends in climate, lifestyles, and the use of the countryside, widely acknowledged in recent scenarios,[8] could have considerable implications for AONBs. Some examples are illustrated in Plates 46 to 48.

CLIMATIC CHANGE

Global warming, perhaps by a mean of 1 degree centigrade (possibly two degrees in the UK) in the next 50 years, may gradually result in the high summer temperatures in the UK, theoretically occasional events, becoming a common occurrence, with accompanying drought. An associated trend could be a marked increase in winter storms. Likely impacts on AONBs could include:

- Sea level rise, probably up to 30cm, more in some parts of the coast; this would affect the landscape character and biodiversity of estuaries and other low-lying coastal habitats, reduce the recreational capacity of beaches and less stable cliffs, and cause continuing pressure for coast protection.

- Low summer flows in rivers. This would reduce the quality of wetland habitats and landscapes and would require long-term, comprehensive management of hydrological change, including much storage of water for needs such as farm irrigation.

- A wider range of crops being used by farmers, with a longer growing season. This could intensify agricultural methods, damaging habitats and the traditional pastoral landscape.

- Increased damage to natural vegetation from fires, drought and gales. Heath and woodland, both of which can have high ecological and landscape value, would be particularly at risk during summer, and woodland in winter.

- A continued drive by government towards renewable energy. Uplands and the coastal landscape would especially be threatened by wind-farms, onshore and offshore.

- A similar drive for more afforestation, with species capable of absorbing greenhouse gases. If well planned, this could be of benefit to landscape and ecological quality.

CHANGES IN LIFE-STYLE

Advances in telecommunications and information technology, coupled with increasing difficulty in urban travel, will cause continued pressure for development in villages and the countryside. Equally, more varied working patterns, early retirement, longer and fitter lives, and implementation of the Government's proposals for access, are already increasing leisure demands. The likely impacts on AONBs could include:

- Further inflation in rural property prices, reflecting growing demand for living and working in the countryside. Attractive inland and coastal areas would be particularly affected by increases in second homes and holiday lettings, to the disadvantage of less well-off local residents and community life generally; remoter areas, however, could gain socially and economically from an infusion of new residents. In either case, new development might reinforce the current tendency for the countryside to become 'suburbanised'.
- Considerably increased and more widely distributed recreational pressure, a trend also resulting from global warming. This would apply especially in areas with attractive landscape, wildlife and cultural resources, inland and coastal. Peak use-levels, such as now experienced at major holiday times, could become a frequent occurrence, although information technology may become an important management tool in efforts to redistribute pressures. There would also be a wider seasonal spread of visitors, even in remote areas. 'Activity' recreation, such as watersports, camping and caravanning, trail walking, and cycling, could show continued rapid growth.
- Overall there would be a very considerable build-up of traffic on rural roads. An increase of 75 per cent, merely between 1981 and 1997, was noted earlier in this chapter. The loss of tranquillity has been, and will be, most noticeable.

CHANGES IN MAJOR LAND USES

Some consequences for farming and forestry have been noted above, but market conditions and agricultural policy may well have other significant effects. The farming industry itself could continue to experience serious economic problems; it is suffering from a long-term trend of falling incomes, and pressures from major food retailers and from liberalisation of world trade may well continue to drive down prices, possibly raising production costs too. These problems would be compounded by uncertainty about the future scope of agricultural policy. Forestry, too, is likely to be under continuing pressure to increase the area of woodland, for a variety of social, economic and environmental reasons. The impacts of these trends on AONBs, some of which are already being experienced, could include the following:

- Continued restructuring of the agricultural industry, with more emphasis on business methods, closer integration of production

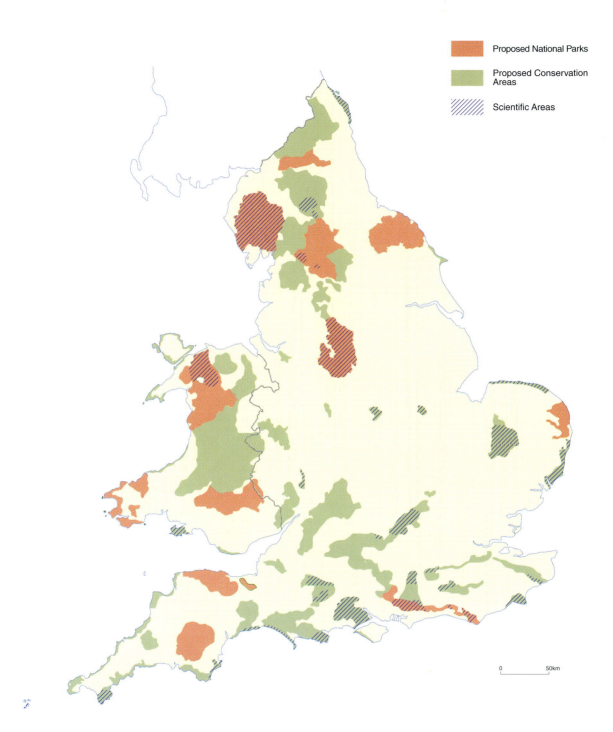

0   50km

Plate 1   Map of National Parks, Conservation Areas and Scientific Areas as proposed by the Hobhouse and Huxley Committees, 1947.

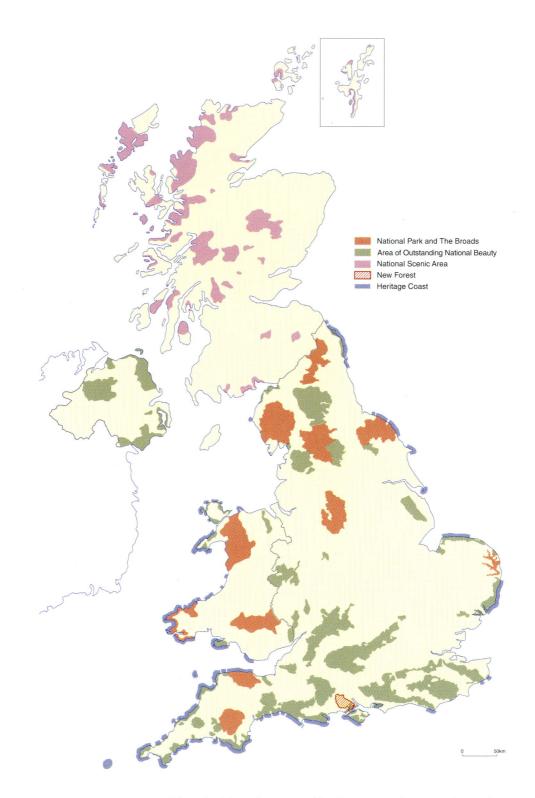

Plate 2 Map of protected landscapes in the United Kingdom, 2000.

National Park and The Broads
Area of Outstanding National Beauty
National Scenic Area
New Forest
Heritage Coast

0   50km

(a)

Protected landscapes in the United Kingdom (1)

Plate 3 The National Parks and AONBs of England and Wales are of the same high quality and are often of a similar character, Dartmoor National Park (a) and Nidderdale (b).

(b)

(a)

Protected landscapes in the United Kingdom (2)

Plate 4   The same qualities are displayed in the National Scenic Areas of Scotland, e.g. Loch Lomond, now proposed as a National Park (a), and in the AONBs of Northern Ireland, e.g. Mountains of Mourne (b).

(b)

Plate 5 Map of Areas of Outstanding Natural Beauty, Heritage Coast, and National Trails in England and Wales, 2000.

Character of AONBs – upland moors

Plate 6 The moors of northern England and north Wales have a very particular character, a sense of wilderness and tranquillity, as shown in the North Pennines (a) and the Clwydian Range (b).

(a)

(b)

**Character
of AONBs –
lowland heath**

Plate 7 The extent of lowland heath has diminished greatly. Its value, particularly for nature conservation is now recognised internationally. Most of the significant areas that remain are within AONBs, e.g. in the Surrey Hills.

(a)

Character of AONBs – woodland

Plate 8 The extent of woodland in AONBs is often considerable, e.g. in the Kent Downs (a) and the Howardian Hills (b). The need to ensure their proper management is a major task.

(b)

(a)

(b)

Character of AONBs – river valleys

Plate 9 River valleys are focal points of a number of AONBs and are often associated with extensive woodlands, e.g. the Wye Valley (a) and the Tamar Valley (b).

(a)

(b)

**Character
of AONBs –
estuaries**

Plate 10   Estuaries, particularly the drowned valleys of south-west England,
are not only key elements of the landscape but are often popular for
recreation, e.g. South Devon (a). In some places, e.g. the Isle of Wight (b),
tidal creeks with mudflats provide peace and tranquillity.

(a)

Character of AONBs – hard coast

Plate 11 Dramatic cliffs and rocky coves are an essential element of the coastal AONBs found in south-west England and in Wales, e.g. North Devon (a) and Lleyn (b).

(b)

(a)

(b)

**Character
of AONBs –
soft/low coast**

Plate 12   Low cliffs, sweeping bays backed by sand dunes and coastal
marshes are typical of many of the AONBs on the east and south coasts
of England, e.g. Northumberland (a), and South Hampshire (b).

(a)

Character of AONBs – Downs and Wolds

Plate 13 Rolling downland or wolds, with extensive arable fields and a feeling of open space, are the bases of a large number of AONBs in southern and eastern England, e.g. Sussex Downs (a) and Lincolnshire Wolds (b).

(b)

(a)

Character of AONBs – pastoral mixed farming

Plate 14 Pastoral, mixed farming landscapes are often thought to be the essence of AONBs. They are an important component of some but by no means all, e.g. Dorset (a) and Cotswolds (b).

(b)

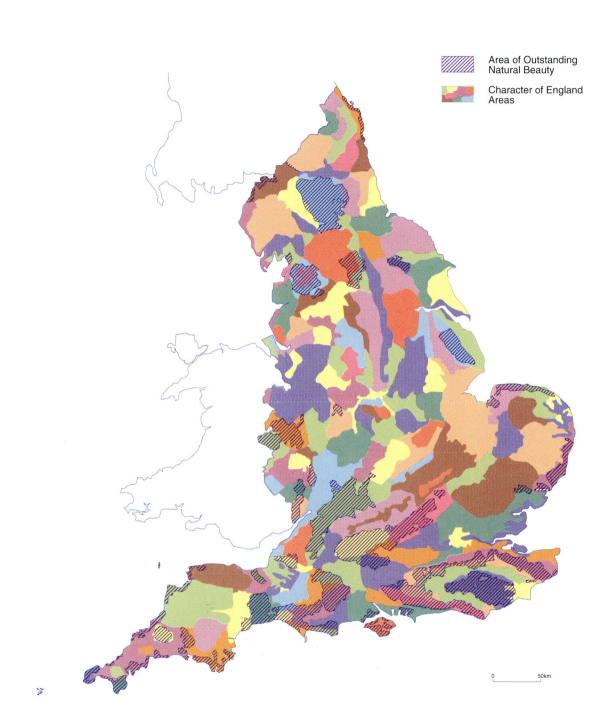

0   50km

Plate 15 Map of Areas of Outstanding Natural Beauty and Character of England Areas.

(a)

(b)

Character Areas and AONBs

Plate 16 Some AONBs are very similar in extent to those defined by the Countryside Commission and English Nature as Character Areas, e.g. The Isles of Scilly (a), which is exactly the same, and the Chilterns (b).

and retailing, larger farms, contract working, and diversification of enterprises. Major restructuring could further weaken links between farmers and communities as more local jobs are lost in the industry. Increasing scale and intensity of farming operations could place continued pressure on landscape and biodiversity, and the use of large machinery and delivery vehicles would make more demands on narrow rural roads. Diversification, on the other hand, even though it could have occasional traffic consequences, should be beneficial to local economies and communities, especially in remote and upland countryside, where the alternative might well be the abandonment of land in marginal areas.

- An increase in the area of land devoted to forest and to farm woodland. As noted above, this would often be a bonus to landscape and wildlife quality, also to recreation and tourism, especially if accompanied by better standards of woodland management.

- The possibility that future agricultural policy could reinforce the existing sectoral approach, and further reduce price support. This would place even greater economic pressures on farmers to intensify production, with continuing well-known damaging effects on the environment.

- The alternative possibility that agricultural policy might give greater priority to integration between farming and other rural policies, giving worthwhile support to rural development and environmental initiatives and encouraging farmers to take on new roles. This would bring clear benefits to the countryside and its communities.

- The use of genetically modified crops. If proved to be safe and if properly regulated, GM crops could be advantageous to society and be introduced without serious environmental damage. On the other hand, there are justifiable fears that, if grown on a large scale without a proper understanding of the consequences, GM crops could have a profoundly adverse effect on biodiversity, and on the relationship between agricultural systems and landscape quality. Of all the trends affecting agriculture, GM is perhaps the most unpredictable.

Commentary: adverse change and growing pressures but the total picture is missing

Any discussion of change and pressures on the landscape tends to assume that it is for the worse. This is not surprising when agriculture and forestry have destroyed some of the key landscape features, inappropriate development has intruded into the scene and large numbers of visitors with their cars impose themselves on fragile sites. However, as the Countryside Commission pointed out in its Advice to Government[9] (see Chapter 4), the picture is not all negative: there has been considerable success on the planning front; agricultural policies, after years of being unhelpful, are now helping to manage and restore the landscape through agri-environment schemes (ESAs/CS/Tir Cymen); and forestry grants are more sympathetic.

Nevertheless, there is no doubt that the landscapes of AONBs have changed and that the change has all too frequently been for the worse. This is a point that will be picked up in later chapters. There is also no doubt that the principal agent of change in AONBs is the result of agricultural activity, recreation, and development. Furthermore it is clear that their communities are under considerable stress too. The similarity between AONBs and National Parks in terms of visitor numbers is striking and raises the very real question of whether AONBs should have an explicit statutory recreational purpose.

It is a sad indictment of the world of AONBs that the exact amount of change has not been recorded, whether for the better or worse. The nature of the evidence to support this view is not comprehensive in the sense that each AONB has a database. However, a perusal of each landscape assessment and management plan will reveal a high degree of commonality of the issues. What is clear is that AONBs need a much more thorough understanding both of the landscape and the way it is changing and of the pressures being exerted on it, both from within by their own communities and from outside, particularly from visitors, and the extent to which change is for the better or worse.

As was pointed out earlier, there is a great deal of uncertainty about long-term forecasts of trends such as those mentioned above. This extends to their nature, their overall effects, and their timing. Some, such as those concerned with changes in life-styles, may be predicted with more confidence than others, for example those affecting major land uses such as agriculture. Some may be relatively immediate in their consequences; others may only be experienced gradually over many years. Although the trends listed here, if they materialise, are likely to affect the countryside generally, their impacts could be more pronounced in protected areas because of the high quality of their landscape, wildlife and cultural resources. The message for AONBs is twofold. First, national scientific and socio-economic research into environmental futures will continue to be of the utmost importance to policy for these areas, and their managers must maintain a constant watch on the implications of research findings. Second, with so much uncertainty about the trends themselves and their effects in particular situations, sustainability and flexibility will continue to grow in importance as criteria to be met by all policy decisions, national and local, for AONBs. To this end, the need for up-to-date systematic knowledge of the natural and community resources of each area, advocated in this book and elsewhere, becomes all the more important. It will help the trends to be anticipated and effectively guided as they arise.

References

[1] Countryside Commission, *Landscape Change in National Parks*, CCP 359, Cheltenham, 1991.

[2] Council for the Protection of Rural England and Countryside Commission, *Tranquil Areas Map*, 1995.

[3] *Tranquil Areas: Sussex Downs*, report for the Sussex Downs Conservation Board by the ASH Consulting Group, 1997.

[4] Rural Development Commission, *1997 Survey of Rural Services*, Salisbury 1997.

[5] Countryside Commission, *Areas of Outstanding Natural Beauty: Providing for the Future*, CCP 523, Cheltenham, 1997.

[6] Countryside Commission, *Areas of Outstanding Natural Beauty: Providing for the Future, an Analysis of Responses to the Countryside Commission's 1997 National Consultation*, CCWP 08, Cheltenham, 1998.

[7] *Protected Areas Funding Study*, report by Environmental Resources Management for the Countryside Commission, London, 1998.

[8] For rural areas see for example:

Countryside Commission, *Climate Change, Air Pollution and the English Countryside*, CCP 458, Cheltenham, 1995.

Countryside Commission, *Fit for the Future, Report of the National Parks Review Panel*, CCP334, Cheltenham, 1991, pp.137-142.

Lloyd, R., paper to the Countryside Agency Enterprise and Agriculture Seminar, Cheltenham, 1999.

Cadbury, J., How might Global Warming affect the UK's Flora and Fauna?, *RSPB Conservation Review No. 9*, RSPB, Sandy, Bedfordshire, 1995, pp.48-52.

RSPB, *Genetically Modified Crops and Bio-diversity*, Sandy, Bedfordshire, 1998.

[9] Countryside Commission, *Protecting Our Finest Countryside: Advice to Government*, CCP532, Cheltenham, 1998.

Part Two
Recurrent Themes

The first three chapters, forming the first and contextual part of the book, have shown that AONBs are important in national terms not only for the value of their landscape, and that they have been, and still are, under widespread pressure from changes which are a source of great concern. Part Two consisting of Chapters 4 and 5, now looks at the response to this threatening situation. It describes the development of policies and management arrangements for AONBs at both the national and local levels, and comments on the important influences over the present situation of these areas. An understanding of this development is essential as a basis for considering later what further improvements are necessary.

The development of national policy for AONBs   4

Chapter 4 now traces the gradual (and as yet unfinished) clarification of policy at the national level. The need for clarification can be directly attributed to the acknowledged shortcomings of the 1949 legislation, but the fact that thirty years were to pass before the first policy review points to the low priority then given to AONBs in countryside affairs. Since then, further interest in policy-making has tended to come to a head at ten-year intervals and each review has been more wide-ranging. That interest says a lot for the increasing recognition of the importance of AONBs and the plight that they have been facing. The chapter concludes with a short account of developments in the international context.

The 1980 AONB review

The whole sequence of events recounted in Chapter 1, especially from the 1960s onwards, and the growing impact of the changes outlined in Chapter 3 must have contributed to the decision of the Countryside Commission (CC) in 1978 to make its first review of AONB policy.

The review began with a discussion paper issued by CC, a national conference on AONBs, and the appointment of Kenneth Himsworth, a former National Park Officer, to report on how far the statutory purposes of designation had been achieved. The discussion paper[1] posed fundamental questions. Should AONBs be scrapped? Should some designations be withdrawn? Should their administration be put on a comparable footing to National Parks? Should agriculture and forestry grants and controls in AONBs be different? Himsworth's report, published in 1980,[2] and the general tenor of the response to the discussion paper, gave the system a relatively clean bill of health, and opposed any major changes in administration, even the establishment of more advisory committees (which existed in only a minority of AONBs). Himsworth advocated the acceptance of recreation as a proper function in AONBs. He thought every AONB should have a management plan, and recommended that exchequer grant, via CC, be increased from the current level of 50 per cent to 75 per cent, and should include core costs. All this was to the good, even if one is left wondering how, without changing the administrative arrangements, the management plans would be prepared and implemented.

On the question of agriculture, however, whose serious landscape impact had been recognised in the discussion paper, there was little that Himsworth could do, having regard to the strength of the lobby against its regulation, other than recommend closer consultation between AONB authorities and the local farming community and its advisers. Could more have been expected?

The review led to the first major policy statement on AONBs proposed by CC and considered by government. In its final form, issued in 1983,[3] it was accompanied by a statement to Parliament by the Secretary of State, Michael Heseltine, giving general support to the Commission's work on AONBs, for which 'the legislation was adequate'. The preface, written by the Chairman, Derek Barber, nevertheless admitted that the benefits of AONB status to rural communities were poorly understood. Against this background, the policies covered:

- completion of the designation programme with a possible further six AONBs, making a total of 39;
- clarification of the purpose of designation, treating recreation as a demand to be met where consistent with conservation, and safeguarding the economic and social needs of rural communities;
- encouragement to the formation of Joint Advisory Committees, including representatives of amenity groups and land-user interests, in multi-county AONBs, and the nomination of an officer to co-ordinate action in each area;
- encouragement to the preparation of Statements of Intent for all AONBs, with an offer of grant-aid for management plans in areas of land-use conflict;
- setting out principles for development control:
  - structure and local plans should emphasise the conservation of natural beauty;
  - major industrial and commercial projects should be regarded as inconsistent with the aims of designation, except when in the national interest and where no alternative is possible;
  - mineral-working and major roads should be examined with particular care, to assess need and environmental effects;
  - small-scale industries, etc., should be in sympathy with the local environment;
  - informal 'notification' arrangements should be made with farmers for agricultural buildings, etc.;

– government departments and agencies should improve their local consultations on major developments in AONBs.

It needs to be said that CC's draft of these policies had been watered down here and there as a result of the Secretary of State's views. Examples of this include the advocacy of Joint Advisory Committees 'only in multi-county areas', and more escape clauses in the wording of policy for major development issues. Another significant alteration concerns the treatment of agriculture. Going much further than Himsworth, CC had wanted to adopt for AONBs the farm capital grant consultation procedures already operating in National Parks, but the Secretary of State, after consulting the Minister of Agriculture, considered that 'the present arrangements are working satisfactorily'. Disappointed by this somewhat partisan view, all that CC could do in the circumstances was to advocate informal notification, backed by the hope that the conservation responsibility laid on government departments under Section 11 of the 1968 *Countryside Act* would be adequate.

Undoubtedly the policy statement was a major step forward, but it had its weaknesses. The pressures mentioned elsewhere in the book were by no means fully addressed. Much would depend, in any case, on the attitude of local authorities, not all of which saw AONBs as a priority in their areas. It was necessary to watch the situation closely, and CC was therefore right to establish a further review only a few years later. Meanwhile its newly published AONB Directory[4] enabled the main characteristics of each area and the administrative position in it to be set out (and updated) on a consistent basis.

The 1989/90 AONB review

For this further review Professor Gerald Smart and Dr Margaret Anderson were engaged to outline progress in AONB planning and management, to note changes affecting the areas (for example, trends in agriculture and recreation, and policy relationships with the wider countryside), and to suggest any new directions for the Commission.

Four main concerns, namely damage to landscapes, habitats and historic resources, growing recreational pressures, difficulties in meeting the needs of local communities, and resource problems provided the background to their work. They saw the main strength of AONBs as the value of designation to development control. Of the weaknesses, 'positive conservation was thin on the ground, and hardly affected agriculture (which has caused most change in AONBs)'. They also noted a remarkable lack of consistent data on the fabric of AONBs. They attributed many of the weaknesses to a low level of

public expenditure, itself often resulting from poor public understanding of the needs of AONBs. Only £1.5 million of CC's annual
grant-aiding budget of £12.25 million was being spent on them, at
rates between 25 and 40 per cent of total project costs. This compared
most unfavourably with nearly £20 million contributed to the National
Parks, including supplementary exchequer grant covering more or
less their full administrative costs. AONBs were the 'Cinderellas' of
protected areas.

Smart and Anderson[5] made two sets of recommendations: immediate and longer-term. They sought the urgent establishment of more
Joint Advisory Committees, with their own budgets, and the appointment of a full-time officer (supported by CC grant) in each AONB,
whose main responsibility would be to prepare, implement and monitor a management plan for the whole area. These committees should
not be limited only to multi-county areas; they had a unique value
even in areas with only one or two local authorities because they were
the best means of bringing all management and user interests together
in a working partnership.

To meet their concern about finance, the authors recommended a
new awareness campaign, leading in the longer term to substantial
additional funding. Their view that current levels should be doubled,
focused on a limited number of 'priority' AONBs and was necessarily
subjective, as they were not able to conduct a comprehensive survey
of financial requirements. The point was that substantial investment
was required, and it was thought that local authorities might give
higher priority to their own funding in AONBs if this need was
recognised in central government expenditure controls.

On the difficult issue of farming, AONBs, they said, are 'working
landscapes', the health of which is affected by innumerable decisions, requiring a broad co-operative approach. Professional liaison
had a very important role to play here, especially in conservation-
based farming. They recommended that the concepts underlying the
new Environmentally Sensitive Areas should be applied widely in
AONBs.

Their report concluded with a brief look at the designation programme. This should run its course, after which new AONBs should
be designated only exceptionally, as there was a danger of 'debasing
the currency'. Chancing their arms, so to speak, they hinted that in
the longer term thought should be given to replacing the current
range of countryside designations by a 'more broadly based categori-
sation reflecting multiple resource values and uses'.

As a result of the review, CC issued a new policy statement in 1990
and republished it a year later jointly with the new Countryside Council
for Wales.[6] Michael Heseltine, Secretary of State for the Environment,
contributed a very supportive personal statement, looking forward to

seeing it 'positively applied by all involved'.

The new policies differed from those announced in 1983 in the following ways:

- there should be further efforts to help decision-makers to be more aware of the importance of AONBs, in the interest of greater commitment – these efforts should include the publication of landscape assessments for each area;
- Joint Advisory Committees should be established in all AONBs and, where possible, should manage their own budgets;
- AONB staff units should be set up in the more complex areas, grant-aided for six years;
- schemes for new major roads should avoid AONBs wherever possible;
- management plans are urged for all AONBs;
- management action should aim to encourage more sensitive farming and forestry, to provide for recreation, to improve the environment and to encourage the voluntary sector and local communities in this;
- there should be better staff training ;
- 'pump priming' grants would be considered for management, and further finance would be sought from government for a limited number of AONBs where special attention is needed.

In addition to these improved policies, the statement contained useful explanations of the approach of CC and CCW to the main policy issues, and guidance on their implementation. However, the statement was disappointing so far as the case for improved agri-environment policies was concerned and, as will be seen below, additional finance for AONB management did not materialise.

The 1990s: a further look at the financial and administrative needs

During the next few years CC issued several consultation papers on policy for the countryside generally. These were influenced by another new factor, the wider national and international environmental debate about sustainability and biodiversity. Although not entirely new, these key concepts called for a broader and longer-term perspective to planning, and thus touched upon the future of protected areas, their resource needs, and their place in the countryside as a whole.

This applied especially to AONBs. Responding to policy guidance, many of them now had Joint Advisory Committees, over half had management plans, and a number of AONB Officers had been appointed, admittedly on short-term contracts. Despite efforts by CC to obtain more money from government for AONBs, studies showed that the total amount being spent by it and by local authorities was only increasing at the rate of inflation. No special long-term funding had become available, nor was there secure money to meet continuing needs. There had indeed been considerable progress in setting up administrative mechanisms for AONB management, but apart from the experimental Sussex Downs Conservation Board, a very important initiative which is described in Chapter 5 and in the Sussex Downs case study in Appendix 2, this was being done on a shoe-string, and positive action was still thin on the ground. It was clear to CC and CCW that, without additional funding, the quality of AONB landscapes would suffer from the cumulative effects of different pressures, and much of the value of past public investment would be lost.

Thus, in 1997, CC issued a new consultation paper subtitled 'Improving the Funding and management of England's AONBs'.[7] (Studies were also in hand in Wales, see below.) In this it set its sights at around £14 million required annually, mostly by local authorities, for the 37 English AONBs, as compared with the current total spending of about £7 million. This would bring spending nearer to the total budget of £23 million for the seven English National Parks and the Broads Authority. The paper sought comments on new approaches for obtaining the complementary requirements of secure core funding and additional moneys for special projects: it suggested a special AONB Grant Scheme to cover core costs, a Challenge Fund for priority projects, and the establishment of funding Trusts. An important quid pro quo in the whole concept would be to strengthen legislation to improve long-term management of AONBs: a statutory duty to conserve them, and the ability to promote formal Conservation Boards, based upon the favourable results of the Sussex Downs experiment.

There were nearly 400 responses to the paper. About half came from local authorities and AONB Joint Committees, and there was encouraging interest from voluntary organisations. CC's assessment of pressures on AONBs (see Chapter 3), and the consequent case for more resources commanded much support, but opinions were more varied on the approaches to funding and management. The proposed legislation was widely favoured, although the creation of Conservation Boards raised fears about the danger of a two-tier approach within the 'AONB family', a concern that had been voiced by local authorities at the time of the 1989/90 review. Similarly, the financial proposals received strong agreement as the best way to get long-term secure funding, although there were some reservations about project money; this ought to be settled on need rather than by means of challenge, which could be divisive. Overall, the responses gave top priority to the need for special AONB funding, and the next priority to placing a special duty on local authorities to manage AONBs.

This exercise must have given the Commission a solid base for recommendations to government on resources for AONBs, and on the various ways in which they might be raised. What, however, should be the actual level of funding? The amount of £14 million identified in the Consultation Paper (and noted as being comparable to the need mentioned by Smart and Anderson to 'double' expenditure) had been rapidly assessed by Commission staff. Clearly there was a case for a more formal investigation than had been possible at the time, and to place this in a total context of protected area requirements by including the National Parks. Consultants were therefore engaged in the autumn of 1997 to undertake a 'Protected Areas Funding Study',[8] on which they reported in March 1998.

For National Parks, they recommended additional funding needs of £12.95 million per annum, of which over £5 million would be an additional National Parks Grant (then running at around £17 million), and over £7 million would represent extra spending by other public agencies, principally MAFF and the Forestry Authority.

For AONBs, despite the serious lack of key data (for example, on landscape trends and on recreational pressures – see Chapter 3) total funding of £18.5 million to £19.5 million per annum was recommended, about half for AONB management units and half for project costs. This is somewhat higher than the Commission's earlier estimate of £14 million, due to the amount of detailed study the consultants were able to give to the problem, especially the core functions, for which they had examined a range of management models. It was also clear that they thought further very considerable sums would be required for agri-environment schemes, over and above current Ministry of Agriculture spending of £9 million in just 12 of the 37 English AONBs.

A parallel study was set up by CCW early in 1998 to look at ways in which the five Welsh AONBs might be put on a firmer financial footing to protect them from the pressures they were facing. Reporting in April 1998,[9] this study recommended the formation of AONB units and formally constituted Advisory Committees for each. The total costs, currently £234,000 per annum, would need to be some £877,000 per annum, and it was recommended that, for comparability with National Parks, the level of grant-aid should be increased from 50 to 75 per cent, requiring an additional sum from government funds of £220,000.

It can be seen that 1998 was an important year in the history of AONBs, with very clear messages about their administrative and financial needs being sent from the then Countryside Commission and CCW. These messages, in the form of Advice to Government,[10] were based on detailed examination of their activities and consultation on the issues facing them, and the way forward in the future. Importantly the advice was based upon common agreement as to the issues facing the conservation of these nationally important landscapes. Similarly, as will be seen below, 1999 was also important with the promotion of an AONB Bill in the House of Lords by Lord Renton, the Chairman of the Sussex Downs Board. Although it did not reach the Statute Book it set out some important points for the Government to consider (see page 76). The question is to what extent would these initiatives, if successful, really solve the problems of AONBs and protected areas more generally?

In proffering its advice, the Countryside Commission invited government to endorse the principles which, it argued, should underpin the approach to protected countryside in the future (see Box 4.1). It also set out the core functions that needed to be undertaken in order to address the pressures on the landscape of AONBs (see Box 4.2). While this advice appears to be a comprehensive list of functions there

---

BOX 4.1

Principles for Managing Protected Countryside

- Appropriate and effective management and funding arrangements are essential if protected countryside is to be secured for future generations

- Each area of protected countryside should have the management and funding arrangements appropriate to the varied needs of its locality

- It should be recognised that carrying out statutory functions requires secure long-term support from public funds

- The authorities responsible for protected countryside, in collaboration with each other, should continue to give high priority to securing funding from non-government sources – but non-government funds should be seen as supplementary to this, not as a substitute for them

- The policies and activities of all departments of central and local government should reinforce the statutory purposes of protected countryside

Source: Countryside Commission, *Protecting Our Finest Countryside, Advice to Government*, CCP 532, Cheltenham, 1998.

- Developing the coherent vision for AONB management and the supporting strategy

- In the early stages, delivering pilot and area-wide projects that promote the coherent vision and help to distinguish the AONB from adjacent countryside areas

- Co-ordinating the implementation of the management strategy

- Providing input to local authority policies that are relevant to the AONB

- Co-ordinating or advising on local authority and other organisation activities to ensure they are consistent with the vision and compatible with management objectives

- Promoting the need for value-added local authority services in the AONB, to go beyond the normal level of service in countryside management

- Monitoring and reporting on progress against management strategy targets

- Accessing resources for undertaking management activities, including external financing, project development and proposals, and providing matching funding for special projects

- Tapping into advice, and liaising with AONBs at a national level

Source: Countryside Commission, *Protecting Our Finest Countryside, Advice to Government*, CCP 532, Cheltenham, 1998.

BOX 4.2

Core Functions for AONBs

do seem to be some notable omissions, in particular there is no reference to:

- monitoring of the health of the AONB (as distinct from progress on the implementation of the management strategy);
- engaging the local communities in the AONB;
- the means of securing action amongst the stakeholders as part of the AONB partnership.

Most of CC's advice was aimed at policies of government, statutory agencies and the local authorities. This is outlined in Box 4.3. While the suite of policies put forward make a lot of sense, a great deal would depend on drawing people into partnership, and to persuade others who do not necessarily have AONBs as their top priority to be active in looking after them. Whether the proposed statutory duty for public bodies to have regard to the conservation of AONBs, mentioned in the next paragraph, will be sufficient is open to question.

BOX 4.3

Policy Advice to Government, Statutory Agencies and Local Authorities

- **Planning and Transport** – government should give a lead in its planning decisions to demonstrate to others the very high degree of protection AONBs should enjoy, and highway authorities and the Highways Agency should become active partners

- **Agriculture and Forestry** – all AONBs should be covered by special agri-environment schemes, and incentives for woodland management should be targeted at them

- **Recreation and Tourism** – authorities managing AONBs should have the costs of providing management services for visitors and recreation allocated from the public purse

- **Cultural Heritage** – English Heritage should increase the level of grants for historic buildings and ancient monuments

- **Funding** – 50% of funding should come on a regular basis from central government, and a special-projects fund should be established administered by the Commission

Source: Countryside Commission, *Protecting Our Finest Countryside, Advice to Government,* CCP 532, Cheltenham, 1998.

While experience in the past suggests that only the minimum is done, it is important to record that a number of accords now operate between statutory agencies and the National Parks following the introduction of a similar duty with respect to National Parks in 1995.[11]

There were, however, a small number of important legislative proposals to strengthen the statutory basis of AONBs:

- statutory duties for local authorities to pursue the objectives for which AONBs were designated and for producing statutory management plans;

- local authorities, where they wish, may discharge their duties to administer AONBs through the formal constitution of Conservation Boards. The purposes of the Boards, their power and membership, including powers to levy locally, should be proposed locally and confirmed nationally, through secondary legislation; the responsibilities of the Board to include being:
    - statutory consultees on planning matters, with the right to be heard by the local planning authority;
    - consultees on the development of recreation policies and plans;
    - consultees on agricultural policy and the delivery of agri-environment schemes as they affect the area.

- an explicit statutory obligation on all public bodies (including local authorities) in exercising their functions in relation to or so as to affect an AONB, to have regard to the need to conserve and enhance the natural beauty of the AONB, similar to the obligation introduced for National Parks in 1995.

The importance of these proposals should not be underestimated. Sadly, however, they fail to address a number of key issues, which can only be dealt with through the legislative process. Most significant is the silence on extending the statutory purposes of AONBs, at least to be the same as National Parks, that is, to embrace wildlife conservation, the cultural heritage, recreation and socio-economic issues. Similarly, despite lengthy discussion of development issues, there are no proposals to make a formal link between AONBs and the statutory planning system, for example, by making the Joint Advisory Committees statutory consultees on development control and development plan issues, and giving management plans a place in the development plan process. Finally, apart from the proposals for Conservation Boards, which are only likely to be adopted by a small minority of AONBs, and the suggestion of a range of management models, the advice does not advocate any requirement for an organisation to deliver the core functions. Given the scale of the core functions which need to be undertaken, and the proposals for long-term funding of AONB administration, such an omission is somewhat surprising.

The paper also made specific recommendations for extra protection of the South Downs (the Sussex Downs and East Hampshire AONBs) and the New Forest, both of whose future had been of long-standing concern nationally and locally. As shown in the case study for Sussex Downs (see Appendix 2), CC recommended a statutory Conservation Board (as proposed for AONBs generally), rather than designation as a National Park, which could not be justified against the criteria of the 1949 Act. For the Forest, their advice was in line with the results of extensive consultations by the existing New Forest Committee, that special legislation should set up a tailor-made Authority which can build upon existing accepted arrangements. This would recognise the status of the Forest as equivalent to a National Park, and would provide it with secure resources, as for other National Parks. Interestingly, the proposal for a New Forest National Park raises the question of what to do with the South Hampshire AONB, part of which is in the New Forest Heritage Area. This is discussed below.

An interesting sting in the tail is contained in the Commission's advice to the effect that, if these arrangements (duties for local authorities, management plans and conservation boards) cannot be achieved, the only mechanism available to confer the needed protection for AONBs would be through the use of the National Park provisions of the 1949 Act. While the CC was not keen on the ideas for reason of extra demands on the public purse, and administration in excess of the needs of AONBs, implicit behind the thinking must be the similarity between the needs of quite a number of AONBs and National Parks, a point made in this and earlier chapters.

The CCW Advice to Government[12] differs from that of the Countryside Commission in a number of important ways, reflecting the fact that there are only four AONBs wholly in Wales and they are relatively small by comparison with those of England. While it does not go into the same detail as the CC's advice, it was based on a fairly critical look at each AONB in Wales. Its advice matches that of the Commission in a number of respects: duties for local authorities to manage AONBs and to prepare management plans. The main differences are the suggestion of 75 per cent rather than 50 per cent funding from central government and the absence of any discussion of Conservation Boards. CCW also introduced the concept of 'State of the Environment' reporting for AONBs as a basis for management plans. There is a further difference in the nature of the discussion in Wales: the position of the new Welsh Assembly. It has a duty to pursue sustainable development. Accordingly there is much greater emphasis in its advice on the integration of policy between landscape, biodiversity, cultural and socio-economic functions, and on the use of protected landscapes to act as test-beds for sustainable development.

Both advice papers have been widely welcomed, and the reception from government has been promising. Local authorities have commented favourably upon the importance placed upon secure central support of core funding, and the higher status that establishment of a formal Conservation Board can give to English areas. This will bolster leadership 'from the front', and attract greater commitment and support from local authorities, public agencies and voluntary sector bodies, such as The National Trust. Nevertheless, a number of AONB authorities appear to feel that a too formal approach to organisation may ruin the very informality that brings their partnerships together.

The Renton Bill 1999

In May 1999 Lord Renton, Chairman of the Sussex Downs Board, introduced a private members bill into the House of Lords that addressed some of the shortcomings of the 1949 Act in relation to AONBs.[13] It was introduced more with the aim of creating awareness of the issues in Parliament and trying to engender some urgency into government thinking on the matter than in the expectation of it reaching the statute book. The main elements of the Bill survived the committee stage, with a small number of amendments upon which there was no disagreement. It is important to note that for the first time :

- AONBs would be given statutory purposes, that include not only the conservation of natural beauty but also of wildlife and the safeguard of those areas from intrusive development, and that all relevant bodies (government departments, public bodies, statutory undertakers, etc.) are given a duty to have regard to the need to conserve and enhance the natural beauty of AONBs in performing their functions;
- local planning authorities would be given a duty to promote the conservation and management of AONBs;
- there would be provision for the establishment of Conservation Boards and Advisory Councils to advise them;
- the preparation of management plans for AONBs would be mandatory;
- local authorities would have a duty to contribute financially and the Secretary of State for the Environment the power to do so though only in the case of Conservation Boards;
- local planning authorities would be required to incorporate the provisions of the management plan in preparing their development plans, and to consult a Conservation Board on the plan and on planning applications.

If such a Bill were to receive Royal Assent, it would clearly represent a major step forward for the conservation of AONBs. However, there are a number of matters that it did not address. While it introduced purposes relating to the conservation of landscape and wildlife, it did not address cultural matters, which are recognised as being of great importance in many areas (see Chapter 2) and are very much interwoven with the other purposes. No reference was made to public enjoyment, recreation and access. Given the acknowledged importance of the areas for such activity (see Chapter 2), this was surprising. In the Committee debate Lord Renton indicated his support for an explicit reference to this activity, but he had been persuaded by the CC not to introduce it in the Bill. The Bill was also silent on socio-economic matters, local communities and sustainability. This was recognised in the House of Lords debates and was a matter which the Government indicated considerable sympathy. CC's Advice to Government was modified by the new Countryside Agency in June 1999 to include reference to socio-economic issues in relation to AONBs – an important early decision for it. Given the inextricable link between the high quality resources that form the basis of AONBs and the local communities and local economy, this recognition could mark a turning point in their history. Whether there should be a primary or subsidiary purpose relating to these matters will be considered in the final part of the book.

A further shortcoming of the Bill was the different way that Conservation Boards, of which only a few would be established, and the remainder of AONBs were treated. That may not be surprising given the provenance of the Bill in the South Downs. However, it is very important that the right framework is established for all AONBs, rather than for just a few. The key points are these. First, in AONBs where no Conservation Board is established, there would be no requirement for any form of joint committee or advisory body, which not only brings together the local authorities but also all those who have a stake in the area (landowners and farmers, local communities, national organisations, and so on) and could play the role of 'champion' for the AONB. Second, the financial provisions related solely to Boards, thus leaving the local authorities in the rest of the AONBs with a duty but, seemingly, no finance from central government. Finally, the existence of a Board would lead to much stronger representation of the AONB in the planning process, that is, there would be an organisation to be consulted and to make representations to the Secretary of State. This would not be the case in AONBs with no Board.

The response of government

The response from government has taken a long time in gestation. By the time of the Queen's speech in November 1999, no conclusion had been reached on AONBs as a whole, despite very encouraging words from John Prescott and Michael Meacher, the Ministers involved.[14] The only conclusions reached were in relation to the South Downs and the New Forest, for which National Parks in the terms of the 1949 Act are the Government's preferred solution. Subsequently, in June 2000, in response to amendments to the Countryside and Rights of Way Bill tabled by Gordon Prentice MP, Mr Meacher announced that the Government would bring forward amendments to the Bill in the House of Lords to strengthen the conservation and management of AONBs. He also referred to the threefold increase in government funding for AONBs over the three years 1998 to 2000 and said that government funding would continue to be available for work with local authorities in managing AONBs in partnership.[15] The implications of this are promising, though the outcome, especially in terms of legislation, is as yet uncertain. However, the two National Park proposals raise an interesting issue about the family of protected landscapes in relation to their enjoyment by the public.

In the case of the South Downs, CA has been asked to reconsider its interpretation of the criteria for designation of a National Park. The main reason for the South Downs not achieving National Park status in the past has been the failure to meet the criterion for recreation, because of a lack of 'wilderness areas'. In asking the Agency to review its interpretation of the criterion (not the criterion itself) the Government has said that it is no longer appropriate to restrict National Park-type management of protected countryside to predominantly open and rugged countryside. It has suggested that more account should be taken of the need to provide improved open-air recreation for the population at large, and close to where people live.[16]

In the New Forest the proposal for a National Park raises a similar issue in relation to recreation, with the need to consider whether the South Hampshire AONB meets the criteria for National Park status and therefore is capable of being absorbed within it. There is no doubt that the quality of the landscape is on a par with the New Forest, and indeed much of the AONB is within the New Forest Heritage Area. Although none of the open forest, the 'wilderness' that would be at the heart of the Park, is within the rest of the AONB, the area is popular for recreation, including sailing; nature conservation is of international importance, and the coastal birdlife and open views over marsh and saltings are enjoyed by increasing numbers of visitors. The National Park boundary proposed in July 2000 by CA for consultation rightly includes the whole AONB.

This questioning of the interpretation of the designation criteria throws into doubt the difference between National Parks and AONBs. As shown in Chapter 2, AONBs are very popular with visitors despite the lack of the 'wilderness' experience that is the hallmark of National Parks. A reassessment of the kind of recreation experience appropriate for a National Park would leave their respective administrative arrangements as the only difference between National Parks and AONBs.

Scotland

As mentioned in Chapter 1, England and Wales were not alone in considering the future of protected landscapes. In Scotland, Scottish Natural Heritage (SNH) has recently provided advice to government on how it might proceed with the designation of National Parks, and how the management of National Scenic Areas (NSAs), which are similar to AONBs, might be improved.[17,18] A number of very useful points have emerged from the advice, which are, as suggested in Chapter 1, relevant to the discussion of AONBs and to protected landscapes generally.

First is that a common vision for National Parks in Scotland seems to be gaining currency, which brings together a range of social, economic and environmental objectives that should be delivered through an integrated approach. In its advice SNH suggested that the vision for National Parks should include the following:

- provision of a greater clarity of purpose for some of Scotland's most special areas;
- higher standards of environmental stewardship;
- engendering of trust between national and local interests in the delivery of conservation and community objectives;
- pioneering of techniques of sustainable development.

Second, in considering the purposes of National Parks, an integrated approach is adopted, which has led SNH to propose the following purposes:

National Parks in Scotland are areas of outstanding natural heritage of special importance to the nation where management in perpetuity will:
- safeguard and enrich the biodiversity, natural beauty and amenity, the natural systems which support these qualities, and the cultural heritage of the area;
- promote the sustainable use of its natural resources;
- promote the social well-being and economic prosperity of its local communities; and
- provide for and enrich the enjoyment and understanding by the public of its natural and cultural values.
- These purposes should be pursued in ways, which are mutually supportive. The resolution in the event of any conflict between them shall be guided by a precautionary approach in favour of the long-term conservation of the natural resources.

Third, SNH has suggested that, in addition to defining the purposes of National Parks, legislation should define the broad criteria to inform the development of proposals for potential National Parks (see Box 4.4). In addition to the requirement for the area to have outstanding qualities, there is an emphasis on local support for any proposals and for an integrated approach to be relevant and of benefit to the area.

Fourth, there is no intention to make the National Parks planning authorities, as they are in England and Wales. This is particularly interesting since the question of planning is prominent in the debate over National Park status for the South Downs, and whether the responsibility for this should stay with the local authorities or be exercised by the National Park Authority. It is also interesting in the light of known difficulties that National Parks have with their local communities over planning.

- **Natural heritage importance:** the area should be of outstanding importance to the nation for its natural heritage, or for the combination of its natural and cultural heritage

- **Coherent identity:** the natural resources of the area should have both a distinctive character and a coherent identity

- **Support:** there should be local and national support for the area to be designated a National Park

- **Needs and benefits:** the integrated and focused approach to management provided by National Park designation should meet the special needs of the area and provide more benefits than other approaches

- **Scale and complexity:** the area should be large enough to secure the long-term future of the natural resources and to enable the pursuit of multiple objectives through integrated management.

Source: Scottish Natural Heritage, *National Parks for Scotland, Advice to Government,* Perth, 1999.

BOX 4.4

Criteria for National Parks in Scotland

Fifth, and somewhat surprisingly, the advice that goes to the Government in Scotland in relation to NSAs does not seem to embrace the kind of integrated approach that is being advocated for their National Parks. It seems likely that the single purpose of NSAs will be retained.

Parks for Life and the European Landscape Convention

While this chapter has focused on the development of policy for AONBs and for other designations in Scotland, it is important to recognise at this stage that there is a developing international context. Indeed over the last century or more, there has been a world-wide movement towards the establishment of national systems of protected areas, including protected landscapes. The most recent edition of the *United Nations List of Protected Areas*[19] reveals a global network in excess of 30,000 protected areas. The 41 AONBs designated in England and Wales are part of this network.

Of particular importance is the programme developed by IUCN, 'Parks for Life', following the World Congress on National Parks and Protected Areas held in Caracas in 1992.[20] It aims to put Protected Areas at the centre of strategies for sustainability rather than promoting them as areas apart from the rest of the world. The UN Conference on Environment and Development held in Rio de Janeiro in June 1992 also confirmed the importance of protected areas in the sustainable development process. The link between protected areas and people was firmly forged.

Parks for Life: Action for Protected Areas in Europe was published in 1994[21] in response to the call of the Caracas Congress for regional plans to be prepared to help link the global with the local. For the first time there is a protected area programme for Europe. Its purpose is to ensure an adequate, effective and well-managed network of protected areas in the region. It sets out the policies and actions each country should take to look after and improve its protected areas, and outlines the action needed at an international level. The programme was the result of a unique partnership. Over 200 organisations and individuals contributed to its preparation and agreed a shared vision. Its main messages and action points are:

- Protected areas include some of the most beautiful landscapes and finest wildlife sites, but equally important is their role in reflecting different cultural heritages, sustaining local communities and providing educational and recreational – even spiritual – experiences for millions of people;

- The isolationist view of protected areas – seeing them as capable of surviving, as oases in a desert, set aside from the main stream – should be buried; instead they should be seen as 'jewels in the crown', where both the jewels and their setting can be devalued by the desecration of the other;

- Protected areas cannot alone achieve a nation's sustainability and biodiversity objectives, but they can play a significant part; they should not be considered in isolation from broader economic and social policies but, instead, they should be integrated into policy decisions across the whole range of government activity and brought to the centre of strategic thinking and planning at local, national and international levels;

- The planning and management of protected areas should be strengthened through an effective legal framework, effective institutions, management plans, adequate funding, training and information and monitoring systems;

- A European network of protected areas should be developed to secure an adequate coverage of landscape and habitat types and to cover the needs of flora and fauna;

- Protected areas cannot co-exist with communities that are hostile to them; new partnerships are needed – involving local communities and promoting the benefits of protected areas more widely will increase public and political support and create the climate necessary for their long-term survival.

The programme called upon each country to set up a national forum to promote the European Plan at national level. Following its UK launch in 1994 by the Secretary of State for the Environment, a Task Force was set up under the auspices of the IUCN-UK Committee to examine the implications for the UK. The Task Force, with representation from all four UK countries, published a report in 1996.[22] Among the six action projects suggested in the report was one to produce a vision for protected areas (including protected landscapes) in the UK in the twenty-first century and to advise government on the strategic framework necessary to achieve that vision. At a subsequent workshop it was agreed that better sense should be made of the present system of protected areas and that in the long term, there will need to be a review of the protected area system to improve delivery, reduce misunderstanding and clarify the overall rationale.[23]

Although the UK was the first nation to follow up the European Action Plan, its recommendations have yet to be taken any further by the IUCN-UK Committee or indeed by the Government or its agencies. Given the amount of discussion about these issues at present – AONBs in England and Wales, National Park Status for the South Downs and the New Forest, National Parks and NSAs in Scotland and SSSIs throughout Great Britain – this is clearly a missed opportunity.

One of the main recommendations of the European 'Parks for Life' programme was for the Council of Europe to implement a convention on rural landscape protection in Europe. This idea, which had already been suggested by the European Environment Agency in its report 'Europe's environment, the Dobris assessment', has now been adopted by the Council of Europe's Congress of Local and Regional Authorities of Europe (CLRAE). It is actively pursuing a European Landscape Convention, with a planned starting date of 2000.[24]

The emphasis is on what each signatory state should do to foster landscape protection, management and planning. The extent of Europe-wide programmes seems to be limited merely to the establishment of a list of Landscapes of European Significance, a European Landscape Prize and the exchange of experience and ideas. There does not seem to be any move towards the kind of regulatory regime introduced under the Habitats Directive nor towards the introduction of any financial support towards action programmes.

Much of the general thrust of the Convention will be familiar, at least to those closely involved with landscape issues in the UK, where these have been recognised by government for many years, though they have not always been given the highest of priorities. The significance of there being such a Convention and of the UK signing up to it is the Europe-wide recognition of the importance of landscape as an integral part of life and a crucial element of the sustainability process. The Council of Europe is aiming for landscape to become a mainstream political subject, with it no longer being acceptable for technical and economic changes to have total policy dominance. Furthermore landscape is not perceived as a narrow theme, to be treated as a specialist sector of public affairs. It is a wide, encompassing concept and reality, and it can be affected for good or ill by actions across many sectors. It is seen, therefore, to be necessary for governments to ensure that the objectives related to landscape are taken into account across all sectors of public life – a very important principle when looking at something like the Common Agricultural Policy, programmes of public works, transport, forestry and tourist development.

So far as protected landscapes are concerned, the implementation of the Convention would seem to be a very positive move. Not only would the whole climate towards landscape issues be changed for the better but also the attitude towards protected landscapes would be strengthened. First, the Convention would aim to incorporate landscape issues in the policies that apply to areas that have already received some form of protection on account of their importance as natural or cultural sites. It is argued, quite rightly, that landscape is a wider concept than some of the objectives that are applied to such areas; it embraces culture and nature, and incorporates the idea of sustainable development.

Second, while the thinking behind the Convention embraces the whole of the area of any state and a whole range of measures are suggested for implementing it, it is recognised that some landscapes should be given special status. This might be justified on account of the rarity or special quality of the landscape, its cultural or natural interest, or some other specific reason which implies a high degree of protection. Equally special status, it is argued, could be given to an area where the landscape is despoiled and requires special concentrated action. The important point is that the process required by the convention will identify those areas requiring special attention. Indeed their relevance is manifest in the requirement of the Convention for the list of landscapes of European importance to be drawn from the areas of national importance defined in each state. Whether this concept will form part of the final convention is in some doubt because of the difficulty in agreeing what the landscapes of European significance really are. Nevertheless the convention will give some momentum to the overall status of protected landscapes.

Commentary: recurrent themes

Thus the pace of policy development for AONBs had been gathering momentum for some time at national level. Before examining how local government and other public bodies with responsibilities in

AONBs are reacting to this and to pressures on the ground, it would be useful to summarise the more important trends in policy affecting their work.

Chapter 1 has already traced the problem-ridden evolution of the very purpose and status of AONBs from the origin of the concept in Dower and Hobhouse. As to their protection, there was little appreciation of the need for active management of conservation in these areas, The aim was to deter inappropriate development: a statutory job for planning control. The impact of agricultural change and of recreational pressures, usually outside the scope of planning, had not been foreseen, and little attention was given to how the economic needs of local communities could be met in a way that was beneficial to the landscape. As to their selection and administration, Hobhouse's sensible requirement for local government to set up Advisory Committees was dropped and no specific duty was placed on CC to initiate designation. Consequently, progress in the 1950s and 1960s towards the kind of approach envisaged by Hobhouse and Huxley was painfully slow. Given the weaknesses of the legislation, the priority assigned to National Parks, the constraints upon public expenditure, and increasing pressures on the wider countryside, especially the urban fringe, this is hardly surprising.

In retrospect the 1980 review was disappointing, although Himsworth's recommendations[25] on the role of recreation in AONBs and on the scope and level of financial support raised issues that are now once more under consideration. The eventual policy statement was right to clarify the purposes of designation and to give guidance on major development issues, but its approach to AONB administration and funding was half-hearted, and the agricultural issue was ducked altogether. It is not surprising therefore that, forty years after the enabling legislation, the 1990 review, hampered as it was by an acute shortage of qualitative data, should still find it necessary to highlight a serious lack of positive conservation. Smart and Anderson made firm recommendations to boost awareness, resources and administrative structures, and environmentally friendly agriculture.[26] The resulting policy statement took most of this on board (even if it were vague about how more sensitive farming would be delivered), and was followed by other measures by CC to tackle the problem of lack of awareness.

Somehow, nevertheless, CC's intention to seek more money from government for at least a limited number of AONBs did not produce the goods. Maybe this was due to other priorities within the Commission, for example on National Parks, or even to misgivings about the continued validity of designations, such as AONBs, when the focus of interest was being broadened to the whole countryside. Perhaps the local authorities themselves were too cautious in pressing their own case, other than in Sussex, where the efforts to set up an effective organisation for the Downs received generous financial support from the Commission, as will be shown in Chapter 5 and in the case study (see Appendix 2). Meanwhile the success of other imaginative initiatives by CC, and its ability as a pressure group, gave it a prominent role amongst national and international voices seeking higher standards of countryside conservation and more sensitive policies for agricultural production. This gathering momentum and its political effect must have assured the Commission that by 1998 the time was at last ripe for a convincing case to be made to government on the importance of protected areas and the need to put their finance and administration on a sound footing. To do this meant revisiting the shortcomings of the 1949 Act, to see in particular how these might be rectified in order to give management of AONBs as much importance as the long-established planning responsibilities for them, to a quality broadly comparable to National Parks. The response from government has been positive so far in terms of finance for the immediate future and of possible legislation.

In other words, while the earlier history of AONB policy development is a disappointing story, more recent moves by CC, CCW and the Government have been encouraging. After fifty years there are still many problems. There is in fact nothing very new about them; they were identified at least ten years ago, and some can indeed be traced to the original legislation. In some respects things have come full circle and, depending on the government response, may present a golden opportunity for local authorities to show how, given the resources and a greater incentive to complement them with their own contribution, they can act vigorously to enhance the environmental quality of these nationally treasured areas. This opportunity should now be grasped, though experience, for example in the Cotswolds (see case study in Appendix 2), shows that major reorganisation takes time.

Indeed, AONB local authorities have already shown a collective interest at national level by initiating, in 1998, their own partnership – the Association for AONBs – to secure a better future for these very special areas of England and Wales. Together with the AONB Staff Forum, set up in 1995, and supported by the AONB Charter (promoted for all AONBs by Swansea City Council), the Association could mark a turning point in the campaign to improve the management of AONBs, to advance their cause, and to help secure national investment in their long-term future. Both organisations have welcomed the two Advice Papers, adding their weight to the case for a 75 per cent rate of grant in England as well as Wales.

The very explicit set of criteria for designating National Parks in Scotland gives an indication of the manner in which the need for multi-resource management has become widely recognised during recent years. These advances may well be a reflection of the fact that both SNH and the Welsh Assembly have duties to promote sustainable development. Perhaps there is a lesson here for protected landscapes generally and AONBs in particular.

'Parks for Life' is significant because it stems from a world-wide movement for protected areas (including protected landscapes), which helps to set standards to be achieved by every nation. For example, the 'Parks for Life' European Plan was very critical of Scotland for having no National Parks. It would probably now be critical of the fact that so much debate about particular forms of protected area is going on in the UK without an overall review, for which there does not seem to be any great enthusiasm. Although 'Parks for Life' has no statutory basis as the Convention on Biological Diversity has, there is no doubt that landscape issues are rising on the agenda. The proposal for a European Landscape Convention reinforces the importance both of landscape in its broadest meaning, embracing natural and cultural elements, and protected landscapes in particular. Well-managed and well-resourced AONBs could well play a leading part in the implementation of these initiatives, acting as exemplars. Equally they could benefit from following the principles put forward and learn from interaction with others in the same field.

All this is encouraging, but the assessment of the ability of AONBs to meet current and future challenges undertaken in Chapter 8 will show that there is a need to go considerably further than the present proposals for their future. Meanwhile, what has been happening on the ground is examined in the next chapters of the book.

References

[1] Countryside Commission, *Areas of Outstanding Natural Beauty, a discussion paper*, CCP 316, Cheltenham, 1978.

[2] Himsworth, K.M., *A Review of Areas of Outstanding Natural Beauty*, report for the Countryside Commission, CCP140, Cheltenham, 1980.

[3] Countryside Commission, *Areas of Outstanding Natural Beauty, Policy Statement*, CCP 157, Cheltenham, 1983.

[4] Countryside Commission and Countryside Council for Wales, *Directory of Areas of Outstanding Natural Beauty*, available only on the Countryside Agency website www.countryside.gov.uk

[5] Smart, G. & Anderson, M., *Planning and Management of AONBs*, report for the Countryside Commission, CCP 295, Cheltenham, 1990.

[6] Countryside Commission and Countryside Council for Wales, *Areas of Outstanding Natural Beauty, A Policy Statement*, CCP 356, Cheltenham, 1991.

[7] Countryside Commission, *Areas of Outstanding Natural Beauty, Providing for the Future*, CCP 523, Cheltenham, 1997.

8   *Protected Areas Funding Study*, report for the Countryside Commission by Environmental Resources Management, London, 1998.

9   *Areas of Outstanding Natural Beauty in Wales*, report for the Countryside Council for Wales by Heritage Management Services, Wrexham, 1998.

10   Countryside Commission, *Protecting Our Finest Countryside, Advice to Government*, CCP 532, Cheltenham, 1998.

11   *Environment Act* 1995, Part III.

12   Countryside Council for Wales, *Advice to the Welsh Office on Protected Landscapes in Wales*, CCW paper 98/74, Bangor, 1998.

13   *Areas of Outstanding Natural Beauty Bill (HL)*, 1999.

14   Michael Meacher, Environment Minister, Speech to the AONB Association Annual Conference, Cirencester, September 1999.

15   DETR, News Release 416, 13 June 2000.

16   Countryside Agency, *Possible National Park Status for the South Downs*, Cheltenham, Paper AP99/34, 1999.

17   Scottish Natural Heritage, *National Parks for Scotland, Advice to Government*, Perth, 1999.

18   Scottish Natural Heritage, *National Scenic Areas, Advice to Government*, Perth, 1999.

19   IUCN, *United Nations List of Protected Areas*, Gland, Switzerland, & Cambridge, UK, 1997.

20   IUCN, *Parks for Life: Report of the IVth World Congress on National Parks and Protected Areas, Caracas, 1992*, Gland, Switzerland, 1993.

21   IUCN, *Parks for Life: Action for Protected Areas in Europe*, Gland, Switzerland & Cambridge, UK, 1994.

22   IUCN-UK Committee, *Action for Protected Areas in the UK: A Response to 'Parks for Life'*, 1996.

23   IUCN-UK Committee, *Action for Protected Areas in the UK: From Islands of Conservation to Models of Sustainability: Moving the 'Parks for Life' Process Forward*, 1998.

24   Congress of Local and Regional Authorities of Europe, 'Recommendation 40 (1998) and Resolution 62 (1998) on the draft European Landscape Convention'.

25   Himsworth, K.M., op. cit.

26   Smart, G. & Anderson, M., op. cit.

The evolution of
AONB management 5

It has been shown that, after a slow start, the policy of government, CC and CCW for AONBs developed both in pace and scope, and that the local authorities themselves have recently begun to show their collective concern about the need to enhance the status and management of these areas. Continuing with the theme of this second part of the book, this chapter now looks at the steps being taken, primarily by local authorities on the ground, to look after the widening range of AONB heritage, and for which considerable responsibility is shared with other organisations and interests.

Active measures to conserve and enhance an AONB depend primarily on three factors: the political will of central and local government to lead and to give financial support; co-ordinated management mechanisms; and the active involvement of public, private and voluntary bodies. In practical terms this requires the establishment, long advised by CC, of an AONB-wide Joint Advisory Committee (JAC) with its own budget, the appointment of an officer or unit devoted full-time to producing and implementing a management plan, and the willing participation, preferably through representation on the committee, of stakeholders (government departments, official agencies, landowners and farmers, and environmental and community groups) interested in the area. A veritable partnership; to what extent does it exist in practice?

**Administration:
the framework
of partnership**

Progress towards setting up JACs was initially slow. In the circumstances outlined in Chapter 1, this is hardly surprising; the designation programme itself only began in 1956. Nevertheless, more than ten years were to pass before the first JACs were formed (in the Cotswolds and Chilterns), and despite encouragement by the Commission during the 1970s, only eight were in existence by the time of the 1980 AONB review. The need for JACs, at least for multi-county areas, was re-emphasised in CC's subsequent policy statement,[1] but even by the time of the 1989 review, the total had only reached 12. Thereafter, with the encouragement given to all AONBs in the 1991 policy statement by CC and CCW,[2] and with better understanding of the importance of AONBs, the pace increased, and by 1998 the total number of JACs or equivalent organisations in England and Wales was 28.[3] The Guide for Members of Joint Advisory Committees, published by CC and CCW in 1994[4] must also have been a factor in this growth. Nevertheless, the case studies in Appendix 2 and experience elsewhere shows that a great deal of preparation and negotiation is necessary before a JAC can begin (or even continue) to operate effectively.

The purpose of these Committees, sometimes expressed in a written 'partnership agreement' (see Box 5.1) which is almost an informal contract between the various parties, is to prepare, monitor and review a management plan; to agree a programme of work which the partners aim to carry out; to raise funds, supported by CA or CCW grant, for the 'core' expenses of AONB staff and for projects; and to

---

BOX 5.1

The Chilterns Partnership Agreement

The ten-page Partnership Agreement for the Chilterns Conference (which is equivalent to a JAC – see case study) aims to clarify roles and responsibilities, to increase commitment of members, and to ensure an equitable and transparent relationship between contribution to the work of the Conference and influence over its direction.

In this large AONB with a population of 100,000 and a wealth of natural resources the agreement emphasises the importance of each partner committing itself to the aims of the Conference and to achieving the national and local objectives of the AONB. The Management Plan provides a common framework for action, and the Partnership Agreement (made in 1997) provides the complementary framework to determine how the Conference and its members should operate to maximum effect.

Members of the Conference are expected to:

• Make an appropriate financial contribution

• Support the aims and priorities of the Conference

• Participate fully in its planning and operations

• Harmonise their own policies and plans to the AONB Management Plan

The Conference is served by a smaller Executive Group, the AONB Officer and a Technical Advisory Panel.

Source: Chilterns AONB, *Chilterns Conference Partnership Agreement.*

act as a forum for discussing issues affecting the area. This should include advice to planning authorities on development proposals. Where an AONB administered in this way contains a section of Heritage Coast, the responsibility for its management, including financial arrangements, has usually become merged with that of the JAC and its officers.

In practice, JACs vary considerably in form, composition and size, depending on local circumstances and the roles that they aim to carry out (see for example, Boxes 5.2, 5.3, and 5.4). Most are voluntary assemblies, from which a partner could in theory 'walk away' if it wished; this has indeed happened, and a great deal of time and effort

---

South Devon AONB is an important coastal holiday area entirely within one local government district. Here the JAC consists of 18 member organisations: South Hams District Council, Devon County Council, Torbay Council, six government agencies and nine voluntary bodies, served by the AONB Officer, an officers' group, and a joint County and District Countryside Management Service. There is also an annual forum for a wide range of organisations. The JAC has responsibility for preparing the Management Plan and annual work programmes, advising on how structure and local plans and the programmes of constituent bodies might be co-ordinated with the Management Plan, promoting awareness, and seeking to ensure that countryside, towns and villages are conserved in line with AONB objectives.

Source: Information from AONB Officer.

BOX 5.2

South Devon Joint Advisory Committee

This was formed under the *Chichester Harbour Conservancy Act* 1971, to manage the harbour and surrounding land for the benefit of recreation, the conservation of nature and to have regard to natural beauty. It is a statutory harbour authority and also functions as the JAC for the AONB. The Conservancy has 15 members, 12 appointed by the local authorities and 3 by its statutory Advisory Committee representing various interests in the area. Its total budget is over £800,000 and it is entitled to levy up to 25 % of this on the two county councils (West Sussex and Hampshire). Most of the income is from harbour dues, etc., the use of which is limited to harbour management. The Conservancy has a consultative role in the planning system.

Source: Chichester Harbour Conservancy, *Chichester Harbour AONB Management Plan*, Chichester, 1999.

BOX 5.3

Chichester Harbour Conservancy

BOX 5.4

Solway Rural Initiative

The Solway Rural Initiative, established in 1992, is an independent organisation and a company limited by guarantee. It is managed by a group with representatives from the three local authorities, as well as English Nature, Solway Firth Partnership, Environment Agency and the Countryside Agency, in co-operation with business leaders and representatives from a variety of community groups. It initiates and assists countryside projects and rural development in the Solway plain and coast, an area that is wider than the AONB. It also acts as a 'single door' opening to a one-stop information and guidance service for all those living and working and interested in rural issues. It is responsible for the management of the AONB, the preparation of the management plan and the operation of a countryside management service. It has a staff of 5, an AONB Officer (part-time), two countryside staff, a rural development officer, and a person to run the rural resource centre. In 1998 the core costs of the unit were £110,000, which were met by the Countryside Commission (£40,000), Allerdale DC (£28,000), ERDF(£22,000), income from the resource centre (£10,000) and Carlisle City Council (£10,000). The initiative is looking to be free of public funding within five years by generating income from a range of tourist enterprises making use of the natural assets of the area.

Source: Solway Rural Initiative.

---

has had to be put in to rectifying matters. Few have any legal status: the Sussex Downs Conservation Board is a statutory Joint Committee; the Chichester Harbour Conservancy has its own Act of Parliament. The Malvern Hills Conservators, established by 1884 legislation, and the Isles of Scilly Environmental Trust, a registered charity, also have important management responsibilities, but not as JACs. Some are composed of members from a wide range of organisations from the public, private and voluntary sectors; the largest have up to 60 representatives, mainly living or working locally. Size is a problem at meetings, as a result of which a few JACs have two types of membership, full and associate, or specialist sub-groups. Some smaller but no less important JACs consist primarily of local authorities and national agencies; they, like some of the larger ones, keep in contact with other essential interests by having regular consultative forums, community conferences and events, annual reports, and by publishing their own newspapers. Most meet quarterly, but the busier ones have small 'strategy groups', including leading local authority members, who can steer the JAC generally and take interim decisions, for example, responding to consultations on planning applications. Several are drawn from local authorities with different political loyalties, but although members are always conscious of political undertones, for example, when negotiating expenditure priorities, this apparently does not cause serious conflict in decision-making – which says a lot about the commitment of these councils to making a success of AONB management, taking a pride in their special areas. Like so many other aspects of local government, however, the extent of this commitment often depends on the enthusiasm and leadership of just a few dedicated elected members and officers who may be there today but gone tomorrow.

Staffing: the core of the partnership

The need for staff dedicated full-time to the management of an AONB has long been advocated in reports to CC and in its policy statements, although progress has been slow by comparison with National Parks. None was in existence at the time of the 1980 review, other than for Heritage Coast parts of AONBs, and the Commission's subsequent policy statement consequently recommended that 'in each AONB the local authorities should nominate an officer to have general oversight and responsibility for co-ordinating management plans'.[5]

By the time of the 1989 review one AONB Officer, as such, was in post (in Gower), but 11 areas had the undivided attention of project officers, mostly on short-term contracts. Despite rolling three-year grants from CC, lack of commitment by local authorities was clearly a problem and the need for staff was not always perceived. Nevertheless, the existence of technical working parties set up by local authorities to prepare management plans and give a wide range of professional advice meant that the total effort was considerably greater than that of a few individuals. The policy statement by CC and CCW[6] recommended that AONB Officers be widely appointed at a senior level, supported by grant for six years, and assisted by interdisciplinary units in the largest areas. Box 5.5 indicates the role and skills required.

Nearly three-quarters of AONBs now have their own Officers,[7] usually attached to a lead authority for 'pay and rations', but on a contract usually far shorter than the six years suggested by CC and CCW. They mostly come from countryside management backgrounds, and are dedicated to their work in every sense of the word. About half the AONBs, those where the pressure is greatest, have management services of various kinds. There is only one widely staffed interdisciplinary AONB unit as such (in the Sussex Downs, see case study), though there are several small units of two or three people (Chichester Harbour also has an inter-professional team for its specialised maritime role). Several of the rest are served to a greater or lesser degree by countryside management teams; a few of these are directly supervised

BOX 5.5

The role of the AONB Officer, and the skills needed in an AONB unit

The policy statement by CC and CCW suggested a model job description for an AONB Officer. This included:

- Management Plan preparation and monitoring
- Co-ordination of implementation
- Fund-raising and budgetary control
- Production of an annual report
- Initiation of research.

It also indicated the range of skills needed within a unit, or accessible to it:

- Finance and administration
- Planning and economic development
- Skills relating to the area's resources (ecology, agriculture and woodland management, landscape conservation, archaeology)
- Skills related to activities (practical countryside management, rights of way, recreation, interpretation and publicity

Source: Countryside Commission and Countryside Council for Wales, *Areas of Outstanding Natural Beauty, A Policy Statement*, CCP 356, Cheltenham, 1991.

BOX 5.6

Countryside Management Services (CMS) can include:

- Landscape maintenance and enhancement, including environmental advice to farmers and landowners (encouraging the use of enhancement tiers in ESAs, promoting CMS, encouraging take-up of woodland and other grants, training and mobilising volunteers in hedgerow and dry-stone wall management, etc.)
- Specialised ranger work on land owned by local authorities or by agreement with other owners (e.g., habitat creation)
- Visitor management, interpretation, guided walks, and promotion of events
- Rights of way management, maintenance, fencing, signing, etc.
- Car park management
- Leadership of voluntary warden schemes
- Day-to-day liaison with public agencies, communities and landowners on management issues

Source: Communication with AONB Officers and *Protected Areas Funding Study*, report for the Countryside Commission by Environmental Resources Management, London, 1998.

by the AONB Officer but the majority operate as county or district teams who may have responsibilities outside the area as well.

Those AONBs that run their own countryside management service or have very close liaison with a local authority service have found that rangers (including voluntary wardens) working on the ground can be of immense value as a point of two-way contact between the AONB partnership, on the one hand, and farmers, landowners, local communities, residents and visitors, on the other. The better the team is versed in policy matters, including economic and social issues, in addition to its own work programmes, the more effective this contact can be. Where the countryside management team is not an integral part of the AONB organisation, this liaison may be difficult to establish. Box 5.6 gives an outline of the functions of a countryside management service.

Organisation of AONB management

The arrangements for AONB management are almost as diverse as AONBs themselves. The arrangements have evolved individually over many years, mainly at a time when the management aims for these areas were necessarily limited and local authorities were searching for practical ways of making a start, constrained by short-term finance and uncertainty as to the extent of commitment amongst potential partners. There was no general guiding principle, except for the need for a JAC, the appointment of AONB officers and, for some AONBs, the establishment of a special unit.

In practice a pattern has emerged, however, that can be broadly regarded as ranging from relative independence, on the one hand, to relative integration with local government, on the other. Among the factors affecting the place of any one organisation would be the account taken by those who established it of considerations such as the size and character of the area and the structure of local government within it, the effect of this and other requirements on the constitution and membership of a JAC, the options available for the location and function of the AONB staff, the need for consultation and liaison, and the financial opportunities and constraints.

Two organisations described in the case studies exemplify the 'independent' end of the range: the Sussex Downs Conservation Board and the Cotswolds Partnership, both of which have a particular need for identity in their large and administratively complex AONBs, and for ability to carry out a variety of functions, especially in a strategic sense. These functions are currently more fully developed in the Sussex Board, the Cotswolds Partnership being comparatively new. The Chichester Harbour Conservancy (see Box 5.3) is a further case in point, with a statutory constitution that gives it a strategic and operational role throughout this unique AONB.

The Solway Rural Initiative, which is a company limited by guarantee, can also be regarded as being near this end of the range. As can be seen from Box 5.4, it functions as a JAC for the Solway Coast AONB but also covers a wider area. So can the Island 2000 Trust, currently being formed in the Isle of Wight on the basis of experience in the AONB which covers half the Island; financed initially from landfill tax, it aims to integrate work on landscape quality, the rural economy, and community action throughout the whole island. Both these examples are in administratively straightforward and relatively small AONBs, but are necessary because the local authorities felt there were special reasons for promoting unconventional organisations, with the financial benefits and independent status that their positions can bring, especially to economic development and tourism.

At the other end of the range, management in Gower AONB, in the City of Swansea, is integrated with countryside work in City Council departments through their Countryside Officer, with advice from the Gower Countryside Forum. There is no JAC as such, policy decisions being the responsibility of the City Planning Committee. These arrangements were no doubt influenced by the development of corporate management in the City Council when it replaced a more conventional AONB organisation at the time when Welsh local government was restructured in 1996.

In the middle of the range can be found a whole variety of arrangements. Some appear to be nearer the 'independent' end of the range; others tend to be more 'integrated'. The case studies in Appendix 2 include five examples of the former. One of these is the Blackdown Hills, where a widely based JAC is served by a very small unit located on its own in a village and giving priority to economic and community work with local groups and individuals. Another is the Chilterns, with a longstanding JAC (The Chilterns Conference) that has established its own identity in a large and diverse AONB, served by a small, centrally located unit necessarily receiving much working support from local authorities; the Conference's intention to become a Conservation Board seems a logical step. In the Mendip Hills a large JAC employs a team with its own countryside management capability that shares accommodation and works closely with a field studies and activities centre. Another example of relative independence is the Norfolk Coast AONB, served by a very small unit located on its own and aiming to play a strategic role on very limited resources; for countryside management it is fortunate that the area's land-owning conservation bodies are extremely active in the more critical parts of the area. Wye Valley AONB is another interesting example, where an English and Welsh JAC has created considerable identity for administration of the AONB as a whole, and its centrally located small team is active strategically; here, however, the countryside management service, carried out by local authorities in liaison with them, has been considerably reduced for financial reasons.

Examples in the case studies that are near the 'integrated' end of the range include the Forest of Bowland and the Purbeck Heritage Area, both of whose AONB Officers are housed in the accommodation of lead local authorities and, while clearly separate in function, are thus in daily contact with the council's specialist advisers and countryside management services. Also at this end of the range is South Devon, where countryside management in the AONB is integrated with that in the rest of South Hams District, in whose headquarters the AONB Officer is located (see Box 5.2).

CC's Advice to Government Paper[8] commended five models for delivering management functions in AONBs.

1) *Integrated* within the leading local authority;

2) *Separate*, but supported by a leading authority that might share some of the responsibilities;

3) *Independent*, having responsibility for most aspects of management, though working closely with all local authorities and partners;

4) Independent, but receiving part funding from an *independent Trust*;

5) Independent, high profile, such as a *Conservation Board*, with links to democratic structures, local officers, and possibly to an independent funding trust.

They were originally devised during the Protected Areas Funding Study as means of costing the management of AONBs, rather than models to be followed closely. Indeed it is not easy to fit what is found in practice into the framework, nor is it really clear what they mean.

Thus there is a whole range of issues to be considered in creating the management structure for an AONB, not least the identity of the AONB and its management, and the functional and economic considerations of providing the necessary skills. While it is not the purpose of this book to evaluate these models or the arrangements found in practice, there is one principle that needs to be adopted whatever the actual arrangements are: the organisation and staff running the AONB need to be identifiable to the public and visible. This is particularly so when only part of the staff's time is spent on AONB matters. Indeed for every AONB there should be at the very least one person who is dedicated full time to its work, and for most a small and seemingly independent unit will be essential, with both a strategic planning and a countryside management capability. Further detailed study of the merits of different types of organisation (not necessarily those indicated in the Advice Paper) would undoubtedly be worthwhile, possibly undertaken by the AONB Association in conjunction with CA and CCW. One important conclusion that can readily be drawn at this stage, however, is that any proposals for new legislation affecting the management of AONBs should be flexible enough to allow for a wide choice of organisation attuned to the specific needs of each area.

Management plans: the means by which partnership can operate

Management Plans for AONBs are not mandatory at present, though CA and CCW attach much importance to them when considering applications for grant. Amongst the proposals for new legislation in the Advice to Government Papers is a requirement that 'Conservation Management Plans' should be prepared and published for every AONB.

CC and CCW issued advice on the content and format of AONB management plans in 1992 (see Box 5.7).[9] They defined a management plan as 'an advisory document prepared by, or on behalf of, all those organisations or individuals with a management role within the AONB, which establishes common aims and objectives of management based on a strategic view of the whole area within a wider planning context, and which recommends area-based proposals that will guide and stimulate management action towards the achievement of these objectives'. The plan was seen as a means of promoting and co-ordinating conservation of natural resources, and appropriate social and economic development, including recreation.

Five years later, in 1997, the two organisations published guidance on National Park Management Plans (see Box 5.8).[10] National Park Management Plans are statutory requirements, but the format of these plans may nevertheless be relevant to AONBs, bearing in mind that many AONB plans are about to be reviewed and that the guidance given by the Commission and the Council is now nearly ten years old.

The two types of document have much in common. However, the National Park Plan places rather greater emphasis on vision (medium to long-term aspirations for the core values of the area), as a basis for awareness, identification of problems and setting of objectives; on the need for an integrated approach to management; on information,

CC and CCW say that a standard management plan format would not be suitable for every area, but that the contents should accord broadly with the following five headings:

- Introduction: descriptive background
- Context: planning, environmental, and management
- Issues, strategic objectives and policies: AONB-wide topics

  Conservation issues: landscape, nature, cultural heritage

  Socio-economic issues: agriculture, forestry, tourism, recreation and access

  Traffic management and parking, interpretation, settlement and community, development and minerals
- Zone strategies and proposals (with an indication of resource requirements, lead agencies and priorities)
- Implementation: participants, organisation and means of co-ordination, financial resources and funding mechanisms, work programmes, arrangements for monitoring and review

Source: Countryside Commission and Countryside Council for Wales, *AONB Management Plans: Advice on Their Form and Content,* CCP 352, Cheltenham, 1992.

BOX 5.7

Advice on the format of Management Plans (1992)

CC and CCW say that a National Park Plan should be the major determinant of vision, land management and resource allocation for the Park, promoting an integrated approach to management within a broader regional context. The contents, while differing slightly from Park to Park, should include the following:

- Introduction
- A vision for the Park
- Conservation: natural environment and cultural heritage
- Promoting understanding and enjoyment: recreation management, information interpretation and education
- Economic and social well-being of local communities
- Development planning and control
- Themes or policies for geographic areas (where applicable)
- Implementation: applying policies in geographic areas (where applicable); management, administration and resources
- Monitoring and review

Source: Countryside Commission and Countryside Council for Wales, *National Park Management Plans Guidance,* CCP 525, Cheltenham, 1997.

BOX 5.8

Advice on the format of National Park Plans (1997)

BOX 5.9

Whole farm plans

A whole farm plan requires a comprehensive assessment of the holding and the development of a long-term plan to integrate production with environmental conservation. Hampshire County Council and East Hampshire District Council have encouraged this concept in East Hampshire AONB, and a few farms have adopted the approach, although it remains at an early stage of development. Lack of financial assistance is the main constraint to its more widespread adoption.

Source: Hampshire County Council, East Hampshire AONB, *Integrated Management Guidelines*, Final Report by Landscape Design Associates, Peterborough, 1998.

interpretation and education; and on community interests.

By 1998 nearly three-quarters of AONBs had area-wide management plans,[11] the majority of which have been prepared within the last five years. Several have been followed up by zonal or project-based plans, and some, with support from the Agriculture Departments, have instigated moves towards 'whole farm plans' (see, for example, Box 5.9). Some, especially in areas with employment problems, have a strong economic and social content. Clearly, good progress has been made in the ten years since the 1989/90 AONB review, when only one-third had AONB-wide plans, but there is still some way to go and, as has been pointed out above, many of the existing plans are due for review. By and large the format of these plans is in line with the 1992 guidance, and most of them have been followed by budgetary statements and work programmes, even in a few cases by comprehensive business plans.

As might be expected, their quality varies. Take, for example, the need for policies to be integrated throughout the spectrum of environmental and socio-economic issues. This was not brought out in the guidance on AONB plans as clearly as in the more recent National Park advice. Indeed, only a few plans set out a 'vision' for the area, usually brief and perhaps a little obvious but leading to a series of inter-linked objectives. Only a few set out in any detail the policy implications of new thinking on sustainability. Nevertheless, some recent plans do show an innovatory approach, for example, using a thematic structure within which the whole sequence of planning, from broad objectives to individual proposals, is comprehensively ordered (see examples in Boxes 5.10 to 5.13). In others, however, especially the earlier ones, the connections are weaker. Some have made imaginative efforts to encourage community participation in their preparation and to feed this through into implementation; in others, size or diversity has made integration of this kind difficult.

Quality also varies in the actual presentation of objectives and

BOX 5.10

Sussex Downs Management Strategy (1996)

In the Sussex Downs the strategy of the Conservation Board (see case study) revolves around four main themes for the AONB:

. • Conserving Natural Beauty (the natural environment, landscape, nature conservation, cultural heritage)

• Towards a Sustainable Economy (agriculture, forestry and woodland)

• Living in the AONB (local needs, development and minerals, roads)

• Enjoying the Landscape (traffic and visitor management, access, specialist recreation, tourism, interpretation and information)

These four themes lead to another: Partnership in Practice, concerned with the plan's Action Programme.

Source: Sussex Downs Conservation Board, *A Management Strategy for the Sussex Downs AONB (revised)*, Storrington, 1996.

BOX 5.11

North Pennines Management Plan (1995)

North Pennines is one of the largest AONBs, and its Management Plan tackles an upland problem, very different from those of AONBs in southern England. After extensive consultations with local communities the plan is based on a vision for the future of the area in which

• Communities and conservation are mutually supportive, and change which avoids over-exploitation is accepted

• The hill farming regime is reshaped but viable

• The local economy is diversified

• An important tourism industry is developed in a low-key manner

• Landscape and natural habitats are maintained and enhanced, but with some change in land management practices

• Historic features and buildings are maintained as far as possible

• Widespread enjoyment of the North Pennines landscape and ways of life is promoted

Source: North Pennines AONB Steeering Group, *North Pennines AONB Management Plan*, Durham, 1995.

proposals. Some plans contain large numbers of very broadly worded objectives; these may be difficult to monitor systematically, and their relevance to decisions by partners, from local planning committees to national agencies, may not be clearly focused. Equally, some of the

BOX 5.12

Blackdown Hills Management Strategy (1997)

Blackdown Hills AONB (see case study) has a Management Strategy that is based upon consensus-building and identifies priorities for community initiatives. In addition to policies for landscape (dependent upon retaining a healthy farming economy as the primary agent for landscape management), and for the natural and historic environments, the plan gives guidance on matters relating to the local economy, housing and community facilities. For housing, it says, for example:

- 'The JAC supports strategies which maintain mixed and thriving communities and are in sympathy with the local environment'

- 'The JAC supports provision in Local Plans for limited development in village envelopes, and, where larger sites are possible, will introduce a quota for local affordable homes'

- 'The JAC supports provision of local housing based on new development in the local economy, to allow for growth'

Source: Blackdown Hills Joint Advisory Committee, *Management Strategy for the Blackdown Hills AONB*, Stockland, 1997.

BOX 5.13

Kent Downs Management Strategy (1999)

During 1996/7 the Kent Downs 'Your piece in the Jigsaw' project was developed as a grass-roots input to the Strategy and other planning documents. Workshops were held with Parish Councils, and many organisations and individuals attended AONB seminars. All 132 parishes in the area were involved, from which 124 responded with illustrated 'Parish Pages' of key issues (transport and infrastructure, planning, community, and countryside). The many photographs reflected local perceptions of the AONB:

- churches, traditional buildings, parkland, villages (62 per cent of the total number)

- ancient lanes and tracks, orchards, grazing livestock (40 per cent)

- significant trees, recreation, nature, archaeology, countryside traditions

Source: Kent Downs AONB Joint Advisory Committee, *Kent Downs AONB Management Strategy*, Maidstone, 1999.

plans tend to be over-ambitious in the number and range of proposals for action; this may make for a degree of difficulty and confusion when the JAC and its partner organisations are setting priorities. Annual reports and regular 'State of the Environment' reports, if linked to a fuller development of monitoring, would help to clarify the

Sussex Downs Conservation Board and Nottingham University have been given a £130,000 grant by the European Union as part of a wider European project focused on national parks and other protected areas. In Sussex the key themes relate to countryside access, development pressure and agricultural change (including loss of downland), and to the integration of remotely sensed data with other geographical information from a range of agencies. The project will help the Board to create a data framework for use in the sustainable management of landscape.

Source: The Primavera Project, School of Geography, Nottingham University, Nottingham, 1999.

BOX 5.14

Satellite Imagery (the Primavera Project)

focus (see Box 5.14). Unfortunately the analytical work required to identify the necessary indicators of change (in land use and the environment, visitor pressures, the local economy and community structure, etc.) requires a level of input from specialist staff or consultants which has not normally been affordable.

Indeed, despite the use of Partnership Agreements, (an example was given earlier in Box 5.1), the links with work of partners, even the local planning authorities, tend to be generally weak. A few of the more recent plans, however, go further than the official guidance, embracing the widening scope of environmental concerns: biodiversity, air quality, water resources, and matters such as sustainable energy, traffic reduction, promotion of quiet zones, etc. This is to be welcomed, as is their inclusion of guidelines for acceptable development in the AONB, including matters such as design and landscape criteria, and treatment of 'buffer zones' adjoining the AONB, for the local authorities to use in their own development plans and when determining planning applications.

Management plans, though not a statutory requirement and not always of immediate practical advantage to organisations with sectoral responsibilities which may affect AONBs, are nevertheless firmly established as sources of AONB-wide guidance. Their preparation, and that of business plans(see Box 5.15), is a key process in welding together the partnership approach and involving the local community. They also give essential support to bids for grants, whether from the Commission (CA) or other sources such as the Heritage Lottery Fund.

Having regard to the huge variety of AONBs, these plans should avoid too much standardisation. They should be encouraged to explore new formats that meet the requirements of each individual area, giving full play to developments in policy formulation, in the ever-widening range of environmental issues, and in the relationship between countryside management and rural planning. Together with

BOX 5.15

Business Plans

AONB Business Plans (of which there are not many as yet) usually cover a rolling three-year budget period, updated annually. A typical plan starts with a brief look at the current organisational structure, 'customers' and their service requirements, and considers strategic priorities for the partnership as a whole and the options available. From this it develops an action plan (listing the partnership 'leader' for each task), estimates of income and expenditure and possible funding sources, leading to an apportionment of financial contributions between local authorities and other funding partners. Its preparation and negotiation is a major undertaking for the JAC, usually through a group of its leading members.

Source: Information from discussions with AONB Officers.

National Park Management Plans they should serve as models for the management guidance that will increasingly be required in the countryside at large, for example, for Character Areas or Natural Areas.

Finance and new sources of funding

Total net expenditure in individual English National Parks ranged from £2 million to £6.4 million in 1997/8.[12] This, of course, includes the cost of their planning functions and a considerable management role. Nevertheless, what is known about total expenditure on management in AONBs suggests that in 1997/8 the amounts were tiny by comparison, ranging from around £40,000 (although it is likely that several areas fall well below this) to about £0.5 million.[13] Only one AONB came above this level: the special case of the Sussex Downs Conservation Board, with its core expenditure of £1.3 million (it is now about £1 million – see case study). Excluding this, the average level of total expenditure in some 27 AONBs for whom figures were available was £182,000, of which £132,000 represented 'core' expenditure and £50,000 was for project work. There is no long-term security in any of this, as local authority budgets tend to be settled annually, and CA grant support for projects (up to 50 per cent but usually less) is normally for a three-year term.

Chapter 4 has described the steps being taken by CC and CCW to gain additional financial support for AONB management from around £7 million in 1996/7 to a total of £18.5 million to £19.5 million in England, and from around £0.25 million (1997/8) to nearly £0.9 million in Wales. Chapter 4 also refers to the recent increase in government funding for AONBs. This amounts to £2.1 million rising to £5.9 million over three years for England; £100,000 has also been allocated in Wales for the year 2000. Nevertheless there must be some doubt as to whether, at a time of severe constraint on public expenditure and increasing needs in the countryside as a whole, the 170 per cent increase in costs envisaged in the Advice Papers could all be met from local and central budgets. It was therefore right for the Paper to advocate the potential of other sources for things other than core funding. National Parks have been successful in securing such outside money, and although AONBs have less experience of this, in AONBs there have been just a few notable achievements in obtaining funds, especially for capital projects, from European sources, the Lottery, from a few commercial enterprises, from charges of various kinds, and from local sources including, in a few cases, trusts (see Box 5.16). Ten groups of various sources are usefully assessed in the Funding Study[14] and summarised in CC's Advice Paper. While they

---

The case studies show that sums of £1.26 million have been raised by Purbeck Heritage Committee from the Capital Challenge Fund and £0.6 million from sponsors of a park-and-ride scheme. The Chilterns Conference has raised over £300,000 from the EU. Other successes in fund-raising from the kind of sources mentioned by CC include small amounts from sponsorship (Suffolk Coast and Heaths, Malvern Hills, Mendip Hills, Isle of Wight, Northumber-land Coast, Arnside and Silverdale and Chichester Harbour), and from European Structural Funds (Forest of Bowland, Northumber-land Coast, Nidderdale, North Pennines).

Source: Discussions with AONB Officers.

BOX 5.16

Fund-raising

---

cannot in any way be an adequate substitute for secure core funding, they offer an important and extremely flexible potential, and far more use could be made of them. Nevertheless it requires intensive staff effort to make a successful bid, and not all AONB teams are geared up to this. Furthermore, it may not be easy for some AONB authorities, where in the past they have been extremely parsimonious in their spending, to make a sudden increase in contributions to finance their own share of the total package, essential though this is for core funding.

The roles of the partners: public, private and voluntary sectors

It will be seen from this account of progress in AONB management that the partnership approach is central to the production of workable plans, and to translating them into action. County, Unitary and District Councils, having a democratically accountable presence in their areas and a wide range of responsibilities including environmental and land interests, lead the way. Other public bodies with special countryside responsibilities and funds, such as the Agricul-ture Departments, English Nature, Forest Enterprise and the Environment Agency, should share with them the main driving force of the partnership. It will be seen from the case studies that there is particularly close part-nership between JACs and public bodies with sectoral interests in Purbeck Heritage Area (with MAFF, English Nature and Forest Enterprise), Mendip Hills (with MAFF), and Chilterns and Wye Valley (with Forest Enterprise) in the Forest of Bowland (with MAFF). In these areas there is a joint interest in natural resources of critical importance, but, as will be shown in Chapter 6, where corporate pri-orities and those of the AONB do not happen to coincide with the interest of these bodies they tend to be marginal, and evidence of close working is hard to find. It is unfortunate that some of them have been known to take the line that 'AONBs are not one of our designations'.

It goes without saying that estate owners, public and private, and farmers control the most fundamental resource in any AONB: the land. They, too, should be essential partners in policy-making and action, and they usually are, through their representative bodies. Individually, their contribution can offer important opportunities for positive action, and there are excellent examples of co-operation between AONB managers and owners in conservation and provision of facilities on the ground, especially with organisations whose land-holdings occur in many AONBs such as National Trust, RSPB and the Wildlife Trusts. The map in Plate 49 is of particular interest in this context, showing how the pattern of public land-ownership in the countryside and of access agreements with the private sector relate to the most intensively used parts of the Surrey Hills AONB. In the Norfolk Coast there is a very good example of close working of the National Trust, RSPB, the Norfolk Wildlife Trust and English Nature in their capacity as landowners, with the AONB Unit (see Norfolk Coast case study in Appendix 2).

The National Trust, in particular, whose criteria for land purchase focus on the national importance of an area in terms of landscape, his-toric heritage and nature conservation, owns land in all but three AONBs, over 45,000 hectares in all.[15] Table 5.1 shows that the areas owned in some AONBs are very significant and as is the proportion of the AONB area in a few instances. With its high standards of manage-ment, interpretation and research into visitor needs, the NT can be a huge influence in AONB conservation. In the Chilterns for example, the Trust is working with the AONB Unit in preparing a Preservation Policy Plan that explores its holding in the context of all the policies operating in the area, and sets out its role in the protection of the Chilterns. In a similar way the Trust is particularly active in Purbeck

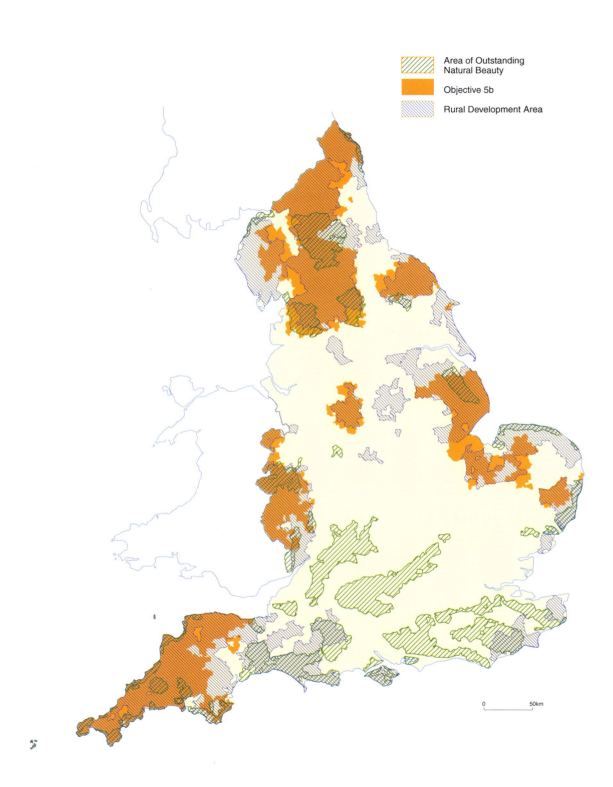

Plate 17 Map of AONBs and areas with priority for rural economic development in England, 1999.

Legend:
- Area of Outstanding Natural Beauty
- Objective 5b
- Rural Development Area

0 50km

(a)

The rural economy

Plate 18 A significant number of AONBs are all or partly designated as Rural Development Areas. In these areas the future of rural communities is of utmost importance, particularly in the more remote ones, e.g. North Pennines (a) and Cornwall (b).

(b)

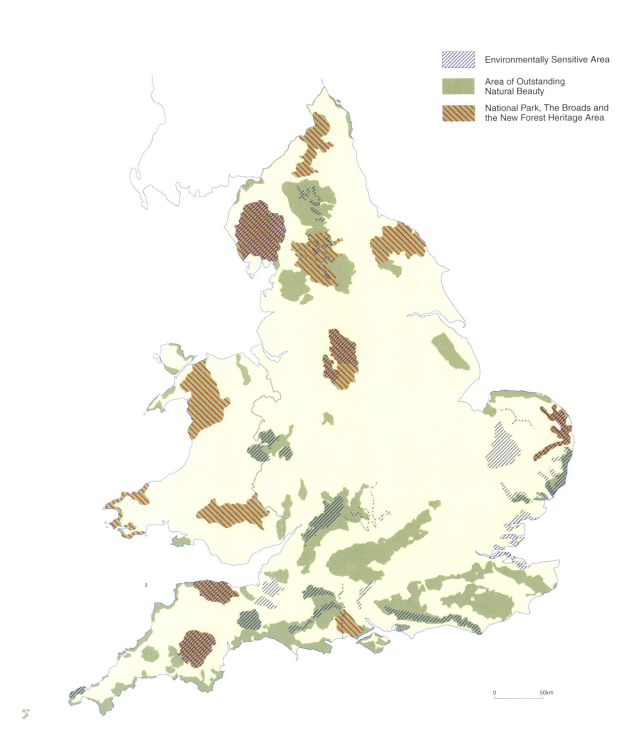

Plate 19   Map of Environmentally Sensitive Areas and protected landscapes in England. Note that a different scheme, Tir Gofal, applies in Wales.

Agriculture   **Plate 20**   Agricultural activity has shaped much of the character of the landscapes of AONBs. This relationship has been recognised by the designation of parts of some AONBs as Environmentally Sensitive Areas, for the purpose of securing EU funding, e.g. Blackdown Hills.

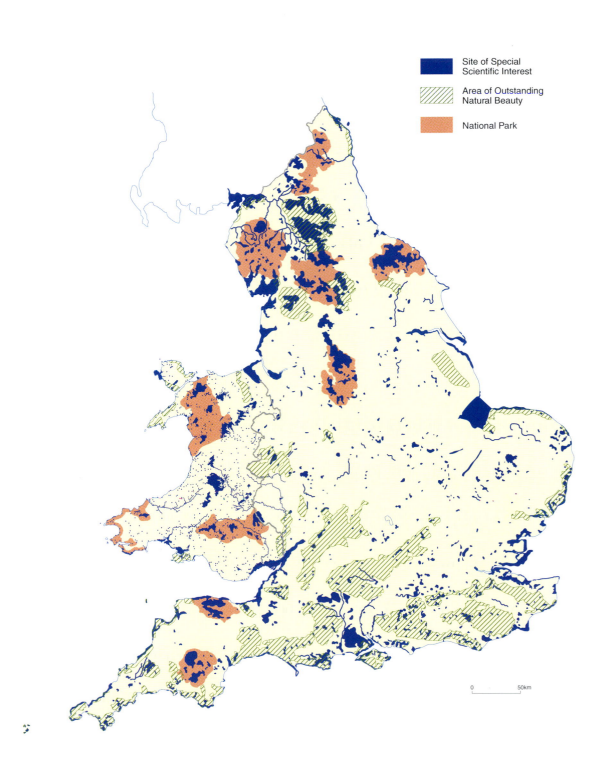

Plate 21 Map of Sites of Special Scientific Interest and protected landscapes in England and Wales.

(a)

(b)

**Wildlife and
AONBs (1)**

Plate 22 AONBs have many important wildlife habitats, e.g. chalk flora in the Chilterns (a), raised bogs in the Solway Coast (b) and coastal marshes and birdlife on the Norfolk Coast (c).

(c)

(a)

Wildlife and AONBs (2)

Plate 23 AONBs have many important wildlife habitats, e.g. ancient woodlands in the Wye Valley (a), heather moor in the Shropshire Hills (b) and limestone pavements in Arnside & Silverdale (c).

(b)

(c)

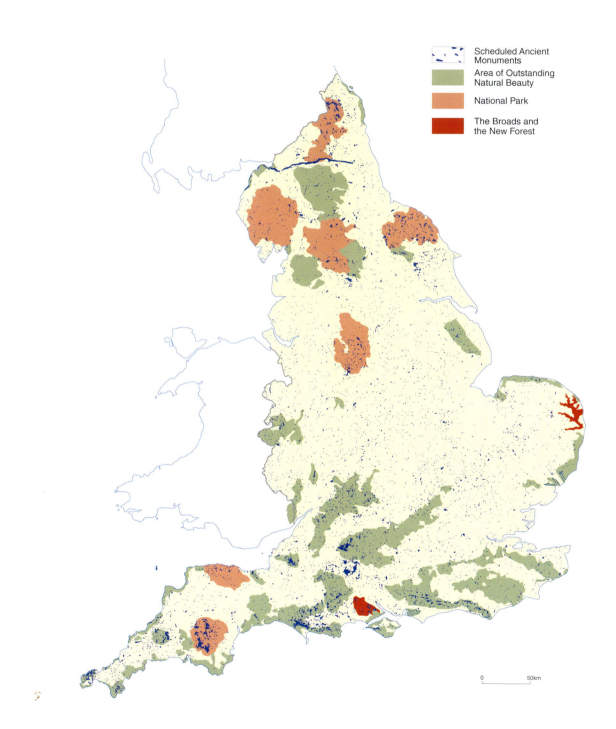

Plate 24 Map of Scheduled Ancient Monuments and
protected landscapes in England.

Scheduled Ancient
Monuments

Area of Outstanding
Natural Beauty

National Park

The Broads and
the New Forest

0   50km

(a)

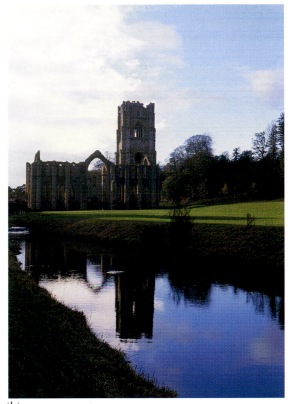

(b)

(c)

Historic and cultural features of AONBs (1)

Plate 25 Features of historic interest abound in AONBs, e.g. Bamburgh Castle on the Northumberland Coast (a), Fountains Abbey in Nidderdale (b) and ancient ritual stones and ancient field patterns in West Penwith, Cornwall (c).

(a)

(b)

Historic and cultural features of AONBs (2)

Plate 26 Features of historic interest abound in AONBs, e.g. the Iron Age Maiden Castle in Dorset (a), historic quays at Cotehele in the Tamar Valley (b) and more recent tin mine engine houses in Cornwall (c).

(c)

(a)

(b)

(c)

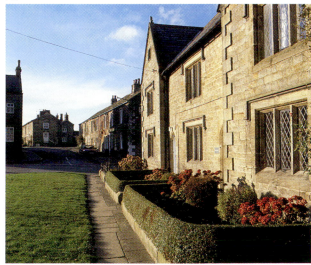

Buildings as part of the character of AONBs

Plate 27 Traditional buildings provide a particular sense of place in many AONBs, e.g. half-timbered houses in the Kent Downs (a), the distinctive stone of the Cotswolds (b) and Nidderdale (c).

(a)

**Villages in
the AONB
landscape (1)**

Plate 28 Villages, too,
add to the character
and quality of AONBs,
e.g. Cley on the Norfolk
Coast (a) and Slaidburn
in the Forest of
Bowland (b).

(b)

Villages in the AONB landscape (2)

Plate 29 Villages too, add to the character and quality of AONBs, e.g. Tollard Royal in Cranborne Chase and West Wiltshire Downs.

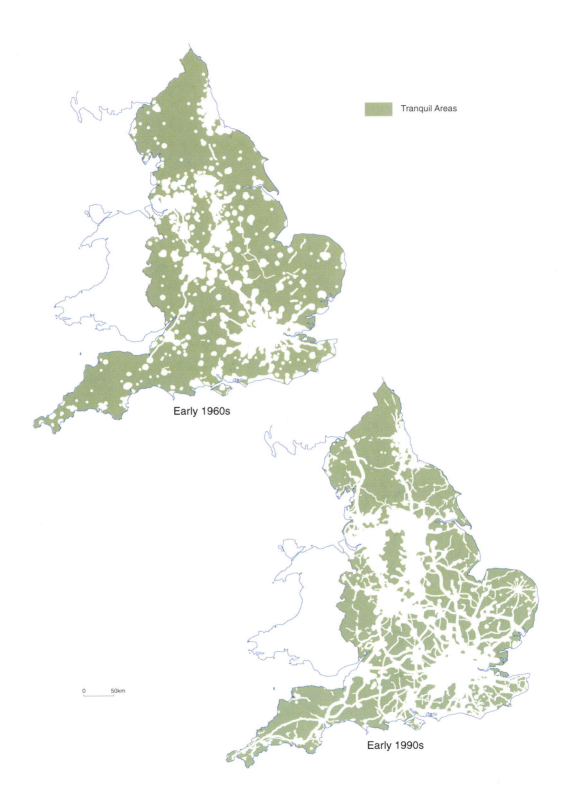

Tranquil Areas

Early 1960s

Early 1990s

0   50km

Plate 30   Map of Tranquil Areas in England, early 1960s and early 1990s.

Plate 31 AONBs, just like National Parks, are havens of tranquillity with open spaces, e.g. the beaches of the Norfolk Coast.

AONBs – Havens of tranquillity and wide open spaces (2)

Plate 32 AONBs, just like National Parks, are havens of tranquillity with open spaces, e.g. the extensive moors of the Forest of Bowland.

Table 5.1 Main National Trust Ownership in AONBs

AONB	Area (hectares)	% of AONB
Cannock Chase	363	5.40
Chilterns	2446	0.03
Cornwall	5429	5.60
Cranborne Chase	4464	4.70
Dorset	4583	0.10
Gower	1916	0.10
Norfolk Coast	2054	0.04
Shropshire Hills	2522	0.03
South Devon	1655	0.13
Surrey Hills	3605	0.20
Sussex Downs	3943	0.04

Source: National Trust.

where it owns two of the major attractions, Studland Beach and Corfe Castle. It is now an active partner in the Purbeck Heritage Committee, working to help achieve the wider policies for the area.

Finally, voluntary effort has made a very positive contribution in some AONBs, from the countryside management role of voluntary warden schemes, of major importance in Cotswolds and Sussex Downs, to the financial and project-based support of 'friends' organisations such as the Arnside and Silverdale AONB Landscape Trust, Chilterns Society and the Mendip Society (see Box 5.17), and the Society of Sussex Downsmen (see case studies). More similar organisations are being encouraged where there is the will and expertise to set them up as groups, which can both support the work of an AONB in various ways and be ready to offer informed criticism when this is necessary.

Awareness and understanding

The question of the 'profile' of AONBs in the minds of the general public and of policy-makers has come to the fore at the time of reviews of AONB activity. This was very much the case at the time of the Smart and Anderson review in 1989/90.[16] The need for a campaign to 'raise the profile' of AONBs was noted in their report, as part of the process of securing more money for their management. The report urged caution in the use of the word 'profile' because of the implications of encouraging too many visitors into sensitive places and causing damage to the environment. However, in doing so it suggested that 'awareness' was a more fitting way of describing the need for greater understanding of AONBs at a national and local level, and of the policies and actions required to secure their long-term conservation. One of the recommendations was that a well-argued case should be put to the DoE by the Commission, enlisting the support of MPs, the Association of County

BOX 5.17

Mendip Society

A good example of a voluntary group promoting the conservation, enjoyment and understanding of an AONB is the Mendip Society. Set up in 1965, it now has some 800 members. Its activities embrace a great deal more than the traditional, often rather negative, role of such societies – commenting on planning applications.

The Society is represented on the JAC for the AONB and took an active part in the preparation of the management plan for the AONB (1998). It has now launched a 'Mendip Hills Heritage Fund' to provide small grants to local organisations for initiatives such as: village appraisals and design statements; restoration repair and creation of small characteristics features in and around villages; the provision of information and interpretation facilities; publications that celebrate or increase awareness of the Hills and encourage appropriate access; and the acquisition of land or cultural items of Mendip significance.

Each year it runs an extensive programme of talks and walks and publishes books and leaflets about the area. In the spring of 1999 it ran a photographic competition – 'Eye on Mendip' – with a travelling exhibition containing the entries to stimulate awareness of the Hills. The Society also owns a small amount of land.

It is not only the fact that it has a very active and positive approach that is important. It is that it embraces both conservation and the enjoyment and understanding of the AONB. Also of great importance is the very positive relationship with the AONB team and the JAC, that helps to link the 'official' efforts relating to the conservation and enjoyment of the AONB with those of local people (see case study in Appendix 2).

Source: Communication with the Mendip Society.

Councils and the Association of District councils, aiming to raise awareness of the importance of AONB landscapes and their needs in terms of policy and finance.

Ten years on it is apposite to reflect on the progress towards greater awareness of AONBs. Nationally, the Countryside Commission took a number of modest steps to help the process, with the publication of the AONB Directory[17] and a leaflet[18] describing where and what they are and their significance. More important was the start of the process of preparing assessments of the landscapes of each AONB in England, including clear statements of why the particular AONB is nationally important. There is no doubt that these have proved useful, particularly in the preparation of management plans in some AONBs and in the process of development control when an understanding of the landscape has been important, particularly in public inquiries. They were also of considerable use in the designation of the most recent AONBs – the Blackdown Hills and Tamar Valley. While these initiatives were valuable, and indeed continue to be so, they did not add up to a campaign. For example, there was very little activity in terms of influencing the likes of MPs and national agencies. Indeed it took seven years for the Countryside Commission to see fit to put a case to government for more resources, but even that was not on the back of a major campaign. This may not be surprising since the major review of National Parks by the Edwards Committee,[19] followed by legislation for them in 1995 took up significant time and resources. Importantly that process was backed up by considerable energy from managers of the National Parks themselves, who had formed the Association of National Parks, and from the voluntary sector, in particular the Council for National Parks. Indeed there is perhaps a lot to be learned from the experience of the Association of National Parks, which has made significant strides in maintaining the profile of the Parks within government, and through a series of Accords it has agreed operating plans with key national agencies such as English Nature, Environment Agency and Forestry Commission, and the two responsible for the Parks, CC (now CA) and CCW.

Sadly for AONBs, there was no such movement behind them and to bolster the Commission's resolve. At the time of the Smart and Anderson report there seemed to be little enthusiasm for an AONB Forum, despite their having suggested it, and it is only recently that the AONB Staff Forum and the Association for AONBs have been formed (see also Chapter 4, which also refers to the promotion of the AONB Charter). Furthermore there were only a few local authorities with AONBs where councillors appreciated the need for national action. Although legislation was not included in the Queen's Speech of November 1999, the fact that it is now contemplated must in part be due to the growing power of the lobby for AONBs. This had to start from a base that was not nearly as powerful as that which has existed for long over the need for improvements of safeguards for SSSIs.

During this period individual AONB managements were taking a whole range of steps to raise awareness, though it was generally on an *ad hoc* basis rather than to any preconceived plan. Considerable effort has been given to raising the awareness of visitors by the production of leaflets about the area and information about facilities and activities, such as guided walks. In one or two cases information is now provided on websites, for example, Blackdown Hills and High Weald. Less obvious are attempts to raise awareness of what needs to be done to look after the area, although the majority of AONBs seem to have a logo, which is the start of creating an identity for an area. Quite a number of areas now produce newsletters on a regular basis and annual reports of activities of AONB Units are now more frequent. In many instances the very process of preparing the management plan is being used to raise awareness amongst the local population. The Mendips case study in Appendix 2 notes the importance of links with a field education centre (see Plate 50). In a few AONBs, for example, the Chilterns and the Forest of Bowland, road signs have been erected at key entrance points to the AONB (see Plate 50). There is, however, little evidence of AONB personnel actively securing the support of MPs, though some, such as in the Gower and Clwydian Range, seem to have made good progress. In the former the local MP led a debate in the House of Commons, and in the latter all the MPs and Welsh Assembly members have signed up to the spirit of the AONB Charter. A number of AONBs have been helped considerably by local societies formed to promote the interest of the conservation of the area. Notable amongst these are the Chiltern Society, the Arnside and Silverdale Landscape Trust, which was instrumental in securing a management service for the AONB, and the Mendip Society. Unlike the National Parks, each of which has its own voluntary society, the majority of AONBs do not have such spirited support.

A number of AONBs have adopted a more strategic approach to this whole question. For example, in 1995 the Chilterns Conference adopted a promotional strategy, mindful of the need to make more information available to the 100,000 residents in the area. The strategy embraced the production of an Annual Report, a new leaflet about the AONB, a summary of the management plan, a biannual newsletter – 'Chalk and trees' – display boards, regular articles in local newspapers and other journals and a general newsletter for councillors. The use of the logo is promoted amongst the partners and already 41 gateway signs have been erected. The case studies also demonstrate that the Purbeck Heritage Committee has developed a strategic approach, which was particularly valuable in its early years when longer-term political and therefore financial support was being sought. In preparing the strategy it was very clear in defining its target audience: existing and potential partners, the people of Purbeck, key regional and national opinion formers and the local and national media. It was also very clear that the strategy had to address the partnership itself by encouraging ownership of the Committee's activities as well as raising awareness of Purbeck's special qualities amongst local people – hence the adoption of two key messages, 'Working together to keep Purbeck Special' for the former group, and 'Keep Purbeck Special' for the latter group. The key elements of the strategy were the design of a logo, the establishment of a Forum, the regular publication of a newsletter, the running of 'Purbeck Aware' weekends, member briefings, display material and leaflets, publicity materials such as posters, car stickers, a planned programme of press releases and local community projects.

At this local level, the whole process of developing and implementing such a strategy is clearly a time-consuming and specialist affair. In the case of Purbeck, they were fortunate to have specialist advice from the Countryside Commission's Regional PR adviser. In the case of the Suffolk Coast and Heaths, a specialist is employed as member of the Unit. All too often, however, it is seen as just another tedious task, whereas it should be seen as an integral part of any AONB unit's work, if greater awareness of the importance and needs of AONBs is to be achieved, and the long-term support for what is being done to look after them is to be secured. Equally at the national level, particularly through the Association of AONBs and the National Agencies (CA and CCW), a much greater effort is needed if AONBs are to be accorded the kind of profile that National Parks have. Indeed there is a major opportunity for the Association to test its mettle in promoting the need for AONB legislation in the forthcoming Countryside Bill amongst MPs.

Commentary: a patchwork quilt

There is no doubt that the policies of CC, and latterly CCW, on administrative organisation for AONBs, their financial support for staffing and project work, and their guidance on the contents of plans has advanced the state of the art of AONB management. So has the surprisingly cross-party response of the leading AONB local authorities. This, and the strength of voluntary sector support in some areas, has been one of the features of the AONB system, though much still needs to be done in creating greater awareness and understanding of the importance and purpose of the designation, nationally and locally.

Nevertheless there is a considerable divergence between those areas that have a recognised management organisation and those (about a quarter of all AONBs at the time of writing) where nothing has been done other than the normal work of local planning authorities. Experience has shown that establishing an organisation takes a long time, not only to get the necessary agreement amongst the leading local authorities, but in creating a working partnership with the many organisations concerned (see, for example, the Cotswolds case study). By their very nature, most JACs are unwieldy and depend for their success on a few key personalities and the dedication of minimal staff on very short-term contracts. Partnership is not always as close as it might be. Countryside management services are integral in only a few areas, and delivery is not necessarily fully geared to JAC objectives and lines of communication. Similarly, at the time of writing about one-quarter of AONBs have no Management Plans as yet, and those that are in existence could be in some need of improvement, especially in treatment of sustainability issues and in monitoring.

Herein lie some of the weaknesses of the system. The statutory duty to conserve an AONB, proposed in the CC's Advice Paper,[20] is to be welcomed, but the weaknesses cannot be rectified properly without far more generous financial support and a generally higher profile for AONBs.

References

[1] Countryside Commission, *Areas of Outstanding Natural Beauty, Policy Statement*, CCP 157, Cheltenham, 1983.

[2] Countryside Commission and Countryside Council for Wales, *Areas of Outstanding Natural Beauty, A Policy Statement*, CCP 356, Cheltenham, 1991.

[3] Countryside Commission and Countryside Council for Wales, *Directory of Areas of Outstanding Natural Beauty*, available only on Countryside Agency website www.countryside.gov.uk

[4] Countryside Commission and Countryside Council for Wales, *Areas of Outstanding Natural Beauty, A Guide for Members of Joint Advisory Committees*, CCP 461, Cheltenham, 1994.

[5] Countryside Commission, CCP 157, op. cit.

[6] Countryside Commission and Countryside Council for Wales, CCP 356, op. cit.

[7] Countryside Commission and Countryside Council for Wales, *Directory of Areas of Outstanding Natural Beauty*, op. cit.

[8] Countryside Commission, *Protecting our Finest Countryside: Advice to Government*, CCP 532, Cheltenham, 1998.

[9] Countryside Commission and Countryside Council for Wales, *AONB Management Plans: Advice on Their Form and Content*, CCP 352, Cheltenham, 1992.

[10] Countryside Commission and Countryside Council for Wales, *National Park Management Plans Guidance*, CCP 525, Cheltenham, 1997.

[11] Countryside Commission and Countryside Council for Wales, *Directory of Areas of Outstanding Natural Beauty*, op. cit.

[12] *Protected Area Funding Study*, report for the Countryside Commission by Environmental Resources Management, London, 1998.

[13] Ibid.

[14] Ibid.

[15] Communication from the National Trust.

[16] Smart, G. & Anderson, M., *Planning and Management of Areas of Outstanding Natural Beauty*, Countryside Commission, CCP295, Cheltenham, 1990.

[17] Countryside Commission and Countryside Council for Wales, *Directory of Areas of Outstanding Natural Beauty*, op. cit.

[18] Countryside Commission, *Areas of Outstanding Natural Beauty in England and Wales*, CCP 276 (revised edition), Cheltenham, 1994.

[19] Countryside Commission, *Fit for the Future, the Report of the National Park Review Panel*, CCP 334, Cheltenham, 1991.

[20] Countryside Commission, CCP 532, op. cit.

Part Three
Wider Countryside Issues

Any discussion of the conservation of AONBs as nationally important landscapes must embrace land management and rural development. Part Three of the book, comprising Chapters 6 and 7, now examines how the many issues currently affecting the whole countryside interact with these two closely linked driving forces that need to be harnessed to secure the great value of these areas for the future. The chapters are concerned with land-based activity (agriculture and forestry, recreation and tourism, traffic and transport), and with rural development (especially the implications of planning and sustainability), and how those who manage AONBs have begun to tackle the tensions that exist. The fact that these concerns are inextricably linked is never far from the surface.

Land management 6

As Chapters 2 and 3 have already shown, it is agriculture and forestry that are the two most significant land uses in AONBs. While some land is used primarily for the conservation of wildlife and cultural resources and for recreation, it is nevertheless essential to the conservation of the finest landscapes that the area used for farming and forestry, holding a very significant proportion of the key features, is managed in such a way as to promote conservation. In other words there is a very strong element of multi-purpose land use. Indeed even where conservation is the primary purpose of management, success will often depend on the right form of agricultural management to secure conservation objectives. It is the activity of farmers and landowners over the years that has moulded the character and sustained the great value of AONBs. Conversely though, they have been the agents of change, often encouraged by government policy and incentives, that has not always been for the good of the nationally important resources that make up these areas. A key part of this chapter, illustrated in Plates 51 – 54, will be the examination of the interplay between agriculture and forestry on the one hand and conservation on the other. Accordingly it will explore agriculture and forestry policy, and the activities of MAFF and FC. The chapter will also focus on the work of the conservation agencies, especially English Nature and the Environment Agency, as essential members of the AONB 'partnerships'. This is illustrated, along with the environmental work of other partners, public and voluntary in Plates 55 – 57. The remainder of the chapter considers the challenges and opportunities for managers presented by the popularity of so many AONBs for recreation and tourism and the associated traffic and transport problems, illustrated in Plates 58 – 61. It will also explore the contribution to all these issues of land ownership in the public and voluntary sectors.

Agriculture

As has been described earlier the founding fathers of National Parks and AONBs relied on benign agricultural practices to look after the landscape. In the event an ever-increasingly efficient agriculture, fuelled by financial support for food production from central government and the EU, was the agent of dramatic changes in the landscape (and of course wildlife): hedgerows were removed, wetland drained, chalk down and moor or heathland ploughed, and woods grubbed up.

The managements of the fledgling protected landscapes, especially of AONBs, were not in a position to influence things. Even those of the National Parks were not really powerful enough (witness the ploughing up of large parts of Exmoor). However, from the 1970s onwards, with the growing understanding of what was happening, there has been a gradual change from agricultural policies that were not in the interests of the landscape towards those that foster a more sympathetic approach. The major milestones were:

- The 1981 *Wildlife and Countryside Act* – with stronger arrangements for protecting SSSIs, the introduction of management agreements, but no controls over landscape change (except where it happened to be an SSSI);

- The 1986 *Agriculture Act* – introduced ESAs (see Box 6.1), with their direct link to nationally important areas, and the duty of care for Ministers;

- In the 1990s the introduction of schemes such as Countryside Stewardship in England and Tir Cymen or Tir Gofal in Wales and the evolution of CAP to embrace environmental measures (see Box 6.1).

This evolution has been very important for both National Parks and AONBs, as some very useful tools have been developed with which they can begin to influence the way features of the landscape are managed. However, they depend on the voluntary co-operation of farmers, there being no compulsion to enter schemes, nor any cross-compliance with other parts of agricultural support. Further, the extent to which landscape features that have been lost are capable of restoration remains a moot point. Only time will reveal whether the attempts to re-create, for example, chalk downland or heath are successful.

While they are both schemes for paying farmers for managing land in a particular way, ESAs and Countryside Stewardship have evolved in different ways. ESAs rely on the designation of an area within which the scheme operates. As has been indicated earlier, an ESA has to be defined on the basis of its importance for conservation nationally (landscape, wildlife and archaeology), there has to be a close relationship with agriculture, and the area must be a discrete and coherent unit of conservation interest. Designation as an AONB is but one of the measures of national importance that is considered. As a

BOX 6.1

Agri-Environment Schemes in England and Wales

Environmentally Sensitive Areas (ESAs) – introduced in 1987 to help protect those areas where the landscape, wildlife or historic interest, are of national importance, from the changes brought about by the development of more intensive farming methods. The areas subject to the scheme are selected by MAFF with advice from the national conservation agencies. The 22 ESAs range in character from coastal marshland and rolling chalklands, to river valleys and open moorland. Farmers who enter the scheme are offered a 10-year management agreement to carry out agricultural practices which conserve or improve the landscape, wildlife habitats and historical features, in return for payments according to the amount and type of land they enter.

Countryside Stewardship (CS) – this scheme targets the conservation and enhancement of some key English landscape features and habitats and, where appropriate, improvements in public access to them. The targets are chalk and limestone grassland, lowland heath, watersides, coasts, uplands, historic landscapes, traditional orchards, old meadows and pastures, the countryside around towns including community forests, traditional field boundaries and the margins of arable fields. Ten-year management agreements are offered at the discretion of MAFF, with annual management payments ranging from £15/ha to £2580/ha and a wide range of capital grants. Unlike the position for ESAs, agreements are available anywhere in the country and to any owner or manager of land, subject to the priorities of the scheme as a whole and targets set out in statements prepared for each county.

Tir Gofal – introduced in 1999 to replace ESAs in Wales and to extend the operation of the experimental scheme Tir Cymen. It is a 'whole farm' scheme, available throughout Wales to farmers or others who have responsibility for, and control over, farmed land. The scheme offers 10-year agreements. Under the scheme there are certain mandatory requirements over the whole farm, for example, the retention of all existing traditional field boundaries, retention of trees, protection of ponds and streams with a one metre strip, maintaining stocking at 1998 levels and allowing public access to all unenclosed moorland. It also allows for optional restoration or creation of certain habitats or features, and the creation of new permissive access. In addition capital payments are made for work to protect and manage habitats and features.

result 11 AONBs in England have part of their area so designated (see Table 6.1 and Plate 19).

In contrast the eligibility for CS depends on the existence of a particular landscape feature or features on the property. A report on the uptake of CS between 1991 and 1997 prepared by FRCA for MAFF in

Table 6.1 AONBs in England with ESAs

AONB	ESA	Eligible area sq.km	Uptake at 1.1.98 sq.km	Payments pa at 1.1.98 (£ million)
Blackdown Hills	Blackdown Hills	n/a	n/a	n/a
Cornwall	West Penwith	69.0	78.0	0.55
Cotswolds	Cotswold Hills	661.0	437.0	2.65
	Thames Tributaries	n/a	n/a	n/a
Dedham Vale and Suffolk Coast & Heaths	Suffolk River Valleys	326.0	97.5	1.52
Dorset and Cranborne Chase & West Wiltshire Downs	South Wessex Downs	383.0	205.0	0.677
East Hampshire and Sussex Downs	South Downs	517.0	127.0	1.79
North Pennines	Pennine Dales	n/a	n/a	n/a
Shropshire Hills	Clun & Shropshire Hills	n/a	n/a	n/a

Source: *Protected Areas Funding Study*, report for the Countryside Commission by Environmental Resources Management, London, 1998.

1998,[1] shows that of the 7,239 agreements entered into during the period, AONBs and Heritage Coasts account for 1,824 or approximately, 25 per cent of the national total. Given that AONBs cover just 14 per cent of England, the representation of CS within them is significantly above the pro-rata distribution. In one sense this is surprising, as the idea behind the scheme was to embrace all parts of the countryside and there is no formal link with the existence of protected landscapes. In practice, however, there has been a close link with AONBs because there is a concentration of these features within them. Furthermore the targeting process has led to all or parts of them being the focus of investment. This is in part due to active lobbying by AONB services and to the existence of clear ideas of what to do. As shown in Box 6.2 and the case study in Appendix 2 the Mendip Hills AONB has been particularly active in relation to CS. A recent report to the AONB Joint Advisory Committee[2] concluded that key issues in the management plan are being addressed through the use of the scheme; the targeting of historic landscapes and heritage features, sites of nature conservation importance and boundary features like stone walls and hedgerows has been particularly successful.

Most AONBs appear to have been involved in one way or another with these agri-environment schemes and with agriculture generally.

The kind of involvement was highlighted by the Protected Areas Funding Study,[3] and by discussions with AONB staff during research for the book, as shown in Box 6.3. The study stressed the importance of the provision of advice to farmers by AONB teams to the success of agri-environment schemes. It also indicated the significant amount of time spent by AONB Staff on giving advice, for example, in the Forest of Bowland the equivalent of 0.5 full-time staff and in Howardian Hills 0.8.

By the very nature of AONBs, interaction with farming will always be a central task for their managers. It is clear that these schemes or their successors will be vital to their future and it would be appropriate for each area to have its own scheme tailored to its particular needs – a point made in the Commission's Advice to Government.[4] However, it will be a bold move on government's part to target certain areas to the inevitable detriment of others. It will also require increased expenditure. The Funding Study estimated that some £60 million per annum might be needed in AONBs – a small sum compared with other elements of support going to agriculture. Whether or

---

Key Stewardship Objectives

BOX 6.2

Applications should satisfy at least two of the following key objectives:

Countryside Stewardship in the Mendip Hills AONB

- Conservation of neglected limestone grasslands, old meadows and pastures or heathland
- Restoration of dry-stone walls and hedgerows as characteristic field boundaries
- Arable land measures – either the re-creation of permanent grassland or heath from arable land and the creation of uncropped grass margins around fields

Applications are likely to be enhanced if they include the provision for new permissive public access, conservation of archaeological earthworks and features, restoration of neglected orchards and traditional farm buildings.

Achievements

- 43 agreements between 1991 and 1998
- 1250 acres (9% of the AONB) of semi-natural grassland and heathland managed under the scheme
- 15 km of stone wall restoration
- 20 km of hedge restoration
- 15% of the AONB is covered by agreements

Source: Report to Mendip Hills JAC, March 1999, by Ben Thorne, Somerset FWAG.

BOX 6.3

Activities carried out by AONB Units and supporting Local Authorities to manage agri-pastoral schemes

- Influencing the direction of and operation of agri-environment schemes, e.g. Sussex Downs, Dorset, Cotswolds, Dedham Vale

- Encouragement of farmers to take up schemes, especially where enhancement can be achieved, e.g. Suffolk Coast & Heaths, Solway Coast, Norfolk Coast

- Providing advice through signposting and production of leaflets and conservation days

- Countryside management services and mobilising volunteers, to assist in repair of stone walls, laying hedgerows, etc., e.g. Cotswolds and Arnside & Silverdale, and training on hedgerow management, e.g. Blackdown Hills

- Provision of environmental advice

- Development of landscape guidelines with other partners, e.g. Sussex Downs

- Liaising with other countryside bodies and establishing agricultural or forestry working groups

- Running their own scheme for the AONB, e.g. Chilterns and East Hampshire

- Commissioning studies to demonstrate the need for schemes and suggesting pilot projects, lobbying MAFF and countryside bodies for change, e.g. High Weald, Kent Downs and Mendips

- Running conferences and seminars, e.g. High Weald

Source: *Protected Areas Funding Study* and communication with individual AONBs.

not such a proposal is accepted, it will be very important for the management of each AONB to have a clear idea of what can be done for conservation through agricultural activities with advice and support.

Forestry and woodlands

Afforestation, in particular extensive conifer planting, was for many years a significant threat to protected landscapes, especially the National Parks. The threat has now largely disappeared following a change of government policy in England in the early 1980s, which effectively brought an end to such planting. AONBs were never under quite the same threat. However, there was a period in the 1950s and 1960s when conifer planting was affecting them too. A particular example was the Cotswolds, where much of the ancient and semi-natural woodland was converted to intensive forestry during this period. Perhaps of greater importance was the loss of woodland altogether in some areas such as the Kent Downs, and the fact that so much of existing woodland was not managed at all.

In recent years forestry policy has been much more sympathetic to issues such as landscape and wildlife. Indeed the Woodland Grant Scheme run by the Forestry Commission is now strongly biased towards the planting of broad-leaved trees and offers assistance for providing public access to woodland, and it also encourages forms of management that will implement the forestry aspects of the UK Biodiversity Action Plan. Generally speaking, however, the Forestry Commission has never focused its attention on AONBs, though the case studies show that it has been active in places such as the Wye Valley and the Chilterns, and there are many woods owned by the Commission within AONBs. Similarly, policies for grant aid have generally applied to the whole countryside and have not been targeted to areas such as AONBs. Recently, however, schemes have been introduced to target grants to specific areas. So far these have included National Parks, Community Forests and places like the South West Forest, where particular emphasis is being given to woodland matters. Thus far, AONBs have not been amongst the specific targets.

Significantly the Forestry Commission now has a special accord with the Association of National Parks[5] relating to Native Woodlands in National Parks. Its aim is to encourage the appropriate management and extension of semi-natural woodland, and to identify areas where it is appropriate to encourage new woodland that emulates semi-natural woodland. In practice this means that the Forestry Commission is working very closely with each National Park, providing advice and training, undertaking research and, most importantly, deploying funds under the woodland grant scheme to assist in the practical management of woods.

The recently published Forestry Strategy for England[6] is silent on protected landscapes, except for mention of the challenge fund for new native woodlands in National Parks, but it is very strong on the links with biodiversity. However, the thrust of the strategy towards sustainable management of existing woods and forests, and towards a steady expansion to provide more benefits for society and the environment is one which should indirectly benefit AONBs. Indeed the multi-purpose approach, linking rural development, economic regeneration, recreation, access and tourism and environment and conservation, is something to which some AONBs are already attuned.

Quite a number of AONBs have become closely involved with forestry and woodland matters, particularly those that have a significant woodland cover (see Chapter 2). The involvement ranges from the development of management guidelines, for example in the Wye

Valley (see Box 6.4) and the Howardian Hills, to the encouragement of management through advice and initiatives for marketing and the use of timber, for example in the Chilterns and the High Weald (see Box 6.4).

One of the problems for managers is that some AONBs are often not sufficiently large to warrant their own marketing initiatives, and with no economies of scale. Fortunately there are increasing numbers of initiatives covering much wider areas which can be latched on to. A typical example is the Howardian Hills, a small AONB that has been associated with the North York Moors National Park and

---

BOX 6.4

Woodland Management Initiatives

Wye Valley – The AONB Committee, together with the Forestry Commission and others, has produced guidelines to encourage good management practice. The main objectives are seen to be the perpetuation of the wooded landscape, nature conservation, wood production and recreation. The relative importance attached to each will vary from place to place but in most woods they will all need to be considered. The guidelines help to strike the right balance. Typical of the principles established are:

- When broad-leaved trees are felled they should be replaced with another broad-leaved crop – usually oak, ash, beech, cherry or lime

- Ancient semi-natural woods should be regenerated with species native to the site, preferably natural regeneration by seedlings

- Shelterwood helps to perpetuate the wooded appearance – old trees are left standing over a regeneration area to provide seed and shelter for the next generation of trees

- The size of felling areas should be in scale with the landscape – small fellings in small woods or intimate landscapes in the gorge, larger fellings in the wider landscapes on the plateau above

- Where conifers are grown, they should merge gradually with other species

Source: Wye Valley AONB Joint Advisory Committee, *Woodland Management Guidelines* (2 ed.) 1996 and see also Wye Valley AONB Case Study in Appendix 2.

Chilterns Woodland Project & the TWIG project

The Chilterns AONB Case Study (see Appendix 2) shows that for many years the woodlands of the Chilterns have been the focus of the AONB Conference. Its own plan includes detailed objectives, principles and proposals for forestry management. The Chilterns Woodlands Project, initiated in 1983 by the Chilterns Society, continues to be one of the cornerstones of

thence with the county-wide 'Yorwood' project. Similarly the Forest of Bowland is linked to the wider Lancashire Woodlands Initiative. This kind of connection with the wider world is an important management principle not just for woodlands but in dealing with many other issues, such as recreation and traffic. It will be vital for AONBs to make such links.

Forestry and woodland management are clearly very important matters for AONBs, not only because of their contribution to the landscape but also because they can achieve a wider range of benefits – for recreation, for wildlife and as a source of economic activity.

---

practical work, having become a registered charity. As well as providing advice to owners of small woods, it helps the marketing of local timber as the local co-ordinator for WOODLOTS, a national exchange and mart advertising parcels of timber and woodland produce for sale. It has also helped raise awareness of the need to manage woodlands through its own newsletter and the organisation of conferences. More recently the AONB Conference has inaugurated an Annual Chilterns Woodlands Award for excellence in woodland management. In 1998 the TWIG project (Trans-national Woodland Industries Group) started following a successful bid to the EU RECITE II programme for grant aid by a consortium of international partners (from Sweden, Greece and Germany), created by the Conference. The project aims to promote woodland management by enhancing the commercial value of local timber and other woodland products. Some £312,000 are available to the Chilterns over the 3 years of the project for a variety of research, marketing and development initiatives.

Source: Chilterns AONB Conference Annual Reports and Newsletter.

High Weald Design project

The project was set up in 1993 under the auspices of the High Weald Forum, aiming to conserve the traditionally managed woodlands of the AONB by promoting the use of local hardwoods for the production of indoor and outdoor furniture, using contemporary and innovative designs by local craftsmen. It has demonstrated how local wood can be used to provide high value, robust and long-lasting everyday furniture. A company limited by guarantee that was established for the purpose has now taken on the work of the project.

Source: High Weald AONB – Newsletter, project promotional brochure.
See also High Weald case study in Appendix 2.

Although AONBs have not been targeted in the same way as National Parks, there is no reason why they should not have similar treatment, with specific programmes of grant support. What will be important, though, is for each area to be absolutely clear as to what it wants to achieve through the management of existing woodland, and how the expansion of woodland fits in with its character. In this way they could then benefit from such programmes that are developed.

The wider environment

In the 1940s when the idea of setting aside special landscape areas was conceived, little thought seems to have been given to the relationship to their wider environment. The focus was very much on the quality of the scenery as distinct from the quality of the air and water, protection from flooding, water supplies, waste disposal and the like. In recent years the quality of the environment has moved centre stage, driven by such concerns as health, global warming and the conservation of wildlife.

At a national level one very important expression of the concerns about the wider environment was the creation of the Environment Agency in 1995. The new agency has a central role in addressing climate change, improving air quality, managing water resources, enhancing biodiversity, managing freshwater fisheries, delivering integrated river basin management, conserving the land, managing waste and regulating industrial pollution.[7] Its principal aim, set out in the Action Plan for its conservation function, is 'to help protect special conservation assets and to help enhance and restore degraded areas, for the benefit of current and future generations'.[8] Indeed the principle of protecting the best conservation assets and improving the rest is central to the Agency's overall environmental strategy.

The Agency's conservation remit embraces wildlife, landscape and physiographical features, plus sites, objects and buildings of archaeological, architectural, engineering and historical interest that are directly or indirectly affected by its regulatory and operational activities. The Agency is not responsible for site or species protection, but in using its regulatory duties and powers it has a major influence in preventing and controlling pollution of air, land and water, and in the management of the water environment and resources. The Agency's Action Plan for Conservation identified the relationship between the key environmental issues it is concerned with and conservation. This is set out in Box 6.5.

Although the Action Plan focuses heavily on nature conservation issues, in particular the protection of sites and the delivery of the UK Biodiversity Action Plan, it also relates to the broader landscape such as

- **Addressing climate change** – Impact of drought, sea level rise on species and habitats

- **Improving air quality** – impact of acid rain on plants animals and buildings

- **Managing water resources** – impact of over-abstraction on wetlands

- **Enhancing biodiversity** – obligations under the UK Biodiversity Action Plan and implementing the EU Birds and Habitats Directives

- **Managing freshwater fisheries** – stocking policy, disease, exotics

- **Integrated river basin management** – catchment-based conservation objectives

- **Conserving the land** – impact of soil erosion on landscape, habitats and archaeology

- **Managing waste** – impact of spreading waste on special wildlife habitats

- **Regulating major industry** – effective conservation criteria for consents

Source: Environment Agency, *An Action Plan for Conservation*, Bristol, 1998.

BOX 6.5

Conservation and the Environment Agency's Key Environmental Issues

the improvement of river landscapes wherever the opportunity arises.

Many of the issues addressed by the Agency are of immediate interest to those managing AONBs, for example coastal protection will be a major issue for those with low-lying coasts as in Norfolk, Suffolk and South Hampshire; also most AONBs have river valleys that are of significance for the landscape, as well as for wildlife, and the way rivers are treated in engineering terms will often be important; equally the quality of water in rivers and on the coast will be of great importance to recreation users and wildlife. Of less immediately obvious interest is the quality of the air, which will have an impact on the conservation interest as well as people's enjoyment of the area. It is evident, however, that few AONBs have addressed or engaged in these issues to any great degree.

At the local level the Agency is preparing a Local Environment Agency Plan (LEAP) for each river catchment. These plans are a way of producing a local agenda of activities for effective environmental management and improvement, with the accent on the Agency working in partnership with a range of stakeholders. A number of common themes have been identified in LEAPs,[9] including the management of waste and effluents, of particular importance on the coast and

BOX 6.6

The Accord between the Environment Agency and the Association of National Parks

Common objective:

The Parties to this Accord have a mutual interest in furthering the protection, conservation and enhancement of the National Parks and the Broads, and opportunities to understand and enjoy them, while safeguarding the economic and social well-being of the Park and Broads communities. Through this Accord, they commit themselves to co-operate to these ends and to aim for the highest standards of environmental quality and sustainability in these protected areas.

Commitments

The Parties will together:

1. consult as appropriate on the preparation of statutory and non-statutory plans at regional and local level;

2. co-operate in the implementation of conservation programmes including the UK Biodiversity Action Plan;

3. liaise, and where appropriate, collaborate to develop and improve opportunities for the public to understand and enjoy National Parks and the Broads;

4. through partnership seek understanding and awareness of their actions by the local communities;

5. co-operate in research, monitoring and data exchange of relevance to each other's programmes;

6. develop local links, shared training and staff development opportunities.

Working Arrangements

Each National Park Authority and the Broads Authority together with the appropriate Areas of the Environment Agency will work in partnership to develop and take forward specific action programmes.

The Parties agree that all land and water within a National Park and the Broads is of particular importance for consultation under Section 8 of the *Environment Act*, 1995. They will develop appropriate working arrangements regarding specific impacts and actions at a local level.

Progress on both the implementation of this Accord and the development of local action plans will be reviewed annually at a national meeting between the Environment Agency and the Association of National Park Authorities.

Source: Accord between the Association of National Park Authorities and the Environment Agency, 1996.

in rivers; water abstraction and low flows in rivers; flood defence; protection and restoration of habitats; and the improvement of recreational access. So far it is not evident that AONBs have been closely involved in their preparation or that their interests are being taken on board, despite the former Countryside Commission preparing advisory notes for the Agency on how to consider landscape issues.[10]

Clearly a very important range of work on rural resources is being undertaken by the Environment Agency. However, it is not under the same obligations towards AONBs as it is towards National Parks. AONBs are covered by the general requirement that the Agency should promote conservation work. In contrast there is a specific duty in the 1995 Act[11] for the Agency to work with the National Parks, with which it now has an accord (see Box 6.6). This is a reflection perhaps that AONBs are not tuned in to the opportunities that they present; equally it may be a reflection of the emphasis that the Agency gives to biodiversity rather than landscape. However, there are a few instances of close working between the Agency and AONB managers on both conservation and recreation matters as shown in the examples from the case study areas of the Chilterns and the Sussex Downs in Box 6.7. It is clear that there should be a very close relationship between the Agency's work, in particular the planning processes it goes through, and the well-being of AONBs. Indeed there is a major opportunity for AONB managers to enlist a very valuable partner that has resources to bring to the table. However, AONBs will need to be fully geared up to help develop such a partnership and will need to be clear about what they want to achieve, particularly through the clarity of their own objectives and plans and the use of staff and financial resources, so that a genuine partnership can be struck.

Wildlife conservation

The wildlife resources of AONBs are very important as shown in Chapter 2. Indeed the wildlife interest is often, though not always, similar to that of the landscape. As shown elsewhere in the book, nature conservation has tended to focus on sites (SSSIs, etc.) rather than areas or the countryside as a whole. More recently with the publication of the joint character map by English Nature (EN) and the Countryside Commission in 1997[12] the focus has widened to the whole countryside. Through the use of their Natural Areas EN has laid the foundations for the conservation of wildlife, with targets for which purpose certain Natural Areas are seen as more important than others. Some of these coincide with AONBs, for example, those with lowland heath as a prime target for conservation and restoration.

BOX 6.7

Examples of AONBs working with the Environment Agency

Sussex Downs: The Ouse Valley Project – It is a partnership between the Agency and the Sussex Downs Conservation Board, which aims to conserve and enhance the nature conservation, landscape and amenity value of the Ouse Valley. By pooling resources and experience this partnership ensures an integrated approach towards all aspects of the management of the valley – landscape, wildlife, recreation, farming and water. A project officer acts as the catalyst for activity working with farmers and landowners and the local community. The post is paid for by the Agency, with the Board providing office space and administration. A project budget of £11,000 each year has been supported by the Countryside Agency, English Nature, Sports Council and the local authorities. The wide range of initiatives being pursued includes canoe access to the river, building otter holts, an interpretation plan using the work of local artists, linking farmers to Countryside Stewardship, the preparation of landscape guidelines, the development of circular routes with links to bus and train services. The work of the project is integrated with the Ouse Valley LEAP and the Sussex Biodiversity Plan.

Source: Leaflet prepared by Sussex Downs Board, and communication with the Board.

Tamar Valley – The Tamar Valley Discovery Trail has been developed by a partnership between the Tamar Valley Countryside Service, Cornwall and Devon County Councils, several district councils, the Countryside Commission and the Agency. A 30-mile trail between Plymouth and Launceston through the AONB has been established. It runs through a variety of landscapes: tidal mudflats and salt marshes, broad-leaved woodlands and the river bank. Circular routes allow the visitor to explore local villages and to gain access to the railway that passes

Perhaps one of the most far-reaching influences has been the Convention on Biological Diversity, not least for the process it has stimulated throughout the UK. It was one of several major initiatives stemming from the 'Earth Summit' in Rio de Janeiro in 1992, which together form an international agreement on sustainable development. Signatories recognised that action must be taken to halt the global loss of animal and plant species and that each country should take action to conserve and enhance its own biodiversity. They agreed that each nation should develop a national strategy, plan or programme for the conservation and sustainable use of biological diversity.

The UK response to the Convention is set out in *Biodiversity: the UK Action Plan* that was published in 1994.[13] It sets out the broad along the valley. Environmental benefits include hedging, tree planting, orchard development and production of farm conservation plans. Socio-economic benefits include the promotion of local produce and support for local transport.

Source: Discovery Trail leaflet and Environment Agency Conservation, Access and Recreation Report 1997/8.

Chilterns: Misbourne and Chess Valleys Project – These valleys form part of the heartland of the AONB. Low rainfall and water abstraction have lead to the disappearance of the River Misbourne. The River Chess continues to flow through one of the most distinctive landscapes of the AONB. The project aims to restore and maintain river flows, conserve all aspects of the environment of both valleys and to show how rivers can be managed throughout the Chilterns. Local demand for water is one of the causes of low river flows. The project aims to help people understand the water cycle, and how they can use water wisely. A major part of the project, being undertaken by the Agency and the water companies is the transfer of water from the River Colne to the two valleys, thus reducing the amount of groundwater taken from the aquifer beneath the rivers. These works have been complemented by the Project led by the AONB, with a budget of £32,000 over two years. It has developed a range of education and interpretation initiatives based on the landscape and wildlife of chalk rivers, and small-scale landscape and wildlife projects. The success of this project has led to the development of similar initiatives elsewhere in the Chilterns.

Source: Communication with AONB Officer, Project leaflet, Chiltern Society and Chilterns Conference Newsletter Summer/Autumn 1999.

strategy for conserving and enhancing wild species and wildlife habitats in the UK for the next 20 years. The overall goal of the plan is 'to conserve and enhance biological diversity within the UK and to contribute to the conservation of global biodiversity through all appropriate mechanisms'. The objectives of the plan, which are very broad in their scope, are set out in Box 6.8. Since then work has proceed apace on the preparation of costed action plans for 290 species and 29 key habitats. As the Local Government Management Board (LGMB) Guidance Note[14] points out, the concept of quantifiable targets for species and habitats accompanied by monitoring the success of the plan is a new concept in UK rural planning and, perhaps, something that protected landscapes could usefully follow.

Equally important has been the introduction of the Local Biodiversity

BOX 6.8

Objectives of the UK Biodiversity Action Plan

To conserve and, where practicable, to enhance:

- The overall populations and natural ranges of native species and the quality and range of wildlife habitats and ecosystems

- Internationally important and threatened species, habitats and ecosystems

- Species, habitats and natural and managed ecosystems that are characteristic of local areas

- The biodiversity of natural and semi-natural habitats where this has been diminished over recent decades

Source: *Biodiversity: The UK Action Plan*, CM2428, HMSO, London, 1994.

Action Plan (LBAP) as a basis for ensuring that that the national strategy is turned into action locally in a consistent fashion (see Box 6.9). The LGMB advice note goes on to say that there is more to LBAPs than meeting national targets. They provide a means of achieving several aspects of the UK Action Plan that can only be achieved at the local level.[15]

This work has received a very high standing in government priorities. However, it is proceeding on a course that is to some extent detached

BOX 6.9

Functions of a Local Biodiversity Action Plan

- To ensure that national targets for species and habitats, as specified in the UK Action Plan, are translated into effective action at the local level

- To identify targets for species and habitats appropriate to the local area, and reflecting the values of people locally

- To develop effective local partnerships to ensure that programmes for biodiversity conservation are maintained in the long term

- To raise awareness of the need for biodiversity conservation in the local context

- To ensure that opportunities for conservation and enhancement of the whole biodiversity resource are fully considered

- To provide the basis for monitoring progress in biodiversity conservation, at both the local and national level

Source: Local Government Management Board, *Guidance for Local Biodiversity Action Plans*, Guidance Note No. 1: An Introduction, London.

from landscape and other countryside work, with a great deal of energy and resources being devoted to it by a wide range of organisations.

The emphasis on biodiversity does of course embrace the whole countryside, but there is very little recognition of the role that protected landscapes can play in implementing the UK strategy. There is no mention in the UK plan of AONBs (though there is of NSAs in Scotland) and only passing reference to National Parks. The LGMB advice is silent on AONBs, though it does say that National Parks might be amongst many organisations who might want to prepare such a plan. It also suggests that plans such as National Park management plans offer opportunities for assisting with the delivery of biodiversity targets and are often crucial in this respect.[16]

There is clearly an opportunity here for well-organised AONBs to play a part in this process, even if they do not lead it. One example of the kind of role that can be played is provided by the Purbeck Heritage Committee, which together with the RSPB has led the process of preparing a LBAP for its area – a very important and discrete part of the Dorset AONB (see Box 6.10 and the Purbeck case study in Appendix 2). The role has included the employment of an officer to guide its implementation.

While the Biodiversity Convention is essentially strategic in its approach, a number of other conventions and treaties were much more specific. The most important of these are the Ramsar Convention, the EC Birds Directive and the EC Habitats Directive (see Box 6.11). Each requires the designation of sites and their subsequent protection for particular wildlife purposes.

The significance for AONBs lies in the fact that they are specifically aimed at the conservation of species and habitats rather than the wider landscape. One consequence is that political priority tends to be given to the requirements of the treaties rather than to other countryside issues. Nevertheless, for those AONBs with extensive areas designated under these treaties (see Chapter 2), there is a good opportunity to ensure that policies for wildlife management and those for the wider landscape context are compatible.

AONB management plans address wildlife conservation issues to an extent, and with Natural Area (NA) profiles and Biodiversity Action Plan (BAP) targets they should be able to provide a basis for action. However, it is evident from research for the book that the link between EN and AONBs is weak. AONBs are not recognised as providing a wider context for the management of nature conservation sites, nor as agents for co-ordinating or carrying out nature conservation activities; this is evident in relation to BAPs and also to NA profiles which themselves are very light on implementation. That said, there are examples of nature conservation activities with informal joint working between the various partners in AONB management, especially with the voluntary sector bodies

BOX 6.10

**A Local
Biodiversity
Action Plan for
Purbeck**

'Purbeck is one of the most rich and diverse areas for wildlife in the UK. Its wide range of habitats and variety of species make the area unique. However, Purbeck is suffering from a number of pressures, such as changes in land use and rural economy, which are responsible for losses of biodiversity and environmental quality. These general problems are outlined in *Keeping Purbeck Special: a Strategy for the Purbeck Heritage Area*, which recognises the need for action now if Purbeck is to be passed on to future generations in the same state, or better, than it is today.

Purbeck's outstanding wildlife interest, and the pressure it faces, made the area a natural choice for a pilot local biodiversity action plan. During 1996 and early 1997 an audit of species and habitats of conservation concern was undertaken and detailed action plans for habitats and species requiring urgent attention were written by conservation experts.

The Local Biodiversity Action Plan sets out the 'conservationist's agenda' for Purbeck and the next step is to involve landowners, land managers and other organisations in helping to implement the proposals. Successful implementation will require the co-operation of many individuals and organisations which will be facilitated by a Biodiversity Officer based at the District Council's offices in Wareham.'

Key Elements in the Plan Production

Establishment of Steering Group – RSPB, the Purbeck Heritage Committee, English Nature, Dorset Wildlife Trust, Environment Agency, National Trust, Dorset County Council and Purbeck District Council. This group was established to encourage a shared vision for biodiversity conservation in Purbeck.

Choice of Habitat Action Plans – 10 habitats were chosen for detailed plans. Lowland heath, rivers, reedbed, lowland wet grassland, broad-leaved woodland, parkland, arable, calcareous grassland, maritime cliff and slope, and marl beds.

Each plan contained the following sections – definition, current status, nature conservation importance, biodiversity context, problems, opportunities and current action and monitoring.

Choice of Habitat Statements – less detailed than the main action plans, covering dunes, estuaries, standing, open water, unimproved neutral grassland, fens (mires) extensive sublittoral rock and seagrass beds.

Choice of Species Action Plan – embracing those species that would not be adequately conserved by carrying out actions for habitats alone.

Source: Purbeck Biodiversity Steering Group, *A Local Biodiversity Action Plan for Purbeck*, 1998.

Ramsar – Convention on wetlands of international importance 1971. Ratified by the UK in 1976 with a commitment to promote the conservation of particular sites and the wise use of wetlands. All Ramsar sites are SSSIs. Sites can be areas of marsh, fen, peatland or water – natural or artificial and either permanent or temporary, with water that is static or flowing, fresh, brackish or salt. They can also include very shallow areas of the sea. Not only important for birds but also for their plant communities, invertebrates and other animal populations.

EC Birds Directive (1979) – designation of Special Protection Areas (SPAs) to encourage the protection of wild birds and their habitats, in particular the rare or vulnerable species listed in the Directive and regularly occurring migratory species.

EC Habitats Directive (1992) – protection of habitats and species mainly through designation of Special Areas of Conservation (SACs). Protected through very strict control of planning, with the presumption that no development is allowed unless of over-riding public interest, and the requirement to prepare and implement a management plan. Together with SPAs, SACs will form a network of European sites, known as Natura 2000. The aim is to maintain rare or endangered species and habitats at favourable conservation status throughout Europe. The Directive also promotes other measures for the sustainable management of the countryside and marine environment outside designated areas, for without this wider approach the task of protecting nature inside the designated areas becomes very difficult.

BOX 6.11

International Wildlife Commitments

such as the RSPB and the Wildlife Trusts, as shown by the examples in Box 6.12 and illustrated in Plate 57. This is in contrast to the arrangements between EN and the National Parks, where both have a statutory duty to work together and there is a formal agreement between them.[17] The agreement provides for annual meetings of all the signatories to discuss co-operative programmes at national level and policy issues of common interest, and at a local National Park scale for the implementation of agreed measures via an annual action plan. This process has led to a wide range of joint projects being implemented. Typical examples are the preparation of BAPs for Dartmoor and the Yorkshire Dales, moorland management schemes in Northumberland and North York Moors, integrated management plans for the mountain massifs of the Lake District and broad-leaved woodland projects in the Yorkshire Dales.

All in all, there is a very strong sectoral approach to wildlife conservation, particularly where English Nature is concerned. The arrangements

BOX 6.12

**Examples
of Nature
Conservation
activity at the
heart of AONBs**

*(see illustrations
in Plate 57)*

Norfolk Coast Conservation Plan

With over 30 designated wildlife sites the AONB is of exceptional national and international importance, containing habitats, species and landforms which in variety are unrivalled in England. Given the fact that the AONB is a living, working landscape, providing homes, and livelihoods in tourism, agriculture, fishing and local businesses, the need to ensure that nature conservation is fully taken into account in planning the long-term management of the AONB was recognised in the publication below prepared by English Nature, Norfolk Wildlife Trust, the National Trust and the RSPB, all of whom manage extensive sites on the coast. It was jointly funded by English Nature and the Norfolk Coast AONB Project and is now incorporated in the AONB management plan. It is intended to provide a focus for key organisations or individuals within the AONB whose activities affect wildlife. It draws heavily on English Nature's Natural Area approach, by promoting conservation management in the wider countryside, habitat creation outside isolated designated sites, and the integration of nature conservation policies into all aspects of planning and land use.

Source: English Nature, Norfolk Wildlife Trust, the National Trust and RSPB, *A Vision for Nature Conservation in the Norfolk Coast AONB 1997 – 2022*, 1998, and Norfolk Coast AONB Case Study in Appendix 2.

The Gower Commons Initiative

Gower is one of the most significant areas in the UK for lowland heathland. Much of this heathland is registered common land and is grazed by local commoners. Unlike the situation in other parts of the UK this grazing is still an essential part of the farm economy and this represents a unique opportunity for long-term management of these areas. The commons constitute a major resource for public recreation, many of them being immediately adjacent to the urban area of Swansea.

The aim of the Initiative is to reverse the decline of an internationally important heathland resource, to provide opportunities for education and enjoyment and support the local farming community, in partnership with landowners, in maintaining this asset for the future. The initiative is part of the Tomorrow's Heathland Heritage umbrella programme. The bid was put together on behalf of the 21 organisations which make up the Gower

for National Parks provide clear evidence of the kind of co-operation that would be appropriate for AONBs. However, there is a need for more recognition of the role that AONBs could play in achieving a wide range of nature conservation objectives. The managers of these areas are in a strong position to provide much of the framework for the conservation of wildlife habitats and species, especially linking in

Countryside Forum, the Advisory Committee for the AONB and Heritage Coast and major landowners in the area. It consists of the following key elements:

- Management of 1,145ha of heathlands and the restoration of a further 890ha currently overgrown with bracken and scrub. A total of 2,035ha which represents 3.5% of the UK target for the Biodiversity Action Plan

- Providing the necessary infrastructure, such as cattle grids and traffic calming, to ensure that the traditional management of the commons can continue in the long term despite increasing pressures

- Maintaining and enhancing public access and provision of interpretation and education to improve visitor experience

- The appointment of a Heathland Liaison Officer, with seasonal support, to oversee the proposals, ensure their implementation and liaise with local people and visitors

The overall cost of the Initiative over the five years from 1999 to 2004 is projected at £843,958, towards which the organisations in the Gower Heathland Group contribute up to £253,188 (30% of total) and the Heritage Lottery Fund £590,770 (70% of total).

Source: Gower AONB.

Chichester Harbour

The Harbour, the core of the AONB, has been designated an SSSI and, in view of its importance internationally for birds, it is also a Ramsar Site and has been designated an SPA and a cSAC under the EU Birds and Habitats Directives. Nature conservation is therefore a key element in the management of the AONB. This importance is reflected in the inclusion in the management plan of a Biodiversity Action Plan for the Harbour. This consists of individual plans for habitats and some species as well as monitoring and research.

Source: Chichester Harbour Conservancy, *Chichester Harbour AONB Management Plan*, Chichester, 1999.

with the NA and BAP processes, which overlap very strongly. There needs to be more 'joined up' thinking on this. A formal role in nature conservation for AONBs would help, as might a statutory duty for English Nature along the lines of the arrangements for National Parks.

Recreation and tourism   Studies carried out for CC and others have shown that demand for outdoor activities has been growing, nationally, for many years and, as was indicated in Chapter 3, there is little doubt that this will continue in the foreseeable future. The importance of opportunities for people to enjoy the countryside is well known, as, indeed, are the economic benefits to rural areas. In both senses recreation impinges on the aims of land management whether by the public, private or voluntary sectors. This is an ever-widening responsibility for AONBs and not only in the management of land; the relationship with economic development and traffic policies is also important.

Chapter 2 has pointed to the attractions of AONBs for recreation, for example, in Sussex Downs, Chilterns, Cannock Chase, Malvern Hills and Gower, all of which are close to large centres of population and attract many day visitors. Others, on the coast such as Cornwall, South and East Devon, Dorset and Chichester Harbour, and inland such as Wye Valley and Cotswolds, draw tourists, staying visitors and people with special interests more widely from Britain and overseas. It will have been noted that areas like these experience greater numbers of visits than some National Parks. Most of the visitors travel by car; they come to enjoy their outstanding scenic qualities, and are also attracted by the variety of opportunities for active recreation that some AONBs can offer: long-distance back-packing, caravanning and camping, rock climbing, caving, water-sports, fishing, and hang-gliding.

The promotion and management of countryside recreation has for long been an important priority for CC, and is a major component of the strategy and work programme of CCW and the Commission's successor, CA. The emphasis now placed by the Government on access to open countryside has added a new dimension to CA's recreational role, adding to the long-standing experience of provision for this under the 1949 Act in the National Parks. That Act did not, however, make recreation a statutory purpose of AONB designation, as a result of which a cautionary approach has always been followed, despite the obvious pressures. Indeed, in response to the 1980 AONB review, CC and the Government did consider recognising recreation as an objective of designation when consistent with the conservation of natural beauty, but decided at the time that the current legislation was satisfactory.[18] Thus the cautionary approach became well established and was confirmed in the 1991 joint Policy Statement of CC and CCW,[19] and still applies: AONBs should be used to meet the demand for recreation so as far as consistent with the over-riding interest of conserving natural beauty, and also with the needs of agriculture, forestry and other users.

Within this general policy the two bodies have emphasised the importance of managing tourism and recreation in order to provide a high quality experience for visitors, to maintain the fabric of AONBs, and to avoid friction with local communities. The need for a sustainable approach to tourism, in particular, was spelt out in more detail by CC jointly with the English Tourist Board and the former Rural Development Commission in 1993 (see Box 6.13). There is still concern amongst AONB managers at the tendency for some tourism organisations to attract visitors widely without due regard to this approach.

In line with their policy for the countryside as a whole, CC (and now CA) and CCW have for long made grants available for recre-

---

In 1993 CC, together with the English Tourist Board and the Rural Development Commission published principles for tourism in the countryside. They said it should:

- Draw on the character of the countryside itself

- Assist the purposes of conservation and recreation

- Be well designed and in keeping with the landscape

- Support the rural economy and seek wider geographical and seasonal spread

- Obtain practical contributions to conservation and recreation programmes

- Be marketed so as to deepen people's understanding of the countryside

Source: Countryside Commission, English Tourist Board, Rural Development Commission, *Principles for Tourism in the Countryside*, CCP 429, Cheltenham, 1993.

BOX 6.13

Principles for tourism

---

ational projects in AONBs, especially in Heritage Coasts, albeit at a reducing rate. Interestingly, the priority given to projects for the enjoyment of Heritage Coasts does seem to be greater than might be expected from established policy for AONBs; this initiative has been much appreciated, and possibly has a message for the future balance between recreation and conservation objectives in AONBs generally. AONBs have also gained from CC's strategy for the promotion of access, a major feature of which has been the designation of more than 3000 km of National Trails. It will have been noted from Chapter 2 that all but one of them, including the South West Coast Path, the North and South Downs Ways, the Ridgeway and the Cotswold Way traverse AONBs, running the length of them. Another, more recent, policy development has concerned the management of recreational traffic and transport, including the establishment of two demonstration traffic management projects, one of which has been in Surrey Hills AONB (referred to later in this chapter)

The Government's recent proposals for a statutory right of access to the countryside will apply in the first instance to mountain, moor, heath, down and registered common land, and may later be extended to other types of country such as cliffs, foreshore and woodland. The proposals also aim to develop the rights of way system to improve access to the heart of the countryside on foot, horseback or bicycle. CA and CCW will be integrally involved in setting the scheme up, and in preparing guidelines for its administration. Access to open countryside will undoubtedly affect AONBs. As shown in Chapter 2, they contain most of the country's downland, commons feature in several, both upland and lowland moor and heath is very important in northern and Welsh AONBs and lowland heath in the southern and western English ones. Furthermore, if woodland were to be extensively opened up for access, Surrey Hills, Chilterns, High Weald and Wye Valley would be amongst those involved. Local authorities in such areas would have to take on major new responsibilities for the establishment and running of local access forums, and in strengthening the footpath network. The proposals were at an early stage at the time of writing, and the full implications for the amount and location of recreation in AONBs, and for public and private sector management of it, will not become clear until more progress has been made towards the necessary legislation.

THE LOCAL RESPONSE

Apart from the results of the surveys such as those summarised in Box 6.14, systematic data on recreation in individual AONBs is scarce. It is therefore debatable whether the level of provision is indeed balanced in line with national policy for AONBs. The impacts (traffic congestion, parking problems, wear and tear of the landscape and pressures upon visitor facilities) are well known in general terms. They are acute in the areas near to large centres of population or attractive to tourists mentioned earlier in this chapter. Recreation in such locations needs continuous management in the light of practical experience in order to be sustainable, and charging for parking and other facilities can be an important mechanism for achieving a balanced distribution of opportunities away from 'honeypots' and peak times of the year. Even in busier AONBs, imaginative management of land for an increased range of users can offer improvement in the quality of experience for visitors and benefits for local communities, creating new incomes in the recreation and tourism sector. There seems to be confidence that, given adequate resources, this can be done. Equally, in remote areas green tourism

The Sussex Downs Visitor Survey indicated:

BOX 6.14

- 77% of all visits are by local population

- even for a short visit they come by car
- visitors tend to be in age group 25 to 64, and in the more affluent social categories
- walking, enjoying the view and picnicking are the most popular pastimes
- the region may be earning £159 million per annum from downland leisure

Source: Sussex Downs Conservation Board, Sussex Downland Visitor Survey, report by B.E. Osborne, University of Sussex, Storrington, 1993.

Much the same applies in **Chilterns** where a Visitor Survey in 1998 shows:

- 92% of visitors are day visitors, the majority by small groups of family or friends
- 77% come by car
- there is relatively little seasonal variation
- direct expenditure by visitors is around £190 million per annum
- 48% of this is in pubs, cafes and restaurants and it sustains nearly 3,600 full-time equivalent jobs

Source: Southern Tourist Board, *Chilterns Visitor Survey*, 1998.

On Holy Island, **Northumberland Coast**, with at least 350,000 visitors annually, a 1994 survey showed that:

- 85% of visitors arrived by car
- 73% came for general sight-seeing
- 34% were attracted by the Island's historical interest
- 13% were attracted by its religious significance
- 11% by its wildlife
- 43% were repeat visits
- only 10% came as a result of tourist-related advice

Source: Northumberland County Council, *Holy Island Management Plan*, Morpeth, 1998.

can give a major boost to a rural economy that may be over-dependent on agriculture, supporting incomes and jobs on farms, improving local services, and encouraging the conservation of landscape and buildings.

Each type of approach, whether or not based on visitor surveys, can be found in the management plans and programmes for individual areas. The measures vary from general guidelines for the encouragement or restraint of recreation and tourism, sometimes applied on a zonal basis, to more comprehensive strategies that link these topics with proposals for transport and for economic development. Examples of the former include Cotswolds[20] and Suffolk Coast and Heaths.[21] Amongst the latter are Wye Valley,[22] relying upon close co-operation between the JAC and the local tourist industry to improve infrastructure and tourist facilities, encourage holidays based on countryside access, co-ordinate marketing, and reduce environmental impact. Norfolk Coast offers another good example (see Box 6.15[23] and Plate 61) as does the Purbeck area of Dorset improving access to popular areas by park and ride, and assisting the regeneration of small towns (see case study in Appendix 2).[24]

In some cases, for example, North Pennines, Solway Coast and the Isle of Wight, the whole thrust of AONB management gives priority to the development of sustainable tourism. In the North Pennines this has been led by the Tourism Partnership, funded by the regional Tourist Boards, CC/CA and seven local authorities, helped by private and voluntary sector representatives, but the project may now be integrated into a wider AONB strategy. In Solway Coast, AONB management is by Solway Rural Initiative Ltd, an independent body set up in 1992 for countryside projects and economic development in the wider Solway plain (see Box 5.4). It is now funded by CA, three local authorities, Cumbria TEC and the ERDF, and works with business leaders and community representatives. In the Isle of Wight, the unitary council has a long-standing and deep commitment to tourism in

---

BOX 6.15

Norfolk Coast Visitor Management Strategy (1995)

The Visitor Management Strategy for Norfolk Coast (see case study), an AONB with a rich wildlife and cultural heritage, is an important part of the Management Plan. It contains policies for the local economy, traffic and transport, landscape and archaeology, habitats and wildlife, pollution control, information and interpretation, recreation and tourism, and it nominates the lead agencies for each. Aiming to harness the benefits of tourism and recreation and ease the pressures on local communities, it identifies several 'management zones', reflecting the varying sensitivity of the landscape and wildlife of the AONB. These are shown on the map in Plate 61, the colour range from red to green illustrating high to low priority for tackling visitor pressures, and low to high for developing opportunities for quiet enjoyment.

Source: Norfolk Coast Project, *Visitor Management Strategy for the Norfolk Coast*, 1995.

support of the island's economy, giving priority to development of its
resort towns and other tourist attractions and steering it away from the
AONB; on occasions this requires difficult and finely balanced decisions.

All these examples show the close inter-relationship between
recreation and tourism, and the need to integrate provision for them
with other social and economic policies and land management in the
AONB. A strategic framework is required, within which the range of
projects for implementation, such as are described in the case studies,
might include:

- *Access* – recreational public transport, park and ride, small car
  parks and picnic areas, footpaths, bridleways, off-road cycling,
  access to open countryside and woodland and provision for the
  disabled. As has been suggested above, access to open countryside will assume increasing importance in a number of AONBs,
  in addition to the high standard of existing provision to be found
  in some. In Surrey Hills, for example, at least 8000 ha of access
  land are owned by Surrey County Council and the National
  Trust, much of which is almost continuous along the North
  Downs Way (see Plate 49). In Malvern Hills, the Conservators
  have a unique statutory role in administering 11 per cent of the
  AONB, mainly upland and commons. In other areas some 30
  country parks and many Forest Enterprise woodlands are open to
  the public.

- *Information, interpretation and promotion of outdoor activities* – visitor
  centres, education programmes, leaflets, media outlets, information boards, trails and guided walks, farm open days, other spon-
  sored events. One of the most interesting is the Charterhouse
  Centre, at the heart of Mendip Hills AONB, owned by Somerset
  County Council, accommodating the AONB Officer and Wardens
  and run as a residential field studies and activities centre.

- *Environmental care* – at popular viewpoints, villages, and busy footpaths, etc. In Wye Valley, for example, the management plan for
  the very popular area around the Symonds Yat viewpoint is being
  implemented by several private owners, businesses, voluntary and
  public bodies led by the AONB Partnership. In the Cotswolds,
  Cotswold District Council have a Market Towns Initiative that
  includes environmental improvement of critical tourist attractions such as Bourton-on-the-Water. On Holy Island,
  Northumberland Coast, the visual impact of parked cars and the
  pressure of visitors on the fragile environment of natural habitats
  and historic features has resulted in the complete relocation of
  parking areas from the village and the harbour to a new site outside the village, and a programe of measures to manage public

access. Associated with it is a community development initiative for the Island's economy, with the appointment of a community development officer.

- *Support for tourist accommodation and facilities* – farm-based tourism, bed and breakfast, camping barns, etc. This is particularly important in areas such as Blackdown Hills, where the JAC gives research, marketing and publicity support to the Blackdown Hills Business Association's efforts to encourage local services to tourism.
- *Development of cultural and natural resources* – bodies such as English Heritage, English Nature, local authorities, National Trust, RSPB and Wildlife Trusts have done much to enhance historic sites and buildings, parks and gardens, nature reserves etc., under their control.
- *Monitoring trends and impacts* – a process that needs far more attention than AONB authorities are able to give it at the present time.
- *Fund-raising* from a variety of new sources, including private sponsorship and charitable trusts.

Recent expenditure on recreation and tourism by individual AONB authorities appears to have been within a range rising to about £155,000. By comparison, in National Parks the equivalent programmes range up to £1.66 million on recreation, and £1.65 million on visitor management.[25]

Despite the lack of information on the nature and scale of recreation and tourism in AONBs, there is no doubt about the growing attractions that these areas hold for a wide range of activities. The Government's proposals for access to the countryside will further increase their recreational role. Although present policy gives recreation a relatively low priority in AONBs, these areas are *de facto* serving a national interest in enabling people to enjoy their unique scenery, cultural and natural resources. Despite the scarcity of data on the social and economic benefits and the costs in terms of environmental impacts, it is surely right in practical terms that their response to the challenge of managing recreation and tourism should be positive, especially in areas where other prospects are poor. AONBs are as much under pressure as National Parks, in which recreation is a well-financed statutory requirement, despite their landscape quality. Nevertheless, improved funding and monitoring, especially of carrying capacities, will be essential if the use of AONBs for increased recreation and tourism is to be sustainable and their natural resources, especially their landscapes, properly protected. There is a case for a review of objectives to give generous encouragement to the role that AONBs can perform in this field.

Concern about traffic in AONBs has been felt for a long time. In the past this has tended to focus on the effects of national road-building programmes: the environmental damage threatened by individual trunk road and motorway schemes. The concern has now become a more general one of traffic growth, experienced in the countryside as a whole. The increase in traffic on rural roads referred to earlier is expected to continue relentlessly, and is compounded in popular recreational areas, such as AONBs, by additional visitor travel at peak periods. Specific AONB data on this effect is difficult to find, but it is clear that summer traffic flows on main roads in many holiday areas can be several times winter levels. As much or more of a surge can also be found on minor roads which serve hot spots. Despite the lack of quantitative data, the environmental impacts of such traffic are well-known: congestion, noise, loss of tranquillity, pollution, damage to narrow roads, random parking at visitor attractions, safety risks to pedestrians, cyclists and horse riders, distracting to visitors, upsetting and inconvenient to residents and local businesses.

The problem is not, however, only one of 'pressure', particularly for recreational traffic. Nor is it one to which action on the ground, including land management, is necessarily a solution. It applies in a very different way in the less prosperous rural areas, where lower than average numbers of car-owners are very dependent on public transport, but bus services in them can be expensive and infrequent. It should be added that recreational car-users are reluctant to travel on public transport with conventional routing and timing, and these existing services do not therefore contribute much towards reducing the impacts mentioned above.

The development of integrated traffic and transport management planning in the last decade has resulted in more attention being given to residents' and visitors' transport needs in protected areas. This has recently gained further momentum; the Government's Transport White Paper[26] has to some extent clarified the social, economic and environmental context, more funds are being devoted to rural transport, and new responsibilities have been placed upon local highway authorities by the *Road Traffic Reduction Act*, 1997. Moreover, CC's rural traffic initiatives, started in 1993, are beginning to show how to create improved traffic conditions for a sustainable countryside.[27] Transport, in the widest sense, is fundamental to this, and is rightly identified as one of CA's four strategy priorities.

THE LOCAL RESPONSE

Although traffic and transport is ranked as the most serious problem faced by AONBs in holiday areas or close to major cities, in Gower, Cornwall, East Devon, Northumberland Coast, Tamar Valley, Dedham Vale, Kent Downs and Surrey Hills, for example, only a few JACs have so far taken a leading role in turning this from being a threat into a positive opportunity. Their approach, examples of which are illustrated in Plates 58 – 60, includes:

- **The strategic level:**

  Some management plans contain a perceptive analysis of traffic management and public transport needs, put in the context of objectives for the AONB as a whole. For example, the Norfolk Coast Visitor Management Strategy has led to a Transport Strategy which necessarily covers a larger area than the AONB itself. It proposes a route hierarchy (including a new level of quiet lanes), village speed limits of 20 mph, development of the 'Coastliner' bus with rail and parking connections and services for residents, and a more balanced distribution of car parking. The existing Cycling Initiative will be developed further, environmental improvements are proposed, and there will be guidelines on highway design. After wide consultation the strategy is being used as the basis for Rural Package funding bids in the county's TPP.[28]

  In Chilterns AONB the focus is primarily on landscape impacts and the importance of sensitive highway design. This has led to a published booklet on environmental guidelines for road management.[29]

  In Sussex Downs, under the general theme of 'Enjoying the Landscape' in the management strategy, priorities and responsibilities for action on traffic and transport are well developed, and a great deal of effort has been put into the promotion of recreational public transport.[30]

- **Programmes of traffic management action:**

  One of the important STAR (Strategic Traffic Action in Rural Areas) initiatives by CC included the south-west part of Surrey Hills AONB, a tract of countryside which contains several commons and nature reserves as well as National Trust land. STAR objectives were to change travel behaviour, minimise damage caused by road traffic, encourage alternative transport modes, and reduce travel demand. In consultation with District and Parish Councils and many organisations (including local businesses), and in partnership with the CC and CA, the County Council has developed projects in and adjoining the AONB to meet these objectives: an awareness campaign with schools ('Be a Star'), a leisure cycleway, a 'rural box' traffic management scheme, and more detailed schemes for two villages. Stemming from this, the current proposals are for a package of area-based projects: perimeter gateways and an overall 40 mph speed limit within the 'box'; other speed-reducing measures and 20 mph limits in critical parts of villages, and an access-only road; redesignation of roads to encourage through traffic to avoid a village; and additional provision for walkers, equestrians and cyclists. Results so far have been favourable in reducing traffic volumes (including car travel to school), speeds and accident rates. The total cost of the works, over two or three years, is estimated in the Local Transport Plan (LTP) to be £400,000 within the AONB.[31]

- **Car parking policy:**

  The distribution and size of car parks and the level of any parking charges can be a powerful means of relating levels of recreational use to environmental capacity, and charges may contribute towards management budgets. At present it is mainly the parts of AONBs under heaviest pressure, such as Heritage Coasts, scenic, cultural and sports honey-pots, and places close to urban areas, that have demonstrated the greatest need for a co-ordinated parking strategy. Experience gained in these areas on siting, on the value of links with public transport, cycleways, footpaths and facilities for the disabled, on means of discouraging random parking, and on charging mechanisms, will apply more widely as recreational pressures grow elsewhere.

- **Recreational public transport:**

  The case study for the Purbeck Heritage Area, in Dorset AONB, mentions the unique steam train park-and-ride scheme, set up in 1995 through collaboration between the Heritage Committee and many organisations including BP Exploration, Countryside Commission, Dorset County Council, ECC International, English Partnerships, RDC, and Swanage Railway. The £600,000 park-and-ride scheme is a key part of the Committee's transport strategy, running 19 trains a day each way on the six-mile line between the seaside resort of Swanage and Norden, near Corfe Castle. It links with bus, cycle and footpath routes, has parking for 240 cars, and a visitor centre. In 1997 the scheme was used by 20,000 cars. Studies are now looking at the possibility of extending the railway to meet the main Weymouth, Bournemouth and Southampton to London line at Wareham.[32]

Much effort has been put into public transport development in just a few other areas. These include 'Sunday Bus', 'Hopper', 'Rambler Bus' and 'Pathfinder' services in Forest of Bowland, East Hampshire, Malvern Hills, Nidderdale, South Devon, Sussex Downs and Wye Valley; the Surrey Hills Leisure Buses, promoted in conjunction with the train companies, and the Mendip Explorer Buses, partly financed by Bristol City Council; a rail and circular walks project in Tamar Valley, which is essential to the survival of an existing railway line; baggage transport links between night stops for walkers on a 100-mile stretch of the South West Coast Path; and combined bus, rail and 'attractions' leaflets widely published in, for example, Sussex Downs, Norfolk Coast, Mendip Hills and South Devon.

Traffic and transport management is an issue of critical importance to the environment, local economy and enjoyment of AONBs, and although details of expenditure on it are hard to obtain, it is clear that policy and action is at a comparatively early stage of development. Rightly, management plans tend to see provision for movement as a strategic matter, related to environmental, community and recreational objectives, but the level of treatment in these plans is generalised, and only in relatively few AONBs have proposals actually been carried through to implementation. Even in National Parks less than £0.5 million is being spent on traffic and transport, of which £140,000 is staff costs.[33] To an extent this seemingly low-key approach may be due to the funding priorities of highway authorities, dictated as these often are by pressing urban problems and by safety criteria. It may also reflect doubt about what levels of management, including the sensitive issue of charging in congested areas, are acceptable and realistic within the framework of statutory powers available. CC's demonstration projects and experience elsewhere have now begun to show the nature of the task to be done and the difficulties to be overcome, but regular progress reports on achievements and on monitoring of effects are essential if the lessons learned are to be of wide value. A future development that will need particular study is the possibly very influential role of information technology in shaping local and recreational transport policies and management measures.

Among all the management challenges in AONBs, policy and action for traffic and transport is perhaps the most demanding in terms of finding sustainable solutions to very damaging pressures. Partnership and consultation are more than ever essential to ensure that efforts within AONBs make the best use of national funding and are closely integrated with the preparation by the local highway authorities of LTPs and longer-term transport strategies, and reflect community preferences.

**Commentary:
the multi-resource
role of management
in AONBs**

Grouped under the heading of land management, the six main topics of this chapter illustrate part of the wide range of strategic responsibilities that an AONB organisation needs to address, and the scale of the task of co-ordination. Some, such as encouraging a sensitive approach to the agri-environment and relating this to the management of woodland and the opportunities both offer to bio-diversity, to freedom from pollution and to an increasingly generous range of recreational and tourist provision, are strongly interrelated in land-management terms. Others, such as the management of traffic flows, parking and the provision of public transport, are less directly connected with land management, as such, but need to be seen as part of what can be done on the ground for local community life and visitors.

The message for AONB organisations is one of preparedness, an ability to see all these needs in a strategic sense, their interrelationships, and the practical measures, including finance, which are essential to their management. The level of success will depend on the extent to which the right skills are available or can be made so from various sources, and also the effectiveness of consultation arrangements. Each AONB needs a clear idea of what it has to do, and so be in a good position to harness outside forces to this end whether via landscape and recreation enhancement or in activities such as wildlife conservation and archaeology.

Already some AONBs are active across the board in this way, but not all. Engagement is patchy for a variety of reasons including on occasion a low level of priority given by public agencies. A statutory duty for such agencies to have regard to AONB conservation would help to improve matters. Equally, it is vital that all interests, particularly public, private and voluntary sector land managers, are brought together in a forum or JAC, since even the largest AONB management team is unlikely to have all the necessary skills and ability to influence. It is only by integration of this kind that sustainable policies can be created and implemented in a complementary manner.

References

[1] Ministry of Agriculture, Fisheries and Food, *The Countryside Stewardship Scheme Analysis of Uptake 1991-97*, FRCA, Leeds, 1998.

[2] Thorne, B., Somerset FWAG, *Countryside Stewardship in the Mendip Hills AONB*, report to the Mendip Hills AONB Joint Advisory Committee, 1999.

[3] *Protected Areas Funding Study*, report for the Countryside Commission by Environmental Resources Management, London, 1998.

4   Countryside Commission, *Protecting Our Finest Countryside: Advice to Government*, CCP532, Cheltenham, 1998.

5   Agreement between the Association of National Parks and the Forestry Commission on the Native Woodlands in National Parks, 1993.

6   Forestry Commission, *A New Focus for England's Woodlands: Strategic Priorities and Programmes*, Cambridge, 1999.

7   Environment Agency, *An Environmental Strategy for the Millennium and Beyond*, Bristol, 1997.

8   Environment Agency, *An Action Plan for Conservation*, Bristol, 1998.

9   Jones, P., The LEAP approach to environmental management, *Town and Country Planning*, Vol. 68, No. 11, November 1999.

10   Countryside Commission Advice to the Environment Agency, unpublished, 1997.

11   *Environment Act* 1995, Section 62: 'Duties of certain bodies and persons to have regard to the purposes for which National Parks are designated'.

12   Countryside Commission and English Nature, *The Character of England: Landscape, Wildlife and Natural Features*, CCX 41, Cheltenham, 1996.

13   *Biodiversity: The UK Action Plan*, CM 2428, HMSO, London, 1994.

14   Local Government Management Board, *Guidance for Local Biodiversity Action Plans*, Guidance Note No. 1: An Introduction, London.

15   Ibid.

16   Ibid.

17   Joint Statement on Nature Conservation in the National Parks – a Declaration of Intent between the National Park Authorities, the Broads Authority, English Nature, the Countryside Council for Wales and the Countryside Commission, 1993.

18   Countryside Commission, *Areas of Outstanding Natural Beauty, Policy Statement*, CCP 157, Cheltenham, 1983.

19   Countryside Commission and Countryside Council for Wales, *Areas of Outstanding Natural Beauty, A Policy Statement*, CCP 356, Cheltenham, 1991.

20   Cotswolds AONB Joint Advisory Committee, *A Future Challenge*, Gloucester, 1996.

21   Suffolk Coast and Heaths AONB Joint Advisory Committee, *Management Plan*, Ipswich, 1994 .

22   Wye Valley AONB Joint Advisory Committee, *Sustainable Tourism Strategy and Action Plan*, Monmouth, 1995.

23   Norfolk Coast Project, *Visitor Management Strategy for the Norfolk Coast*, 1995.

24   Purbeck Heritage Committee, *Keeping Purbeck Special: a Strategy for the Purbeck Heritage Area*, Wareham, 1995.

25   Countryside Commission, *Protected Areas Funding Study*, op. cit.

26   Department of Environment, Transport and the Regions, *A New Deal for Transport: Better for Everyone*, Cmd 3950, HMSO, London, 1998.

27   Countryside Commission, *Rural Traffic: Getting it Right*, CCP 515, Cheltenham, 1997.

28 *Norfolk Coast Transport Strategy*, 1998.

29 Chilterns Conference, *Environmental Guidelines for the Management of Roads in the Chilterns*, 1997.

30 Sussex Downs Conservation Board, *Public Transport Panel Report for the Sussex Downs AONB*, 1995.

31 Surrey County Council, *STAR Initiative*, Kingston upon Thames, 1998.

32 Information from Alison Turnock, Purbeck Heritage Officer, 1999.

33 Countryside Commission, *Protected Areas Funding Study*, op. cit.

7 Rural development, planning and sustainability

Earlier chapters have served as a reminder that AONBs are not just pretty places, with an abundance of wildlife and cultural resources; that they are places where people live and work and are popular destinations for tourists and day visitors; and that there is considerable potential for tension between the major land uses (agriculture and forestry), recreation, tourism and traffic and the conservation of these areas. Continuing with the theme of this part of the book, this chapter explores further serious tensions: those that exist between rural communities, some of which are struggling to survive, and the conservation of these areas. It considers the policies for rural development, the operation of the town and country planning system and the opportunities for greater harmony presented by the sustainable development process.

Rural development policies

In the same way that the rationale of post-war policy for protecting landscapes stemmed initially from the Scott Report in 1942,[1] one finds that the policy for rural development and rural communities originally stemmed from the same principles. Scott took the view that a prosperous farming economy would not only protect the landscape but also rural communities (*ergo* the rural economy). He argued that if pressure for housing and industrial development could be resisted (and so protecting farmland and keeping labour on the land), farm incomes were boosted and modern services provided in villages, then not only would the amenities of the countryside be preserved but traditional rural life would be retained.

The failure of agriculture to protect much of the landscape, even in the designated areas, has already been described. However, as it went through a major revolution, agriculture also failed to sustain rural communities. The decline in the agricultural workforce led to a drift away from the land. There were few alternative sources of employment for those workers. This was exacerbated by the strict planning controls over non-agricultural employment and by channelling such development that was allowed in to selected centres.[2]

Somewhat ironically the drift from the land did not lead to an overall decline in the rural population. Other factors, in particular the mobility afforded by the car, led to changes in the social and occupational composition of many rural areas. The decline in farming population has been matched by an inflow of middle-class commuters, retired people and second-home owners. This trend, known as 'counter urbanisation' has led to growth rates consistently above the national average.[3]

Thus in the fifty years since the passing of the *Agriculture Act* and the *Planning Act* in 1947, both of which sought to promote agriculture as the mainstay of the rural economy a dramatic change has taken place. The original rationale has been undermined, with the emergence of a rural population less rooted in the countryside and increasingly free of farming as a source of income or employment. This has meant that the numerous and sometimes competing demands for the use of rural areas have an increasingly different framework within which they have to operate, not least the protection of the finest landscapes.

In policy terms there has been a gradual shift in agricultural policy to align it more with the broader rural agenda. As shown in the previous chapter it is being increasingly linked with the rural environment, through the payment of farmers for the management of the countryside rather than production (ESAs and CS). Diversification both at the local farm and at a wider regional and sub-regional level has been encouraged. In 1988 MAFF introduced grants for diversification, with more and more farmers branching out into contracting and tourism enterprises. In some parts of the country, notably the South East, part-time and hobby farmers have incomes from sources totally unrelated to the land.

In parallel with the evolution of agricultural policy, the former Rural Development Commission played a significant role in the diversification process, especially in defined 'Rural Development Areas' (see Plate 17) , which currently embrace some 35 per cent of England (with 6 per cent or 2.75 million of England's population), much of which is in AONBs (see Chapter 2). It adopted a number of measures based on the preparation of integrated rural development programmes for each area. They are aimed at strengthening communities, helping disadvantaged groups and creating the right conditions for economic diversification. It also provided business advice and grants to individual enterprises, for example, for the conversion of redundant buildings and has provided purpose-built business accommodation for rent. Much of this work has been taken on by the new Regional Development Agencies, following the RDC's merger with the Countryside Commission to form the Countryside Agency, which will be promoting the needs of rural communities alongside its remit for landscape conservation and recreation.

Europe is also influencing rural areas, not only through the development of the Common Agricultural Policy. The EU Structural Funds (Objective 5b) have been applied to designated rural areas with below average levels of economic development, high levels of dependence on agricultural employment and low levels of agricultural income (see Plate 17). Significant levels of funding have been applied to solve these issues. Whilst the 5b and Rural Development Area programmes may have helped the economies of AONBs, there is very little evidence that either has achieved much for the conservation of these areas, through the encouragement of activity that actually enhances them. The degree of integration was limited, with very little recognition of the environment as a source of economic benefits for local communities. The problem seems to be twofold. First, the planning processes for these schemes do not embrace the natural environment. Second, because these programmes are driven by the necessities of creating employment, applications have had to demonstrate that they will do so. This has created problems for AONBs where very often the impact on jobs is often only indirect, for example, the effect of managing the landscape will be to encourage visitors to visit the area, where they will probably spend some money. However, there are a few instances where AONB managers have sought and received support from the EU for their own projects, for example in the Chilterns, Nidderdale, South Devon and Tamar Valley. As shown later in the chapter, there is also increasing evidence of the direct and indirect impact of conservation on job creation, which will help future bids.

The Rural White Paper of 1995[4] sought to provide a new policy framework based on a commitment to sustainable development – with the goals of a healthy rural economy and an attractive rural environment reinforcing each other. The major difference from the Scott Report[5] 50 years earlier is that farming as a focal point is now being replaced by a much broader view of the rural economy, local communities and the environment, that requires an integrated approach. The Rural White Paper stated six principles for the future of the countryside:

1. the pursuit of sustainable development;
2. shared responsibility for the countryside as a national asset, which serves people who live and work there as well as visitors;
3. dialogue to help reconcile competing priorities;
4. distinctiveness, approaching rural policies in a way which is flexible and responds to the character of the countryside;
5. economic and social diversity;
6. sound information as the basis for effective policies.

In promoting sustainable development the White Paper emphasised that

> Wealth creation and environmental quality are increasingly interconnected. The appeal of the countryside is central to its economic prosperity, and healthy economic activity in rural areas facilitates investment to protect and improve the countryside. New development should respect, and where possible enhance, the environment in its location, scale and design.

The Department of the Environment's Planning Policy Guidance Note No. 7,[6] in promoting economic diversification in order to adjust to the changes in the rural economy brought about by the changes in agriculture, recognises the interaction with the protection of the countryside in its own right, especially in National Parks and AONBs. Therein lies the essential tension now that the agricultural economy is no longer in the pole position, a matter that will be at the heart of the work of any AONB.

Recent changes in the Common Agricultural Policy serve to illustrate the direction in which the support for farming and the rural economy is now moving. In 1999 the European Council agreed the 'Rural Development Regulation' or 'second pillar of the CAP' as it is sometimes described.[7] The Regulation lays the foundation for a new European framework in which the reforms in the agricultural commodity sectors will be complemented by more closely integrated measures to support rural development and to protect and improve the environment. The twin track approach will bring agricultural and rural policy closer together, recognising that the future of rural areas and communities depends both on farmers' broader role in sustaining the countryside and local economy and on the adaptation and diversification of rural economies through support to non-farming interests. Two important principles that have been established are that, where subsidies for production are reduced, the money saved can be used to implement the measures in the new Regulation, and that cross compliance can be used, for example, by stipulating environmental measures in return for support of the agricultural business.

At the centre of the process is the requirement for each member nation to prepare a Rural Development Plan to cover the seven years of the Scheme that ends in 2007/8.[8] The Plan describes the measures to be used, the geographical areas covered, the proposed expenditure and the economic, social or environmental justification. In their plans member states are required to provide for agri-environment measures throughout their territories. The remaining measures can be adopted at the discretion of individual states. While most of the measures will only be available for farming and forestry or directly related interests, the scheme includes a number of general rural development measures. 'Article 33' defines their scope, including, for example, protection of the environment in connection with land, forestry and landscape conservation, encouragement of tourist and craft activities, renovation and development of villages and the protection and conservation of the rural heritage.[9]

Separate plans have already been prepared for England, Wales and Scotland. In England,[10] the plan has a national and regional component. Of particular interest to AONBs is the intention to expand the agri-environment schemes, mainly through Countryside Stewardship, and also forestry and woodland schemes, through the Farm Woodland Premium Scheme and the Woodland Grant Scheme when it applies to farmland. In addition a new Hill Farm Allowance Scheme is to be introduced in 2001, to replace the Hill Livestock Compensatory Allowance. The objective will be to help to maintain the social fabric of upland rural communities through support for continued agricultural land use, and to maintain the farmed upland environment by ensuring that the land in the less favoured areas is managed sustainably. Furthermore, it also contains a new Rural Enterprise Scheme to provide project-based support for the diversification of the rural economy. This will embrace the kind of initiatives set out in Article 33 of the regulations, described above.

Clearly AONBs and other protected landscapes will benefit from the new scheme. However, the extent to which they will be targets for these programmes remains to be seen. The Countryside Agency in its Advice to Government on the Rural Regulation continued to advocate the need for special levels of payments in AONBs and National Parks, as well as in Natura 2000 sites as already proposed.[11] However, it seems unlikely that this will be considered until the mid-term evaluation of the England Rural Development Plan in 2003.

It is encouraging that the level of resources that are likely to be available is not inconsiderable, at least for some elements, for example, the Countryside Stewardship budget, which will increase from £29 million in 1999/2000 to £126 million in 2007/8. However, projects under Article 33 will only have a modest budget of £8 million in 2001/2 rising to a peak of £36 million for 2004/5 and subsequent years.

The kind of thinking behind the measures is already being piloted in the Forest of Bowland AONB (see Case Study in Appendix 2) and on Bodmin Moor (part of the Cornwall AONB). The basis of the pilot initiatives has been to test two questions at a regional level. First, what kind of measures are required to integrate rural economic activity with positive environmental management and, second, the effectiveness of a single application process and a local delivery mechanism. Key elements of the process being tested are the requirement

Plate 33   Agricultural practices have led to significant change in the
character of the landscapes of AONBs, e.g. the North Wessex Downs, where
extensive areas of chalk grassland have been lost to arable cultivation.

Change in the landscape – agriculture (2)

Plate 34 The Sussex Downs are another example of where extensive areas of chalk grassland have been lost to arable cultivation.

(a)

Change in the landscape – agriculture (3)

Plate 35 Extensive pig rearing in the Mendip Hills (a) leading to the loss of limestone grassland, and the removal of hedgerows in the Shropshire Hills (b), are further examples of the impact of agriculture.

(b)

(a)

Change in the landscape – agriculture (4)

Plate 36 In Dedham Vale (a) arable cultivation has come down to the edge of the flood plain, and in the North Wessex Downs (b) the training of horses has introduced new elements to the landscape.

(b)

(a)

(b)

Loss of tranquillity and pressure for development (1)

Plate 37 AONBs are continually under pressure for development and have lost much of their tranquillity in recent years, e.g. from new and inappropriate housing as in Cannock Chase (a) and industrial activity in the High Weald (b).

Loss of tranquillity and pressure for development (2)

Plate 38 Major developments like power generation in the Suffolk Coast and Heaths (a) and quarrying in the Mendip Hills (b), are a constant cause for concern.

(a)

(b)

(a)

(b)

Loss of tranquillity and pressure for development (3)

Plate 39 The need to dump waste, as in the Isle of Wight (a), and the impact of roads and traffic in the Sussex Downs (b), are further examples of intrusion into the landscape.

(a)

Loss of tranquillity and pressure for development (4)

Plate 40 The need for improved telecommunications, as in Cornwall (a) and the Shropshire Hills (b), is an emerging issue with the potential to cause serious damage to the landscape.

(b)

(a)

Plate 41 Most AONBs are popular for tourism and recreation. The pressures are considerable and are increasing, e.g. crowded beaches and car parks in the Suffolk Coast and Heaths (a & b).

(b)

(a)

Growth in tourism and recreation (2)

Plate 42 Small villages can be overwhelmed with cars, at Blakeney on the Norfolk Coast (a), and caravan parks, as on the East Devon coast (b), can be intrusive.

(b)

Growth in tourism and recreation (3)

Plate 43 New activities, such as parascending in the Sussex Downs (a) and mountain biking on the Norfolk Coast (b), cause a new set of problems for managers.

(a)

(b)

(a)

Growth in tourism and recreation (4)

Plate 44 Walking on the South West Coast Path National Trail on the Cornish coast (a), and sailing, as in Chichester Harbour (b), are increasingly popular, and bring new problems as well as support to the local economies.

(b)

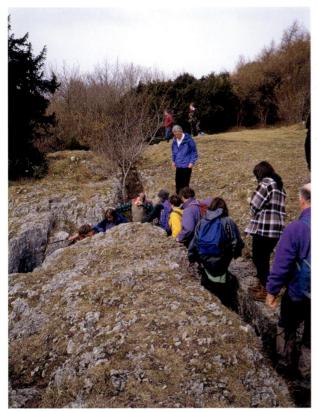

(a)

Growth in tourism and recreation (5)

Plate 45   Visiting AONBs in groups is increasingly popular, e.g. exploring nature reserves as in Arnside & Silverdale (a) and learning to climb in the Mendip Hills (b).

(b)

Long-term trends (1)

Plate 46 Long-term changes in the climate, life styles and in major land uses could affect the character and quality of the landscape, e.g. the demands for new forms of energy, such as wind farms (a), and the gradual loss of land through erosion, as in Suffolk Coast and Heaths (b), could have serious implications.

(a)

(b)

Plate 47   The works required to protect the coast can be large-scale with an inevitable impact on the landscape, carefully limited here in the replenishment of Hurst Spit on the South Hampshire Coast.

(a)

(b)

Long-term trends (3)

Plate 48 New crops, such as oil seed rape, have introduced new colours to the landscape, as in the Isle of Wight (a), and extensive afforestation can change landscape character, as in the Shropshire Hills (b).

The Bowland Initiative is one of two set up by the Ministry of Agriculture early in 1999, in anticipation of the reforms being planned for the CAP under Agenda 2000. It is designed to deliver both environmental and economic benefits to the farmers of the Bowland area. It achieves this by integrating locally developed proposals for business supported from the EU Objective 5b programme with access to existing environmental schemes, in particular Countryside Stewardship. The project is delivered via a local partnership rather than a single national body. Overall the Initiative has a budget of around £3.0 million for the period till June 2001 drawn from Objective 5b, MAFF and some 20 other organisations, and has six full-time and two part-time members of staff.

BOX 7.1

The Bowland Initiative

Key elements of the Initiative are:

- *Improving marketing* – including the development of local brands of beef and lamb through the establishment of a Meat and Livestock Marketing Agency, organic milk, the marketing of Bowland farm accommodation

- *Environmental enhancement* – using Countryside Stewardship, in particular, and financial support for other activities being conditional on environmental safeguards and the establishment of a fund based on tourist and business donations to help environmental improvements in the area

- *Business development* – support for diversification on the farm where it can be demonstrated that there are both economic and environmental benefits; the better management and marketing of Bowland's woods through an added value project

- *Skills development* – particularly in environmental land management, woodland management, animal welfare and IT

- *Community development* – including stress and debt counselling, a farmer health care initiative, and the development of a credit union

The Initiative provides a free farm business and environmental appraisal, which forms the basis of subsequent detailed applications for support. Such applications must include a business element and some form of environmental enhancement. Some element of cross compliance is essential for applications to be successful.

One applicant who enquired about a countryside stewardship grant provides an example of the way in which the scheme operates. The full appraisal of the farm revealed that he ran self-catering accommodation and was hoping to convert a redundant building to expand the business. He also ran a small joinery business. The Initiative has been able to assist with the accommodation, with the expansion of the joinery business through new plant and equipment and marketing and promotional material, as well as the Countryside Stewardship scheme that was enhanced to improve public access.

Source: The Bowland Initiative.

for applicants to undergo a full business and environmental audit and observe conditions and cross compliance to achieve environmental benefits. The scope of the Bowland Initiative is described in Box 7.1. It is too early to judge the success of the pilots. However, if the preparedness of applicants to enter the scheme in Bowland is anything to go by, the required link between business and the environment has not been a deterrent.

The proposals by the EU for LEADER +,[12] an extension of the LEADER II programme, also demonstrates the kind of thinking that is now emerging. It seeks to encourage the implementation of integrated, high quality, original strategies for sustainable development designed to encourage innovation in enhancing the natural and cultural heritage, reinforcing the economic environment, in order to create jobs and to improve the organisational capabilities of their community. The need for active partnerships at a local level is emphasised in the proposals. All rural areas will be eligible under the scheme which is due to start in 2000. For AONBs there is clearly an opportunity under this scheme and the new rural regulation to put themselves forward as the focus for such an integrated approach run by an active partnership. The question is, are they in a position to do so?

Designation and rural development

In many people's view there is an inherent conflict between the designation of an area for its landscape quality and the well-being of local communities. This is understandable in the context of major development, such as quarries, power stations or new roads, but not so easily when small-scale economic activity is involved. A good illustration of this tension is provided by the debate over the designation of the North Pennines as an AONB in the late 1980s. The central point of the debate at the public inquiry was the concern of the local communities (including the local authorities) that designation would stifle any attempts to boost the local economy, which was not in good heart. Indeed much of the area was designated as an RDA.

In his statement to the inquiry, as Director of the Countryside Commission, Adrian Phillips, made a number of important points.[13] He explained that

> at the heart of the Commission's approach is a conviction that development and conservation are not inevitably and universally in conflict. Indeed the Commission is the first to recognise that much of the beauty of today's landscape is due to the way in which its natural qualities have been modified by man in the past. And the Commission readily accepts

that a well-protected, sensitively-managed countryside can be compatible with the objective of providing rural communities with jobs, sustaining incomes and maintaining essential rural services.

By landscape conservation, I do <u>not</u> mean 'fossilisation', but the management of the process of change so that the qualities which make the rural environment appealing are protected, and where possible improved.

Designation is not, therefore, so much about stopping development as securing the right kind of developments which meet local needs and are in keeping with the local environment.

This view was given support by the then Chief Executive of the Development Commission:[14]

Our experience of AONBs is that, whilst potentially restrictive in development terms, there is nothing in these designations which is intrinsically inconsistent with the kind of socio-economic initiatives on rural areas which the Commission wishes to encourage. By this I mean, in our view the designation of AONBs does not require local planning authorities to turn down the kind of small-scale, sympathetic economic development which we tend to sponsor and which is so critical to the well-being of so many rural communities.

He also added that

AONBs can serve as a positive benefit to rural development... the protection they should afford to the environment and the very fact that they have been designated as areas of special merit, can only increase their attractiveness to tourist and day visitors to the benefit of the local economy.

The key lies in how they are interpreted and administered locally. Handled sympathetically and reasonably flexibly, we could see them as bringing benefits to the rural communities they embrace.

In confirming the designation of the AONB, the Secretary of State of the day agreed with these views.[15]

Whether the North Pennine economy has benefited from designation is not really known. However, there have been a number of activities and initiatives that have resulted, at least in part, from the existence of the AONB. The fact that part of the area has been designated an ESA will have helped the farming sector, and the Tourism Partnership, with its focus on the AONB, will have helped the local economy. Furthermore, the management plan has been used in bidding for EU money.

While there may have been accord at a national level some 11 years ago, there still remains the feeling that AONBs stifle the local economy as the debates on the Renton AONB Bill in the House of Lords in June 1999 demonstrated.[16] This tension is also manifest in the operation of the planning system. Indicative of the clash between policies is the statement in the RDC's policy document *Planning for People and Prosperity* (1995)[17] in which it said that:

> The need to integrate conservation and development in rural areas is at the heart of PPG 7. The guidance makes it clear that in areas, such as National Parks and AONBs, greater weight should be attached to the conservation of the landscape. However, the planning authorities are required by PPG 7 to 'have regard to the economic and social well-being' of these areas. As a result, development plans should not contain policies which assume that conservation values automatically override the economic and social needs of local communities.

Behind that standpoint is a very strong feeling (especially in the former RDC) that the preservationist policies for protected landscapes are hindering their economic future. This is despite the fact that there are no 'no-go' policies in these areas and AONB policies have always said that appropriate scale development in the areas is in order. There may well be something in this view that the planners have always taken a strong preservationist line, influenced by local residents who have settled in these areas because of the quality of the environment, not because they want to earn their living in the area. This goes to the heart of the sustainability debate and the principles behind the protection of nationally important landscapes. The operation of the planning system is explored later in the chapter.

Local action for the rural economy in AONBs

The impression that the protection of landscapes hinders economic activity continues despite increasing, though rather patchy, evidence to the effect that there is considerable economic value in the conservation of fine landscapes and wildlife. The contribution to local economies is made in a variety of ways, through direct employment in conservation activities, expenditure by conservation organisations on local goods and services, by visitors attracted by wildlife and produce from the management of reserves.[18]

It is estimated that in Great Britain some 15,000 people are directly employed in conservation, often in the more remote parts where the contribution to the local economy is of greater significance. Substantial sums are spent by organisations involved in nature and landscape conservation on management works – £384 million in England and £44 million in Wales in 1991/2. It has also been estimated that tourism expenditures related to nature and landscape conservation totalled £350 – £450 million in 1991/2[19] in England and Wales, supporting 53,500 full-time equivalent jobs.[20] Recent National Trust and RSPB studies and the South West Coast Path Study show further the considerable contribution made to the local economy (see Box 7.2). Furthermore there is clear evidence from a number of AONBs that a link can be forged between the conservation of the landscape and the future well-being of the local economy and community. The challenge for all AONBs is to harness their inherent economic value to secure their long-term health, rather than unduly to constrain the economy. Box 7.3 and Plates 63 and 64 illustrate a few examples of what might be done. So how does the planning system help resolve these tensions? This is explored in the remainder of the chapter.

Planning guidance

Although the pressures analysed in Chapter 3 and the tensions described above are not all 'development' in planning terms, many of them can be influenced in some way or other by local authorities, whether through formal planning decisions or persuasive countryside management. Thus they often figure in policy statements of the kind broadly expressed in development plans, that is, in regional strategies, structure and local plans.

The rural content of development plans is a matter on which the Government has given general guidance (PPG7).[21] In keeping with the tone of the Rural White Paper,[22] this guidance advocates sustainable development that can be of benefit to economic activity, to environmental protection and enhancement, and to community life. It makes specific reference to designated areas. For National Parks, it highlights the statutory purposes: conservation, public enjoyment, and local social and economic well-being. For AONBs, attention is drawn to established objectives (conservation being the prime requirement, within which provision should be made for recreation when consistent with this and with the needs of agriculture and forestry), and to long-standing policies for potentially damaging development. These policies are prescribed in slightly less exacting terms than for National Parks, but to all intents and purposes are the same. Indeed they have recently been strengthened by a categoric statement from government that the landscape qualities of National Parks and AONBs are equivalent, and that they should share the highest standards of protection. Broadly, the policies say that the environmental effects of all development should be a major consideration (though regard should be had to economic and social well-being), and that in the case of major development there should

BOX 7.2

Evidence of the economic value of conservation

National Trust

In the South West of England 12.6 million holiday trips are motivated by conserved landscape each year. These trips are estimated to last 67 million nights with a visitor spend of £2,354 million. A total of 54,000 full time equivalent jobs (97,000 actual jobs) are supported by landscape-motivated holiday trips.

As an organisation the Trust's activities in the South West are linked to 10,913 full-time equivalent jobs (15,457 actual jobs). These jobs are supported by an estimated spend by the Trust and its suppliers of £313 million on wages, by visitors to trust properties and by Trust tenants spending on wages.

Source: National Trust, *Valuing Our Environment: A Study of the Impact of Conserved Landscapes and of the National Trust in the South West*, by Tourism Associates, 1998.

RSPB

Heathland Conservation in Dorset – the RSPB currently spends £300,000 per annum on heathland management, leading directly or indirectly to 27 full-time equivalent jobs. Overall in Dorset more than £1.2 million is spent by all organisations on this work providing 38 FTE jobs directly and an estimated 67 FTE jobs in total.

The Red Kite and the economy of rural mid-Wales – the Kite country project was set up in 1994 to promote wildlife tourism by providing all-weather viewing facilities and improving the interpretation of wildlife and natural environment of mid-Wales. The red kite has become an important marketing tool and has helped define the image of the area, whose economy has suffered from an over-reliance on agriculture. In 1995/6 the Kite country centres had 148,000 visitors, who were estimated to have spent £5.4 million in the local economy. Of this £2.9 million has been attributed to the project. This expenditure is estimated to have supported 114 full-time equivalent jobs. The Project itself provides 10 FTE jobs.

Source: Rayment, M., *Working with Nature in Britain: Case Studies of Nature Conservation, Employment and Local Economies*, RSPB, Sandy, 1997.

South West Coast Path

A survey of users of the South West Coast Path, which passes through five AONBs, in 1994 revealed that the path attracts over one million visits a year and that 44 per cent of holidaymakers walking the path cited its existence and the high quality of the landscape through which it passes as reasons for their west country visit. Each person using the path spends over £15 on average per day on local goods and services, bringing in more than £15 million annually to the regional economy, and generating the equivalent of over 800 full-time jobs.

Source: South West Coast Path Project Steering Group, *More Than Just a Path: South West Coast Path Strategy*, Exeter, 1997.

Solway Coast – the AONB is managed as part of the Solway Rural Initiative – a rural economic initiative (see also Box 5.4). Opportunities for rural economic regeneration based on the natural assets of the area have been identified. The SRI plans to develop its own income base from parts of the tourism and education infrastructure developed within the AONB. With a commitment to the ethos of sustainable tourism, the initiative expects to be in a good position to protect the AONB from excessive use.

Blackdown Hills – the development of the management plan and the appointment of the AONB officer were supported jointly by the RDC and CC. The future of the rural community is a driving force for the AONB service. The management plan supports new economic activity that creates local employment, fits the community and uses resources efficiently and without compromising the environment. Actions include the formation of a Blackdown Hills Business Association, and an arts association, the production of local skills and business directories, training programmes and the promotion of local products (see also case study in Appendix 2).

Nidderdale – an assessment of the local economy was an integral part of the preparation of the management plan. Underpinning the study was the requirement to identify forms of economic development that will sustain and enhance the AONB's natural assets; those identified included promotion of high-value produce, speciality retail crafts and workshops, a tele centre, green tourism, farm diversification into tourism, land conservation.

High Weald – an initiative is underway to ensure the survival of the nationally important landscape and its associated rural economy by rebuilding an integrated rural land-based economy, which rekindles the strong cultural identity of the area. The AONB is also developing ideas for local products, particularly using local timber and the sale of seed to help re-establish wildflower meadows (see also case study in Appendix 2).

Sussex Downs – initiatives based on local products, re-establishing the networks and markets for hazel coppice and the creation of a brand name for agricultural produce from the South Downs.

Sources: Material provided by AONB Officers.

BOX 7.3

Economic development activity in AONBs

normally be an assessment, as in National Parks, of the need in national terms, the impacts on the local economy, the cost of development elsewhere and the detrimental effect on the environment.[23] The guidance also refers briefly to planning policy for other designated areas: nature conservation sites, historical and archaeological sites, and Rural Development Areas.

Understandably, this guidance is at a very general level, and it does not introduce any new concepts. By contrast, the rural planning advice offered by CC, in conjunction with English Nature and English Heritage, has been more specific and innovative.[24] At the strategic level, policies should be led by environmental rather than developmental considerations, and options should be evaluated by 'state of the environment' assessments. To be sustainable, development should be kept within environmental capacity and demand should be 'managed' to this effect. Special efforts should be made to integrate conservation and development issues, for example, in tourism and recreation, and in rural transport planning. For local planning, the Commission and its partners advocated a 'critical environmental capital' approach, in which cultural as well as natural resources are evaluated according to their level of significance in local, national or indeed global terms. For AONBs, policy should clearly indicate the qualities to be protected, and all development should be required to contribute to natural beauty and have regard to local community needs, enjoyment and access. This guidance has since been updated.[25] It now places a renewed emphasis on the need for a medium to long-term vision for the area covered, integration of environmental, economic and social objectives, design policies, avoidance of cumulative environmental damage, comprehensive monitoring, and effective linkage to non-statutory plans. Importantly, the approach to planning now being articulated by CA,[26] takes this further, rejecting the idea of 'winners and losers' (implying that some considerations are sufficiently important to override losses elsewhere), in favour of 'integration'. Economic prosperity, social well-being, high environmental quality and recreational use of the countryside should be promoted together to bring an overall gain in accordance with criteria to be established in development plans. Mechanisms, such as Village Design Statements, Countryside Character, Environmental and Social Capital, have an important role to play in turning broad planning objectives into policies that are robust and influenced by local communities. To what extent are these guidelines met in strategic and local plans affecting AONBs?

Strategic and local plans

An assessment made during the 1989/90 AONB Review[27] was not encouraging: protected landscapes are of critical importance in regional planning, but there were no useful policies to this effect in Regional Strategies; Structure Plans were weak and very conventional in their approach to countryside matters; and Local Plans tended to treat AONBs on a par with other landscape designations. There was a clear need for better countryside strategies, with closer linkages between environmental policies and with community needs. Studies of Local Plans carried out for CC in 1993[28] and for RDC in 1998[29] also concluded that there was room for improvement, for example in policies for sustainability and environmental capacity, in criteria for recreation proposals, in the use of landscape appraisals, and policy for social needs.

The situation has improved since then. For the regional level, government policy guidance PPG 11 (draft)[30] states the Government's commitment to a living countryside in which the environment is properly protected and preserved, and has genuine access. It emphasises, *inter alia*, the importance of environmental management and enhancement, including 'designated countryside areas'. Special chapters are devoted to nature conservation and the coast, and to social and economic needs. Among the more recent regional statements as such, the one for south-east England,[31] for example, goes further, specifically mentioning AONBs and other protected areas in its geographical analysis of policy needs, highlighting the importance of the Sussex Downs as a constraint upon land for urban development around the coastal conurbation. In the draft statement for south-west England,[32] conservation of the region's protected areas underlies several policies, notably the need for a sustainable approach to tourism and recreational provision. Points such as these are to be found also in the more detailed statements by regional local authority consortia, notably those for the South East, which show a clear understanding of the importance of integrated rural and coastal management.

In Structure Plans, policies for AONBs now contain strong presumptions against unsuitable development, spelt out in accordance with national guidelines, and broadly co-ordinated in multi-county areas. Some plans take a positive as well as a purely protective stance. Bedfordshire, for example, 'will support the following broad policies as set out in *A Plan for the Chilterns*: to conserve and enhance the natural beauty of the area as the prime consideration; encourage agriculture to prosper; manage woodland and perpetuate a healthy broad-leaved forest; limit leisure provision to places of special importance; and give high priority to wildlife conservation'.[33] Similarly, the former West Glamorgan Structure Plan, referring to the Gower AONB, encourages management measures 'in line with the Gower Management Plan' to reconcile the requirements of large numbers of visitors, the needs of the community and protection of wildlife, within the primary objective of protection of the natural beauty.[34] Some also contain policies on specific issues of local importance such as tourist accommodation, coastal recreation including marine berths and moorings, economic diversification and rural community development, design quality, agricultural buildings, provision for quiet roads, and so on.

Unitary Development Plans and district-wide Local Plans vary considerably in their treatment of AONBs. Some merely contain statements reflecting national and county policies. Some establish detailed criteria for matters such as siting and design, use of materials and landscape treatment, conversion of agricultural buildings, location of overhead lines and radio masts, golf courses, etc., against which planning applications will be considered. Here and there these considerations apply also to 'buffer zones', since boundaries can create pressures just beyond AONBs, with a damaging effect on the areas themselves. Some plans go further than establishing policies as such; they make proposals for projects, for example, provision or upgrading of recreation areas, public transport, and rights of way, and the need for special measures ('Article Four Directions') to control damaging small-scale development. The draft Purbeck Local Plan[35] is of particular interest, its whole format being based upon sustainability, through four main themes: conservation, avoiding hazards, quality of life, and social and economic needs. Policies within these themes include requirements for the 'Heritage Area' as a whole and for critical parts such as the coast.

Undoubtedly there has been steady improvement in development plan policies for AONBs. National objectives are followed and elaborated upon, even though there is a tendency for protection to be a more frequent watchword than enhancement, and there is little explanation of the implications of sustainability. The policies also cover a wider range than in earlier days. This tends to occur more in Local Plans; at this level there is more direct experience of needs and pressures and greater scope to respond by practical action through development control and countryside management, especially if policies from Management Plans are included as Supplementary Planning Guidance. Nevertheless there still seems to be a gap to be bridged between the general tenor of development plan policies and the aspirations of CA, particularly for integration.

Control of development in AONBs

It would need a comprehensive study of development control in AONBs to discover the extent to which policies are actually followed in decisions on planning applications. Even broad comparisons of approval and refusal rates in AONBs and in nearby rural areas are hard to obtain. Furthermore, their interpretation would need to take account of the deterrent effect of AONB designation, as such, and of the protective policies being applied. What little data there are, for example, from thirteen responses to a development control questionnaire initiated by Shropshire County Council[36] and from a separate study of appeals by Land Use Consultants,[37] suggests that the rate of approval of planning applications in AONBs is similar to that in nearby non-designated areas, and that the same applies in the case of appeals.

Planning applications are, of course, determined by local planning committees or by their staff acting under delegated powers. Decisions affecting AONBs do not necessarily have any input from people actually engaged in management of the areas themselves. Ideally they should be consulted on all applications, and the decisions should be guided by criteria which take account of the special character of the AONB. There should also be a means whereby AONB staff could appear before the local planning committee in order to back up their points of view when necessary.

In reality there is regular consultation in only a small number of AONBs. This normally takes the form of a weekly list of applications, from which AONB staff can decide whether to inspect any particular application and discuss it with planning officers and key members of the JAC before responding. Some areas, for example Clwydian Range,[38] have established guidelines for the type of application on which the JAC should be consulted (see Box 7.4). On the other hand, in single-authority areas such as Purbeck and Gower where

---

The list of items for consultation includes:

- Two or more dwellings outside settlements
- New mineral and waste locations, extensions and restoration
- Industrial and commercial development outside settlements
- Caravan and camp sites
- Agricultural development
- All road improvements
- Government department proposals

Source: Clwydian Range AONB Joint Advisory Committee, *Guidelines for Planning Consultations*, Mold, 1991.

BOX 7.4

Clwydian Range – guidelines for consultation on planning applications

---

AONB staff are closely integrated with the council's own planning team, there is no need for formal consultation procedures because there is continuous in-house liaison. In a few areas AONB managers are consulted *ad hoc* on applications which planning staff consider important, or the proposals are discussed informally at meetings of technical officers' panels. Only in one case, Sussex Downs, is there an established 'right to be heard' by the local planning committees. This applies when the Conservation Board objects to a planning application which the planning authority may be minded to approve. In practice it has needed to be exercised on only very few occasions each year.

Equally, only a small number of AONBs have environmental criteria to guide decisions on planning applications. These range from a brief list of considerations, for example, scale, precedent and location, to far more detailed statements. The latter can cover matters such as the distinctive qualities of the AONB and the related need for environmental assessments, and criteria for various types of development, conditions to be applied when giving consent, and benefits to be obtained from planning gain. These and other topics are dealt with very fully in the statement used by the Sussex Downs Board and the East Hampshire JAC, an 80-page document[39] that also includes guidance on policies to be written into Local Plans, to protect environmental capital, and for matters such as benefits to be obtained from planning gain and from conditions on planning consents. Chichester Harbour management plan also provides a good example.[40] Box 7.5 gives details of both.

As shown in Chapter 2, the actual case-load of planning consultations varies widely between AONBs. In the busiest, AONB staff find the work demanding, both in the time involved and in the skills required. Only the Sussex Board, dealing with some 1000 applications a year, employs a professional planner on the staff specifically for this purpose. In areas where there is a technical officers' panel, planning issues can usefully be discussed informally between AONB Officers and members of the panel, but this does not match up to the regular dialogue that could take place in-house if there were a planner in the AONB team. All the busier areas should aim to recruit planning expertise when money is available.

It can be seen therefore that, while there is reasonable coverage of AONBs in more recent planning documents, the opportunities for AONB staff and JAC members, backed as necessary by CA and CCW, to influence individual decisions are far from widespread. Despite the views of the RDC and others that planning is too restrictive, there has continued to be considerable concern about the effects of development on AONBs. Difficulties of dialogue must surely be a factor in some of the more controversial developments that have been allowed ostensibly in the national interest (presumably justified as being absolutely necessary, with no alternatives available), in addition to the well-known proliferation of aerial masts and the growing number of wind-farms. On the other hand there have been notable successes in avoiding unsuitable developments, in improving potentially acceptable ones, sometimes as a result of 'planning bargaining', and in removing eyesores. Some of the more significant ones can be gleaned from CC's Annual Reports. From the examples given in

The Sussex Downs and East Hampshire AONBs' planning guidelines include policy advice for:

BOX 7.5

Planning policy guidelines

- Major developments within or adjoining the AONB (for which an environmental assessment is needed)

- Agricultural dwellings and buildings (emphasising the need for testing function, viability and landscape impact)

- Golf courses (unlikely to be acceptable unless in a degraded area)

- Temporary uses (for which a number of criteria are listed)

- Overhead lines (special regard to the possibility of putting underground)

- Minerals and waste (highlighting the importance of the mineral planning guidance tests)

- Signs and advertisements (concern about proliferation, especially of brown tourist signs)

And for detailed topics such as telecommunications development, small-scale agricultural and equestrian uses, re-use of buildings in the countryside, planning gain, policies for development plans to protect environmental capital.

Source: Sussex Downs Conservation Board and East Hampshire AONB Joint Advisory Committee, 1997.

Chichester Harbour Conservancy's guidelines are reflected in local plans covering the area. They are based on the Conservancy's planning aims:

1. To protect, conserve and enhance the natural beauty of the AONB

2. To protect, conserve and enhance the value of the area for wildlife

3. To conserve, maintain and improve the harbour and its associated facilities and marina industries, for recreation, where consistent with aims 1 and 2 above

4. To support sustainable forms of rural industry and agricultural practice where consistent with aims 1, 2 and 3 above

5. To support the economic and social needs of local communities where consistent with aims 1, 2 and 3 above

Source: Chichester Harbour Conservancy, *Chichester Harbour AONB Management Plan*, Chichester, 1999.

Boxes 7.6 and 7, it appears that the number of unacceptable developments that have been prevented has increased over the last twenty years, and that there has been a corresponding reduction in the number of adverse developments allowed. Among the former, not all of which resulted from appeal decisions, are several proposals for intensive recreational development, for energy projects, mineral workings, and a few for major roads. Among the latter, the most prominent are decisions by government, after public inquiries, to allow major roads and developments by the government departments.

BOX 7.6

Some adverse developments which have been successfully resisted or integrated into AONBs

1970s

- planning permission for gravel extraction in South Hampshire (allowed on appeal in the 1960s, but subsequently bought out for nature conservation by Hampshire County Council with financial support from the Countryside Commission, and relocated in a slightly less damaging position within the AONB)
- removal or repositioning of existing caravan sites in South Devon and Dorset coasts

1980s

- oil production in Purbeck, Dorset (award-winning integration)
- yacht marina at Abersoch, Lleyn (dismissed at appeal)
- extension to stock car circuit in Mendips (refused permission)

1990s

- gravel extraction at Hoveringham, Howardian Hills (refused permission)
- A36 to A46 link near Bath in the Cotswolds (after public inquiry)
- North Sea Gas facility on Norfolk coast (resited outside AONB)
- leisure park at former RAF Bentwaters, Suffolk Coast and Heaths (and a policy in the local plan to allow an airport on the site has since been recommended for deletion by the inquiry inspector)
- telecom mast at Stanhope, North Pennines (dismissed at appeal)
- wind turbines on Bodmin Moor, Cornwall
- Channel Tunnel rail link (authorised by Parliament through Hybrid Bill procedures, having been the subject of lengthy negotiations to reduce the impact on the Kent Downs AONB to an acceptable level, and undergoing extensive off-site mitigation measures, for which over £2 million has been budgeted by the promoters of the rail link)

Source: Countryside Commission Annual Reports and information provided by Countryside Agency Staff and AONB Officers.

BOX 7.7

Some developments in AONBs opposed by the Countryside Commission and Local Authorities but nevertheless allowed, normally by the Secretary of State

1970s

- ball clay mining in the Arne Peninsula, Dorset
- M40 through the Chilterns escarpment

1980s

- M25 on edge of Kent Downs
- civil aviation radar site, North Pennines
- military training areas, North Pennines
- A20 and A27 in Kent Downs
- M3 near Winchester, East Hampshire
- wind turbines on the Lizard Peninsula, Cornwall

1990s

- holiday village at Westwood, Kent Downs
- A303/A30 through the Blackdown Hills (allowed by Secretary of State following inquiry, but subsequently dropped from the roads programme)

Source: Countryside Commission Annual Reports.

Sustainable development

As indicated earlier in the chapter, PPG 7 and the CA's advice on planning are based on the adoption of the principles of sustainable development. What does this mean for AONBs?

The need for the most stringent environmental protection to apply within the finest landscapes is highlighted in the UK Sustainable Development Strategy 1999.[41] Special landscape designations, such as National Parks and AONBs are at the heart of the Government's approach. In placing them in this position, the Government has emphasised that in all cases, conservation of the natural heritage will be integrated with local needs for economic well-being, thus making sure that the principles of sustainable development are fully operative in these areas.

This affirmation of the position of protected landscapes in the Government's thinking does much to clarify their importance in terms of sustainable development, that is, in recognising their significance as part of the nation's 'environmental capital' and the importance of maintaining their character. However, turning this seemingly neat intention into practice is a complex task and a big challenge to those responsible for looking after them. The reason for the complexity is the very nature of the sustainable development process, which is one of change rather than some fixed state of harmony.[42] As shown earlier in the chapter it is the very question of change that is at the centre of debate about the planning and management of AONBs. Indeed it was always the view of the Countryside Commission that rigorous protection of these areas should not imply that they are unchanging, though any damage to the qualities for which they were designated should be prevented.[43] The important point is that the nation must have a clear vision for its most important landscapes, in particular to have an understanding of why it is they are so important. For AONBs this has been achieved in part through the series of landscape assessments published by the Countryside Commission. However, these did not define, other than in the most general terms, the limits within which the process of change can take place – a question that is fundamental to the whole process of sustainable development. Nor have individual AONBs started to clarify this question in their management plans, though some have at least recognised that sustainable development has to be addressed, for example, Blackdown Hills, Nidderdale and Purbeck. To do so remains a major challenge, both for AONBs and National Parks. It will require a deeper understanding than hitherto of the nature of the environmental and cultural capital in each area as a basis for establishing the capacity for change and for monitoring such change. It will be vital to identify those elements that are fundamental to the retention of each area's character and quality, either individually in its own right or as part of a greater whole, which is of course what landscape is all about: an amalgam of features the value of which is greater than the sum of the individual parts. Above all there will be a need to ensure that all the stakeholders are fully involved in the process and understand the implications of the definition of limits for change.

The National Parks of England and Wales have been cited as good places to demonstrate sustainability in practice, and to act as 'Greenprints' for the rest of the countryside.[44] This is on the grounds, first, that they are particularly important as reservoirs of the nation's critical environmental capital and other natural and man-made capital; second, that they enjoy legislation with aims that match those of sustainable development, and they each have a special authority, with a blend of national and local representation; and finally, that they already have special national policies applied to them and area-wide management plans setting objectives for the environment, economy and social life of the Park. However, certain prerequisites have been identified[45] before they can play this role:

- All those whose actions have an impact on National Parks need to know more about the natural resources in them;
- The importance of these resources must be explained and emphasised both within the Parks and beyond;
- New policies are needed to ensure that the natural systems and individual economic sectors in them – farming, tourism, etc. – are managed in accordance with the concept of sustainable development;
- The true value of the National Parks' contribution to the economic, ecological and spiritual assets of the nation as a whole should be better reflected in the support given to them;
- The National Park Authorities should guide and co-ordinate the pursuit of sustainable development in them.

There is no reason why AONBs should not be models of sustainability in the same way that National Parks are seen to have the potential, since they too contain a significant proportion of the nation's critical environmental capital. Whether they are capable of performing this role is a matter that is considered in the next chapter.

Commentary: A dilemma

The issues discussed in this chapter reveal clearly the dilemma faced by AONBs over the need for local economic viability, on the one hand, and for protection against unsuitable development, on the other. As to the first, there is no doubt that planning policies are, on the whole, increasingly attuned to economic requirements, even if decisions on actual projects do occasionally appear to be over-protective. As to the second, it has been suggested in Chapter 3 that pressures and trends such as those described are likely to grow, but without adequate monitoring it is difficult to say how much, and to what effect. It can be argued, however, that the higher profile gradually being assumed by AONBs will have a greater deterrent influence. If so, the threats from development lie more in the cumulative impact of small-scale changes noted in Chapter 3 (including those allowable as 'permitted development'), insensitive design (especially in standards for minor roadworks, direction signing, street lighting, overhead wiring, etc.) and unsuitable agricultural buildings, than from major one-off schemes.

The future is none the less uncertain, and no effort should be spared in these days of 'plan-led' decision-making to improve the standards of policy formulation, especially the links, including a common 'vision', between objectives and between development plans and management plans. The widespread impression remains, however, that planning in AONBs and other protected areas stifles worthwhile projects, particularly for rural economic development. The point cannot be proved without systematic research, but we should constantly be trying to improve our understanding of the ways in which well-designed projects can both be of value to the community and, if properly integrated with other aims, can enhance landscape character. AONB management and planning should aim to be more pro-active in encouraging suitable developments, particularly those that combine the recreational attraction and land management needs of these areas with economic viability. A more formal link between AONB plans and the statutory development plans, closer liaison through a more secure system of consultation on forward planning and advice on development control, will go a long way to bring about such sustainability; but it will cost money in staffing.

Application of the sustainable development process should help to lessen the tensions between the local economy and the special environment. Although the need to give high-level protection to the nation's finest landscapes, National Parks and AONBs, is recognised in the UK Sustainable Development Strategy,[46] much greater understanding will be required of the nature of the capital that they represent, its health and capacity for change. To achieve this they will require engagement with the community at large, both local and national, to ensure that there is full understanding and acceptance of these areas as critical parts of the Nation's environmental capital. Whether AONB management has the capability to do this is discussed in the next chapter.

References

1 Ministry of Works and Planning, *Report of the Committee on Land Utilisation in Rural Areas*, Cmd 6387, London, 1942.

2 Allanson, P. & Whitby, M. (eds), *The Rural Economy and the British Countryside*, Earthscan, London, 1996.

3 Ibid.

4 Department of the Environment, Ministry of Agriculture, Fisheries and Food, *Rural England: A Nation Committed to a Living Countryside*, Cm 3016, HMSO, London, 1996.

5 Ministry of Works and Planning, op. cit.

6 Department of the Environment, *Planning Policy Guidance, the Countryside – Environmental Quality and Economic and Social Development*, PPG 7 (revised), HMSO, London, 1997.

7 Council Regulation (EC) No. 1257/1999 of 17 May 1999 on support for rural development from the European Agricultural Guidance and Guarantee Fund (EAGGF).

[8] Article 41 of Council Regulation No. 1257/1999, op. cit.

[9] Article 33 of Council Regulation No. 1257/1999, op. cit.

[10] Ministry of Agriculture, Fisheries and Food, *A New Direction for Agriculture*, London, 1999.

[11] Countryside Agency Paper AP 99/22, Cheltenham, 1999

[12] Draft Commission Notice to Member States laying down guidelines for the Community Initiative for Rural Development (LEADER +) prepared under Article 20(1)(c)of Council Regulation (EC) No. 1260/1999.

[13] North Pennines AONB Public Inquiry, October 1985, Statement by the Director of the Countryside Commission, Cheltenham, 1985.

[14] Quoted in Statement to North Pennines AONB Public Inquiry, op. cit.

[15] Decision letter dated 11 September 1986 from the Department of the Environment to the Countryside Commission following the North Pennines AONB Public Inquiry.

[16] *Area of Outstanding Natural Beauty Bill (HL)*, 2nd Reading, 21 May 1999, Hansard, Cols. 537 to 592 and Committee Stage, 29 June 1999, Hansard, Cols. CWH 1 to CWH 48.

[17] Rural Development Commission, *Planning for People and Prosperity*, London, 1995.

[18] Cuff, J. & Rayment, M., Nature Conservation and the Rural Economy, in *RSPB Conservation Review*, No. 12, Sandy, 1998.

[19] CEAS Consultants (Wye) Ltd, 'The Economy of Landscape and Nature Conservation in England and Wales', unpublished report to Countryside Council for Wales, Countryside Commission and English Nature, 1993.

[20] Ibid.

[21] Department of the Environment, 1997, op. cit.

[22] Department of the Environment, Ministry of Agriculture, Fisheries and Food, 1996, op. cit.

[23] DETR News Release 416, 13 June 2000.

[24] Countryside Commission, *Planning File*, CCP 452, Cheltenham, 1994 and 1995.

[25] Countryside Commission, *Planning for Countryside Quality*, CCP 529, Cheltenham, 1998.

[26] Countryside Agency, *Planning for Quality of Life in Rural England*, CA 21, Cheltenham, 1999.

[27] Smart, G. & Anderson, M., *Planning and Management of Areas of Outstanding Natural Beauty*, report for the Countryside Commission, CCP 295, Cheltenham, 1990.

[28] Tyldesley, D. & Associates for Countryside Commission, 1993.

[29] Rural Development Commission, *Rural Development and Land Use Planning Policies*, report by Oxford Brookes University, RDR 38, Salisbury, 1998.

[30] Department of the Environment, Transport and the Regions, PPG 11, public consultation draft, London, 1999.

31 South East Regional Planning Conference, *A Sustainable Development Strategy for the South East*, SERP 500, London, 1998.

32 South West Regional Planning Conference, draft Regional Planning Guidance for the South West, Taunton, 1999.

33 Countryside Agency, *Directory of Areas of Outstanding Natural Beauty*, available only on the Agency website, www.countryside.gov.uk.

34 Ibid.

35 Purbeck District Council, draft District Plan, Wareham, 1997.

36 Shropshire Hills AONB Joint Advisory Committee, *Study of Development within AONBs*, Church Stretton, 1996.

37 Land Use Consultants, *A Study of Appeal Decisions in AONBs and Heritage Coasts in England*, report to the Countryside Commission, 1995.

38 Clwydian Range AONB Joint Advisory Committee, *Guidelines for Planning Consultations*, Mold, 1991.

39 Sussex Downs Conservation Board and East Hampshire AONB Joint Advisory Committee, 1997.

40 Chichester Harbour Conservancy, *AONB Management Plan*, Chichester, 1999.

41 Department of the Environment, Transport and the Regions, *A Better Way of Life: a Strategy for Sustainable Development for the UK*, Cm 4345, 1999.

42 Brundtland, G.H., *World Commission on Environment and Development, Our Common Future*, Oxford University Press, 1987.

43 Countryside Commission, *Position Statement: Sustainability and the English Countryside*, CCP 432, Cheltenham, 1993.

44 MacEwan, Anne & Malcolm, *Greenprints for the Countryside? The Story of Britain's National Parks*, Allen and Unwin, 1987. IUCN and the Countryside Commission, *Protected Landscapes: Summary Proceedings of an International Symposium, Lake District, October 1987*, 1988.

45 *Sustainable Development in the National Parks*, report of a workshop organised by the Countryside Commission and the UK Centre for Economic and Environmental development, CCD61, Cheltenham, 1989.

46 Department of the Environment, Transport and the Regions, 1999, op. cit.

Part Four

The Future – Landscapes No Longer at Risk?

Previous chapters have examined the way in which the AONB concept has evolved over fifty years and how it has reacted to an ever-changing context. Part Four of the book, comprising Chapters 8 and 9, now considers whether AONBs are fit for the challenges of the new millennium, and concludes from this analysis that a new agenda is required to establish broad principles for their future direction. It makes proposals for improved legislation and for a programme of national and local action to follow this up, and concludes by looking at what AONB experience can offer to the continuing debate about the future of protected landscapes generally.

AONBs: fit for the challenge? 8

This chapter reviews the challenges faced by AONBs as part of the wider family of protected landscapes and asks whether they are adequately prepared to meet them. It then assesses whether the published solutions – the Advice Papers[1], the Renton Bill,[2] and the Countryside and Rights of Way Bill[3] – fit the bill, and it points to the need for a new agenda.

Challenges to protected landscapes

Challenges to protected landscapes and, in particular, to the future survival of AONBs, derive from both international and national activities. Earlier chapters have suggested that the main challenges coming from international activities are as summarised below:

1. Government commitments arising from the Convention on Biological Diversity and the EC Birds and Habitats Directives[4,5,6], have directed priorities towards nature conservation. These documents say very little about protected landscapes, rich though they are in biodiversity resources. The challenge here is to ensure that their key role in delivering these commitments, for example, in implementing Biodiversity Action Plans, is properly understood.

2. The biodiversity measures introduce firm national obligations towards wildlife and carry a degree of international financial support. This is in complete contrast to the pronouncements relating to landscapes which, so far, are not mandatory. The challenge here is for the protection of landscape, a resource of equal national importance, to generate its own powerful impetus.

3. The Parks for Life agenda[7] and the forthcoming European Landscape Convention[8] both emphasise the central importance of protected landscapes, but warn against taking an isolationist view of their planning and management. The challenge is to ensure that their key role in the conservation and enjoyment of natural and cultural resources and in the delivery of social and economic policy

objectives is better understood, and to involve the community in their management.

4. The dominance of production incentives, at the expense of conservation, in the EU Common Agricultural Policy has been well documented. The challenge that remains is to give a far higher priority to conservation objectives, especially in protected areas. There is still a long way to go.

At the UK level, too, challenges to the concept of protected landscapes, especially AONBs, are emerging. These stem from several sources, which are outlined below:

1. The growing emphasis on a 'whole countryside' approach in rural policy has tended to ignore AONBs, which may have suffered in consequence at times of constraint upon public expenditure. The challenge is for these areas of living and working countryside, exceptionally well endowed as they are with natural and cultural resources, to demonstrate their ability to contribute to the wider good and the need for a proper level of financial support to enable them to do so.

2. The UK Strategy for Sustainable Development[9] stresses the need to integrate environmental conservation with social and economic development and, especially in the case of protected areas, to define the limits within which the process of change can take place. It has very important implications for the whole tenor of AONB policy. The challenge is to make sure that AONBs are recognised as providing a crucial part of the national environmental capital and to involve the local community in identifying the sort of sustainable development appropriate for each AONB.

3. The impact of long-term trends resulting from changes in climate, life-styles and land use could have a particularly severe effect upon some protected areas. The challenge is to develop methods which will allow managers to be able to monitor their condition and to anticipate likely pressures.

The greatest overall challenge for those looking after protected landscapes, however, whether in the UK or worldwide, is to be able to manage the changes brought about by the fact that they are living and working landscapes, with all the complex interactions that this involves.

Key requirements needed to meet these challenges

The rural environment is made up of numerous natural and man-made elements that are appreciable as a composite whole, especially as landscape. Within this, there are particular places where the concentration of those elements is such that they are worthy of national recognition and protection. There are certain key requirements that these protected landscapes need if they are to be successfully conserved and able to meet these challenges:

- They need to be underpinned by statute;
- Each of the landscape's component parts – geological, ecological, scenic, archaeological and historic – must be systematically protected and enhanced;
- Areas should be formally identified which recognise and can safeguard key elements of biological, natural, recreational and cultural resources;
- These designated areas should be given a number of purposes that will allow them to protect and enhance each of their component parts in a co-ordinated and sustainable way; this should include an integrated approach to matters such as recreation, agriculture, forestry and economic development and, in each area, a land-use planning overview;
- The system should operate within a policy framework set by national objectives for the sustainability of rural resources in general;
- Each area should have an organisation charged with looking after it in a sustainable way; while these organisations will share common values, their structures will reflect local needs and aspirations and should:
    - be resourced both nationally and locally;
    - be representative of local and national interests, so that all stakeholders – public, private and voluntary bodies, and particularly local communities – are closely involved;
    - have clear links to the planning system;
    - develop a fully-integrated policy approach which aims at sustainability;
    - produce a Management Plan;
- Public agencies should be given clear duties to consider the reasons for designation when operating in these areas;
- The national policy process should recognise these important areas of environmental capital and their ability to deliver sustainability and biodiversity objectives;
- The management of protected landscapes will be successful only if it has the support of the public at local and national levels and the public must be made aware of the need for action at national and local levels.

How does the current system match these requirements?

A review of the protected landscapes system in England and Wales

The protected landscape system appears at first sight to be stable and secure, with a strong legislative base and international recognition. Despite criticism of its apparent complexity, the concept of protecting the nation's best environmental resources has considerable support amongst the general public. This support developed over 100 years ago and has received strong emotional and political commitment ever since.

The 1949 Act contemplated quite a simple system of protected landscapes. However, the one that has evolved has grown in an *ad hoc* way that is neither comprehensive in scope nor consistent in application. From the start, it never fully embraced the UK – hence the variations described in Chapter 1 in the form of designation, policies, funding and implementation methods between England and Wales, Scotland and Northern Ireland.

The selection of areas over the last fifty years has necessarily depended largely on subjective judgement. Policy development and implementation has proceeded well in a limited number of high profile areas in England and Wales, such as National Parks, where the need for funding and statutory administrative arrangements has been recognised. In addition, there is a well-established suite of designated wildlife sites (SSSIs and ASSIs) at UK level, a few of which are extensive, backed by a good base of scientific criteria, an increasing range of protective measures and a powerful political drive, both European and British.

Unlike the designation of protected landscapes, there is no general basis for the identification of areas representing a concentration of sites that are nationally important for their wildlife, in spite of the proposals put forward by the Huxley Committee in 1947,[10] which included the recognition of 35 scientific areas (see Plate 1). In the event, nine of these areas have been embraced within National Parks and 21 within AONBs, with the remainder having no area designation. However, until the recent enlargement of National Park purposes, no formal link of any kind existed between scenic designations and wildlife importance, in spite of their overlapping interest. There is still no such link with respect to AONBs.

Similarly, Chapter 2 showed that there was a strong link between the cultural heritage and landscape. However, the 1949 Act system did not address this and there is no basis for the designation of areas of historic or cultural importance. The focus remains on sites. As a result there has been very little linkage between the two, except more recently in the case of National Parks.

These sites, whether recognised for their wildlife, geological, archaeological or cultural significance, and the protected landscape areas are not mutually exclusive in terms of the land they cover nor in the way in which they are protected, although they are often seen to be. In fact, they should be mutually supportive. As Chapter 2 has shown, it can be expected that there will be significant concentrations of sites within protected landscapes. The broad approach to landscape advocated should be capable of providing the overall framework within which sites are conserved and enjoyed.

As shown in earlier chapters, the whole UK protected landscape system also suffers from a confusing growth in the number of international designations for sites, mainly in relation to wildlife: Ramsar, SPAs, SACs, Biogenetic Reserves and Biosphere Reserves. These international accolades have been accorded almost exclusively to existing SSSIs, but they tend to come with a special suite of rules and regulations which, together with different nomenclature and the lack of public awareness of their purpose and procedures, serves to create an even more confusing picture for protected landscapes.

Further confusion is caused when some lists of protected landscapes include areas that are the subject of agri-environment schemes, such as ESAs, or areas covered by specific environmental protection measures. Agri-environment schemes are not designations. They are essentially mechanisms for channelling funds to farmers and landowners for environmentally friendly management. Environmental protection measures such as Water Protection Zones and Nitrate Sensitive Areas are not defined on the basis of the importance of the area in landscape terms, but on the basis of the management measures required to solve a particular problem. They should not be regarded as part of the protected landscape system.

National Parks and AONBs

Perhaps the most striking anomaly in the system in England and Wales is the somewhat artificial distinction between National Parks and AONBs. Their outstanding natural beauty in national terms is recognised in statute as a reason for designation, but there the similarities end. National Parks have further reasons for designation, namely, the opportunity they afford for open-air recreation and their proximity to centres of population. Their purposes and the administrative structures provided to fulfil those purposes are completely different.

It is generally recognised that their landscapes are of similar quality, although with differences in character, notably in the greater extent and continuity of open land in National Parks. This matter weighed strongly in the 1940s thinking. However, as shown in Chapter 2, the feeling of open wilderness is present in many of the AONBs, particularly those in the uplands, along the coast and in the chalk downlands.

The question of recreation has always been perceived to be the major difference, although the duties of National Parks now also embrace wildlife, cultural and socio-economic matters. National Parks are designated for the recreation opportunities they provide and there is no such requirement for AONBs. However, it is clear from the Dower[11] and Hobhouse[12] Reports, and from the Himsworth Report on AONB performance,[13] that the recreational value of AONBs was at least implied if not set out in legislation. Furthermore, earlier chapters have shown that over the last 50 years, irrespective of legislation, AONBs have taken on a very important recreational role in practice. In some cases it exceeds that of the National Parks and AONBs are often more easily accessible to the public than are some National Parks.

The extensive open country found in National Parks offers a particular form of recreation experience, although in practice it is mainly enjoyed on tracks and paths. This kind of experience was uppermost in the minds of those who originally campaigned for access to open country and is behind the current right to roam campaign. However, AONBs provide a variety of access opportunities, mainly by footpaths, giving a wide range of recreation experiences, often including the feeling of open space. To ignore what is actually happening today, and to rely on a particular view of recreation developed in the 1940s as the main criterion for not giving AONBs a statutory recreation purpose, seems to be outdated and artificial. It is also a pity that much of the debate about the designation of the South Downs as a National Park revolves around the kind of recreation experience that would be provided and whether there is sufficient open country.

The only practical difference between National Parks and AONBs can therefore be said to be in their funding and administration. As a single-purpose designation, AONBs have not acquired an administrative standing, and the funding that goes with it, that is even broadly comparable with National Parks. As a result, there is effectively a two-tier system, with AONBs very much in the second division.

Overall, the protected landscapes system is complex and not well understood and therefore, apart perhaps from National Parks, not given sufficient support. Some of the key requirements identified are missing, particularly in relation to AONBs. The areas still tend to be seen as islands of conservation rather than as part of a much wider policy package. As everyone inches their way towards an understanding of sustainability, the importance of these areas in that process will need to be recognised and acted upon.

Under present legislation and policy, the key aim for AONBs, put simply, is the conservation and enhancement of their natural beauty (defined in such a way as to include 'flora, fauna, and geological and physiographic features'),[14] supported by appropriate and effective management and funding arrangements. This is, to an extent, being met in practice. AONBs have undoubted strengths. There is much to be said for management achievements within them and further efforts to secure their conservation and enhancement can be built up from those accomplishments.

Earlier chapters have shown that the AONB concept has many positive features, including the quality and variety of their natural resources, the extent of public commitment in principle to their conservation and enhancement and the support to these efforts given by the voluntary sector and local communities. They are amongst the finest and most diverse of our landscapes. They contain much of our best wildlife habitats and archaeological sites. They make a significant contribution to meeting society's needs for countryside recreation.

As such, they have attracted various forms of recognition and commitment. They are recognised by a special place in the planning system, through which there has been a good measure of success in protecting them from damaging development. They also feature in about half of the areas of countryside in England and Wales selected for favourable treatment in agri-environment policies.

AONBs have also attracted increasing commitment from organisations primarily charged with their conservation: the Countryside Commission and its successor the Countryside Agency, the Countryside Council for Wales and most of the local authorities in which their boundaries occur. Most receive financial support from these bodies and there has been noticeable progress in the implementation of management projects in certain areas, although the coverage of this is patchy. Three-quarters of them have Management Plans and an AONB Officer.

The commitment of the two countryside bodies has been further demonstrated in the case they have put to government, with a fair measure of success, for strengthened legislation and improved financial support.[15] Local Authorities have also shown collective support by setting up the Association for Areas of Outstanding Natural Beauty, to represent the needs of these areas to government and to advance their general cause collectively.

Some AONBs have forged strong links with local communities. The importance of landscape conservation and of economic development in AONBs has also been recognised by grant aid from the European Union and from bodies such as the National Lottery. The private and voluntary sectors have shown that they can play a very valuable role in the management of some AONBs, by means of investment, fund-raising and practical conservation work.

Nevertheless, in spite of these positive achievements, AONBs have two significant shortcomings in relation to the principles for protected landscapes outlined earlier, which place a question mark over their ability to respond to the challenges identified and, indeed, to their very existence. Their aim or purpose is too narrowly defined to encourage a broad-based and integrated approach to conservation, and there is no statutory framework for their organisation and administration.

The fact that their purpose is limited primarily to the conservation of landscape, with neither a formal link to wildlife and cultural values, nor to people's enjoyment of the areas, nor to local communities and their economic activities, is fundamental. Efforts to conserve and enhance their qualities have been constantly hampered by this weakness in their origin and later development.

It gives rise to problems of co-ordination, particularly in key activities such as recreation and tourism, traffic management and the care of ecological and cultural resources, where organisations with specialist responsibilities tend to have their own priorities that do not reflect the needs of the area as a whole. Issues of development versus conservation are still too often seen in traditional terms of conflict, whereas concepts of sustainability, when more fully developed, could point to benefits from integration.

The lack of a clear requirement in the 1949 Act for AONB management (as distinct from protection under planning powers) to become a public responsibility, has meant that it was optional rather than mandatory. AONBs have often been seen as nobody's responsibility. This has led to shortcomings in the administrative arrangements for their conservation and enhancement and in the degree of commitment by some of the public organisations involved, in the adequacy and security of funds for their management and in the resources needed to define the state of their environmental and socio-economic 'health'.

As a result, only about three-quarters of AONBs have co-ordinating bodies. Those that do usually make use of Advisory Committees that have no firm legal status and depend for their effectiveness on the continuing goodwill of very large numbers of participant organisations. Most of them have little or no influence over planning decisions and there are few opportunities to have their views formally heard by local planning committees.

Despite the efforts of the former Countryside Commission, the Countryside Council for Wales and the local authorities, it has been difficult to obtain the financial resources and expertise that AONBs need. Although the urgency for this was highlighted in the 1989/90 AONB Review[16] and was accepted by the Commission at the time, project funding and the engagement of staff has been dominated by short-term thinking. While good work has none the less been done in several areas in terms of policy-making and generation of good-will, financial stringency has meant that positive action is often thin on the ground, and only in a minority of AONBs is there an integral countryside management service. Where Management Plans exist, they do not necessarily relate to the plans of other bodies, even to those of the local planning authorities, and they are now in need of review. Very few AONBs have business plans.

Monitoring of changes in the fabric and socio-economic conditions of AONBs is far from systematic. There is a widespread feeling that AONBs are being overwhelmed by pressure, especially environmental damage from intensive agriculture, recreation, traffic, poor standards of design and gradual suburbanisation. The scale and frequency of this is far from clear, but there is undoubtedly cause for concern.

These two major shortcomings – the narrowness of purpose and administrative weakness – have led to a lack of awareness by politicians and the general public of the national importance of AONBs, both as landscapes and in their ability to deliver wider policy objectives. This has not been helped by the sheer diversity of these areas and their long and clumsy title – commonly abbreviated into a meaningless set of initials, which are easily misquoted – which expresses fact rather than policy intention. Landscape quality, particularly that of living and working landscapes, can be a difficult concept for people to grasp. All this has meant that the environmental risks that AONBs face have not been fully appreciated, nor have the benefits that their proper management can bring to local communities. There has thus been a somewhat negative and parsimonious approach to the conservation of AONBs. This has also applied to efforts to foster their social and economic value, where they have tended to be seen as 'no go' areas.

It is clear that, notwithstanding the progress that has been made by individual AONBs, major problems remain and require urgent action. This was obviously the opinion of the Countryside Commission and the Countryside Council for Wales when they prepared their Advice to Government, particulars of which are given in Chapter 4.

A review of the Advice Papers and the Renton Bill

While the Advice Papers[17] advocated an approach to the future of the AONBs that leaves the designation criteria and purposes in their present form, they were very positive on the need for improvement of administrative arrangements and financial support. For this purpose, they set a series of objectives for better management and funding, statutory provision for a new, optional, administrative organisation (a Conservation Board) for English AONBs and a duty for local authorities to promote the conservation and management of AONBs.

There are, however, two important ways in which they fall short of the principles for protected landscapes outlined above. Notably, they do not fully cover wider purposes of designation, nor do they prescribe any alternative principles for the administrative organisation to be adopted by those AONBs where a Conservation Board would be inappropriate. Such areas would presumably be encouraged by policy statements and indications of financial support to establish some form of JAC. It is questionable in the light of experience whether this would commend itself everywhere.

The Renton Bill[18] (described in Chapter 4) did introduce new purposes for designation relating to conservation of landscape and wildlife, though it did not address cultural matters, which are of great importance in many areas and very much interwoven with other purposes. There was no reference to public enjoyment, recreation and access. Given the importance of AONBs for such activity, this was a surprising omission. The Bill was also silent on socio-economic matters, local communities and sustainability. This was recognised in the debates in the Lords and was a matter to which the Government showed considerable sympathy. As a result, the Countryside Agency modified CC's Advice Paper to include reference to socio-economic issues in relation to AONBs.

A further shortcoming of the Bill was the differential way that Conservation Boards, of which only a few are likely to be established, and the remainder of the AONBs were treated:

- the Bill contained no requirement for all AONBs to have a joint body, to include stakeholders, to manage the AONB and champion its causes, other than a Board;
- its financial provisions relate solely to Boards, leaving the remainder of AONBs with a duty to conserve but seemingly no certainty of adequate finance from government;
- it would give a Board a strong presence in the planning process, but this would not apply in areas without a Board.

The Government's response to the Advice Paper, described in Chapter 4, includes the proposal that the Sussex Downs and East Hampshire AONBs should become a National Park. This raises once again the question of interpretation of the designation formula, opening up for debate the artificial distinction between National Parks and AONBs, described earlier. If the only practical difference between them in future is to be in their administrative arrangements, a new dimension to the relative importance and standing of AONBs as protected landscapes would be introduced. As indicated in Chapter 4, the response also includes an important promise of legislation to improve the conservation of AONBs. The scope of this is uncertain at the time of writing, but if it were to comprise anything less than the scope of the Renton Bill, there would be cause for concern.

This chapter has suggested that AONB managers have a considerable record of achievement that is to be applauded. But they could do better and, indeed, will need to do so, if the areas are to survive as some of the best living and working landscapes. The serious short-comings that have been identified in the present approach to AONB conservation suggest that managers will find it difficult to respond to the challenges with which they are increasingly being faced.

They have suffered from a lack of political commitment, resulting to some extent from a lack of awareness of the national and local impor-tance of AONBs. This has perpetuated their second-rate status as pro-tected landscapes, has limited the level of funding available for their proper management, and has made it difficult to set up administrative organisations with a strong mandate to initiate and co-ordinate action for their well-being.

These problems are compounded by the limitations in their statutory mandate: a single-issue focus on landscape, which makes it difficult to develop a multi-purpose role in managing their full complement of resources – natural, cultural and recreational. It has also tended to act as a constraint upon the social and economic needs of their communi-ties. The situation is compounded, too, by a notable lack of compre-hensive data about the health of AONBs, making it difficult to identify their needs for new policies and programmes, especially in relation to agri-environment issues.

The problems are also compounded by the inadequate scope of the protected landscape system, which has no basis for recognising areas of wildlife or cultural values. Furthermore, the growth in the number and type of designated areas, sometimes to introduce particular management regimes and sometimes to recognise national or interna-tional importance, has tended to create even more confusion. This has been to the detriment of protected landscapes such as AONBs as they struggle for recognition.

AONBs are at a significant cross-roads. They are neither adequately organised nor financed to be able to move convincingly in new direc-tions of the kind that the future will require of them. There remains an artificial and unhelpful distinction between them and National Parks. Most of the problems mentioned in this chapter were identi-fied some time ago. The fact that they still exist has caused people to question whether the then Countryside Commission, as the only organisation which could have triggered the basic improvement of legislation and resources, had the will to do so. It may well have had other priorities, such as the strengthening of the administration and finance of National Parks. Since then, the Commission and the Countryside Council for Wales have made determined efforts to rectify matters in their Advice to Government. However, it is debatable whether the tenor of this advice, and of the Government's response, goes far enough to overcome the weaknesses in the system, except, perhaps, in the short term. The next chapter explores the kind of statutory framework and implementation measures necessary for a successful negotiation of the cross-roads, which could put AONBs on the right road for long-term success.

References

1   Countryside Commission, *Protecting Our Finest Countryside, Advice to Government*, CCP532, Cheltenham, 1998.

2   *Areas of Outstanding Natural Beauty Bill (HL)*, 1999.

3   *Countryside and Rights of Way Bill (HC)*, 1999.

4   Convention on Biological Diversity was one of several major initiatives stemming from the 'Earth Summit' in Rio de Janeiro in 1992.

5   Council Directive 79/409/EEC on the conservation of wild birds.

6   Council Directive 92/43/EEC on the conservation of natural habitats and of wild fauna and flora.

7   IUCN, *Parks for Life: Report of the IVth World Congress on National Parks and Protected Areas, Caracas, 1992*, Gland, Switzerland, 1993 and IUCN, *Parks for Life: Action for Protected Areas in Europe*, Gland, Switzerland & Cambridge, UK, 1994.

8   Congress of Local and Regional Authorities of Europe, Recommendation 40 (1998) on the draft European Landscape Convention.

9   Department for the Environment, Transport and the Regions, *A Better Quality of Life: a Strategy for Sustainable Development for the United Kingdom*, Cm 4345, HMSO, London, 1999.

10   Ministry of Town and Country Planning, *Conservation of Nature in England and Wales, Report of the Wildlife Conservation Special Committee*, Cmd 7122, HMSO, London, 1947.

11   Ministry of Town and Country Planning, *National Parks in England and Wales*, Cmd 6628, HMSO, London, 1945.

12   Ministry of Town and Country Planning, *Report of the National Parks Committee (England and Wales)*, Cmd 7121, HMSO, London, 1947.

13   Himsworth, K. M., *A Review of Areas of Outstanding Natural Beauty*, report for the Countryside Commission, CCP 140, Cheltenham, 1980.

14   *National Parks and Access to the Countryside Act*, 1949, Section 114 (2).

15   Countryside Commission, CCP532, 1998, op. cit.

16   Smart, G. & Anderson, M., *Planning and Management of AONBs*, report for the Countryside Commission, CCP 295, Cheltenham, 1990.

17   Countryside Commission, CCP532, 1998, op. cit.

18   *Areas of Outstanding Natural Beauty Bill (HL)*, 1999.

A new agenda for AONBs 9

There is no doubt that, after 50 years, a major policy turning point has been reached for AONBs. The previous chapter made it clear that they have neither the organisational framework nor the terms of reference, nor the agenda to meet the challenges of today and the next fifty years. The Advice from the Agencies to the Government only goes part of the way to making them fit for these challenges.

A new agenda is required to address their shortcomings and to ensure that AONBs are firmly at the top of the conservation tree, alongside National Parks, as a key part of the national heritage. This would do much to encourage a new breadth of vision and local leadership, and greater commitment from stakeholders, especially national agencies. To continue as at present, in line with the primarily landscape-based policies established after the 1989/90 AONB review and with current levels of financial support, would not do justice to the importance of these areas. AONBs would remain the poor relations of the protected landscape family, their administration continuing to be somewhat *ad hoc*, low key, and often lacking the ability to co-ordinate policy and its implementation. Their scenic quality and tranquillity would continue to decline under the cumulative impacts of pressures and management shortcomings, and much of the benefit of past public spending would be lost. In time the value of the designation might be seriously questioned.

The fact that AONBs, or rather their present administrative arrangements, are not really up to the challenges begs the question of whether they should be retained at all. Given that the designation 'areas of outstanding natural beauty' is in recognition of the importance of these areas to the nation, such an abolitionist outlook would make little sense. This would be particularly so in a world that is increasingly led by the principles of sustainable development, the pursuit of which requires the identification of environmental capital as part of its process. If the designation were to be abolished, the need to adopt a comprehensive area-based approach would remain where groupings of important assets, like those in AONBs, are found. Thus the wheel would have turned full circle and the definition of special areas would need to be reinvented.

The way forward is to build upon the AONB concept, in accordance with the key requirements set out in Chapter 8, by adopting a more wide-ranging approach than proposed hitherto, involving:

- broader purposes for AONBs, akin to those for National Parks;
- clear duties for local authorities and public agencies to conserve AONBs;
- a suitable organisation for each area, locally derived and nationally endorsed, that involves all stakeholders and has a firm link to communities and the local economy;
- a system of integrated management;
- substantial and secure funding from government;
- a two-way relationship in each area with strategic planning and management for the wider countryside and with other major policy-making organisations.

The three-part agenda set out in the following pages shows how this could be done. Part 1 indicates what needs to be based in statute. Part 2 contains action points for successful implementation in each AONB. Part 3 sets out the action needed in the wider context to allow AONBs to flourish.

Part 1:
A statutory
framework

There is no doubt that key elements of this agenda must be set out in statute. To rely on a fifty-year-old Act that has already had to be supplemented as far as National Parks are concerned, and has been shored up for AONBs by policy statements and financial incentives, may be just acceptable for the short term. However, the national importance of AONBs and the challenges to the very survival of their qualities all suggest that a convincing statutory framework, giving them the same standing as National Parks, is essential in their long-term interest.

The two major policy reviews described in Chapter 4,[1] and the active role of some local authorities, for example in the Sussex Downs, have resulted in some notable progress in AONB conservation in spite of the system rather than because of it. However, the shortcomings in the objectives for AONBs and in the mechanisms for their conservation identified in this book reinforce the view that it is right to propose a new statutory framework. Indeed it is now officially recognised that parliamentary time should be set aside for legislation as soon as possible. The Advice Papers[2] expressed a clear preference for new legislation. This received all-party support in the House of Lords debate on the Renton Bill, and more recently in the House of Commons.

The elements that need to be embraced by legislation are:
- the purposes of designation;
- the duty to conserve;
- the administrative framework.

The purposes of AONB designation

The fact that most AONBs contain nationally important natural and cultural resources and recreational potential makes it essential to develop a comprehensive approach to management of all such inter-related attributes in each area. Effectively this would place the purpose of designation, expressed through aims for management, on a par with that of National Parks, that is, to adopt the twin purposes of conserving natural beauty, wildlife and cultural heritage, and, as far as is compatible with this, promoting understanding and enjoyment of their special qualities by the public. Similarly the primacy of conservation – the Sandford Principle – should be included in legislation, to ensure that there is no doubt about what should happen when the purposes are in conflict

Opportunity should be also be taken to include a secondary purpose, as with National Parks, to foster the economic and social well-being of local communities. However, the constraint of not incurring expenditure for such a purpose, imposed on National Parks, should not be imposed on AONBs. It is essential that an AONB organisation should be able to spend money promoting economic activity, where this is directly related to the conservation of landscape or other natural or cultural resources.

The duty to conserve

A clear duty on local authorities and public bodies with responsibilities in AONBs to promote their conservation and management in a sustainable manner is essential. For local authorities the duty should specifically include the preparation, publication, implementation and regular review of a Management Plan for each AONB. For other public bodies, the duty should be interpreted as a responsibility to recognise the national importance of AONBs when framing their own corporate programmes and, at AONB level, to participate fully in management planning and implementation.

The administrative framework

AONB administration, so often criticised for 'lack of clout' and for containing significant gaps in its coverage, should be given formal national recognition in statute. The arrangements need to include representatives of stakeholders (the main public agencies with conservation responsibilities in the area, landowners and farmers, local communities and voluntary groups). The role should be one of management, normally by consensus; land-use planning should remain a local authority function, for consistency with transportation and other environmental services. It is essential, nevertheless, that the AONB organisation should be empowered to speak formally on the needs of the area when planning and other decisions affecting it are being made.

The approach should be more flexible than those prescribed for National Park Authorities or the proposed Conservation Boards, and should go further than the current ideas for legislation. Essentially it is necessary to establish a procedure whereby, after an agreed period of, say, two or three years, the local authorities in each area should propose an organisation suited to the area's own needs in terms of membership, size, dedicated management responsibility and administrative relationship with existing local government organisation and financial arrangements. The proposal would need to be based upon a set of national criteria for the representation of national concerns (including recreation) and those of other stakeholders, but developed in association with the local communities. In accordance with statute, Ministers would then be required to confirm the proposed organisation, giving national recognition to the body set up to manage the area, as is the case with National Park Authorities.

Part 2: Action points for successful implementation

The establishment of a new statutory framework for AONBs would be just the first step towards fitting them to meet the challenges of the next century. It would not of itself place the landscape and other resources of AONBs completely beyond threat. There are seven key action points for successful implementation within a new statutory framework:

1. staffing;
2. long-term and secure financing;
3. the scope and content of the management plan;
4. new ways of working;
5. awareness raising and communication;
6. research and experiment;
7. education and training.

Staffing

Adequate and appropriate staffing will be crucial to the strategic planning for each AONB and to act as a catalyst for countryside management. The precise requirements will depend on the particular circumstances in each area. However, it is very difficult to envisage an AONB without an officer dedicated to the task of servicing the statutory organisation and developing and implementing the strategy and management plan. Indeed the requirement imposed in 1974 for each National Park to have a National Park Officer could usefully be mirrored in the legislation for AONBs. Although some of the skills required might on occasions be supplied from existing local authority teams, it is equally difficult to conceive of an AONB not, at the very least, having a small unit to act as the focus for the area, particularly given the wider purposes and the much closer involvement with planning that is envisaged. Furthermore it will be crucial to have a countryside management capability that is dedicated to the AONB, so that the benefits of the approach in forging links with farmers and landowners and the local community can be realised.

Long-term and secure financing

Once a suitable organisation had been established for an area, guaranteed financial support from central government for approved levels of core funding would be crucial. There is a convincing case for this support to be given in the same proportion as for National Parks, in recognition of their equivalent national status and to their existing role as managers of tourism and recreation. Some AONB local authorities are having great difficulty in voting enough money to meet a reasonable share of funding. To fix the level of government grant at 75 per cent of core expenditure, as recommended by CCW and the Association for AONBs, rather than the 50 per cent proposed in CC's Advice Paper, would mean a modest additional expenditure for government of about £2.5 million per annum. This would give local authorities much encouragement. They would be expected to contribute 25 per cent of core expenditure. The actual level of core expenditure would be determined in each case, according to the agreed type of administration, the management strategy and the business plan for the area.

The scope and content of the Management Plan

The scope of the Management Plan should reflect the wider purposes of AONBs, not only all aspects of conserving the natural and the built environment but also the enjoyment and understanding of these areas by the public, and the socio-economic well-being of local communities within them. In essence this is all about the sustainable development process, for which the newly strengthened AONBs should be in a good position to act as models. The plans should thus embrace a much wider range of issues than they have normally done, so that the challenges are dealt with in a co-ordinated fashion.

Each plan should set out a vision for the AONB, to which all stakeholders can subscribe, and should provide guidance for all resource management. It should be based upon a thorough understanding of the character of the area and an assessment of the individual elements of environmental capital that make up its overall value. Knowledge of the dynamics of the area and the forces for change operating within it would be of fundamental importance as a basis for systematic monitoring and as a catalyst for innovation, for example in access and transport. The amount of existing information varies, but it will be important to ensure that management plan preparation is not unduly delayed by waiting for all the research to be completed.

The Management Plan should be drawn up in such a way as to guide the main policy content of Development Plans covering the area and Supplementary Planning Guidance. It will be crucial in providing the context for the operation of the planning system, giving guidance on what change is acceptable, thus hopefully making for a more positive approach to planning. Special attention would be required for issues of sustainability, the benefits to be gained from the integration of economic development with conservation, and matters such as design standards and the goals necessary for the operation of the development plan system.

An essential adjunct to the Management Plan would be the Business Plan that guides its implementation. It should reflect the priorities for the AONB, as set out in the Management Plan and contain the operational plans of all partner organisations so far as they affect the area or immediately adjacent areas.

New ways of working
The requirement to prepare a management plan for each AONB will ensure that a means is in place for achieving their wider purposes. While the scope and content of the plan is important, the very process of preparing the plan will be equally important as a means of developing and strengthening partnerships, drawing in all those who have a stake in the long-term good health of the AONB. Implicit in this, and in the new framework generally, is the development of styles of working that are inclusive of all interests, creating a positive climate, that is, active participation rather than merely by consultation, especially with the private and voluntary sectors. The plan should be the vehicle through which the stakeholders (national, regional and local) can express what they will be doing for the AONB. They should 'own' the plan. For the main public bodies at least, regular audit and publication of results of their activities would be an integral part of the process.

The implementation of the plan will be the responsibility of stake-holders individually or in partnership with others. As has already been pointed out, links with the private sector are likely to be strengthened on issues of countryside recreation by means of consultative arrangements with landowners and farmers proposed under the Government's new access policies. This will be especially so in those areas that have much open land, and the need for joint approaches to management, especially wardening, will become critical. Equally, the emphasis on economic development that is emerging in the CAP and in the role of the Countryside Agency will no doubt result in closer co-operation between AONB managers and landowners, private and charitable, and other employers, to diversify opportunities in AONBs generally.

Integrated action will be crucial, with the AONB organisation acting as a one-stop source for advice and financial support across the board and as a catalyst for activity, rather than trying to do everything itself. The public agencies responsible for the key policy areas affecting AONBs, such as CA, CCW, English Nature, Forestry Commission, English Heritage and CADW, the Tourist Boards and the Environment Agency, should enter into simple agreements with the family of AONBs and, where appropriate, with individual areas, in the way they have done with National Parks. They should embrace co-operative ventures, a willingness to second staff for specific projects or to make agency arrangements for specific duties, such as giving advice and grants.

As the case studies have shown, working with the private and voluntary sectors can also be of benefit to AONBs in fund-raising, forging useful links to sponsor or combine resources on a variety of projects, especially interpretation and education, and generally promoting awareness. In order to ensure that everyone, particularly individuals, has a chance to be involved in the AONB, it will be important to promote and support 'Friends' organisations and Local Agenda 21 activities. It will also be essential to make use of countryside management teams to liaise with the local community, farmers and landowners, both at a practical level and as a means of understanding their needs. The creation of 'Friends' organisations, in particular, can bring in a wide range of voluntary expertise, including wardening, and financial support.

Evidence that such processes are in operation may well be crucial in putting together bids (including umbrella bids) for financial support. Economies of scale may point to the need to form partnerships with other AONBs, other Protected Landscapes or, indeed, with initiatives that cover a much wider area, or even with other countries.

Raising awareness and communication

The inclusive approach to the management of AONBs will require efforts to communicate and raise awareness of its purpose amongst the network of stakeholders (including visitors). At national level, the Association for AONBs and Staff Forum could be prime movers, together with the national agencies, in devising and implementing an awareness strategy. This could include national and regional elements aiming to reach, selectively, the general public, professional and scientific bodies, user and interest groups, local authorities, government departments and public agencies, businesses and politicians at all levels. Agricultural policy-makers should be an early target, as should possible funding sources for management projects in AONBs. Landscape is an emotive rallying point and could be used to great effect in campaigns of this kind. Equally important will be the efforts of each AONB to reach all parts of the local community.

The messages that need promotion generally and/or locally include:

- the importance and value of AONBs as jewels in the countryside crown, rather than as islands of conservation – their ability to deliver both biodiversity and sustainability objectives;
- the need to take a broad view of 'landscape', in line with their wider purposes;
- what needs to be done and the link with the management plan process;
- the relevance of an AONB to the various interests within it and to those which affect it from outside;
- the concept of positive change;
- the contribution AONBs make to the wider good – their value in being able to deliver wider policy objectives, for example, economic, education and health;
- progress made in looking after an AONB in a sustainable fashion;
- examples of good practice;
- AONBs' national standing being equal to National Parks.

Research and experiment

The nature of AONBs – places that are constantly changing and evolving – necessitates a good understanding of their dynamics and requires the evolution of new ideas, the very meat of research and experiment programmes. CA and CCW have inherited CC's power to conduct experiments and should use AONBs as valuable test-beds for innovative projects, with possible applications in countryside management generally. For example, the recently completed STAR project in Surrey and in certain National Parks may prove to give a valuable lead in rural traffic management, a topic that is still at an early stage of development. In Chapters 2 and 3, the need for a greater knowledge of trends affecting AONBs and of the effectiveness of management were identified.

The management plan process will need to be supported by research into techniques on such matters as the assessment of environmental capital, indicators of change and definition of limits of change and capacity, monitoring of the health of AONBs and of the nature of the socio-economic fabric, and the economic benefits of AONBs.

Education and training
The nature of the agenda will require a wide range of skills and expertise and is likely to result in considerable growth, medium to long-term, in staff requirements and in the range of skills necessary for both large and small AONB units. The only forecast available is necessarily incomplete and suggests that, over a five-year period, the numbers of core staff across the family of AONBs might rise from over 100 to over 200, plus the extra staffing requirements of countryside management services, which might be around 50.[3]

Even though it is likely that this growth will be compounded by further needs arising in the countryside at large, various course directories indicate that there are now nearly 70 undergraduate courses available in a wide range of relevant disciplines and over 30 courses for postgraduate studies. This suggests that, given flexibility, there could be capacity to meet educational requirements at these levels. Equally important will be the inclusion of this agenda in the numerous education courses for all those disciplines that are deployed in AONBs, such as farming, forestry and business studies.

As to refresher training, CA itself keeps a regular watch on the need for and provision of short course training modules, both for its own purposes and for the continual needs of partner organisations.[4] AONBs, through their Association, will need to address these issues too.

There have been few opportunities for AONB staff to benefit from sharing experience and information with people working at home or overseas in the general area of countryside conservation. At least one AONB is 'twinned' with a French Regional Park.[5] Exchanges of this kind are an extremely valuable adjunct to normal training programmes, and the Association might find it worthwhile to explore with the Association of National Park Authorities opportunities to foster regular links at home and overseas.

It is not only the staff of AONB units that will need to demonstrate a range of skills and expertise. Stakeholders at various levels (residents, farmers/landowners, voluntary bodies, local authorities, etc.) from the individual AONB upwards may well feel a need for greater knowledge of their values and management requirements, if they are to be able to participate in and benefit from the many new ventures that are implied by this widening of the AONB agenda.

AONB managers will need to set aside adequate resources to run programmes of in-house refresher training, exchanges and to help provide the skills needed by stakeholders, if they are to be constructively involved.

Part 3: The wider context

The new agenda for AONBs cannot be implemented successfully in isolation from the broader policy agenda. In this, there are three main actors: the AONBs as a family, the countryside agencies and government.

The partnership role of the AONB family and the countryside agencies
There is great potential in AONBs working together as a family, with common values and common cause. For many years, the family has been represented through the work of the CC/CCW now CA/CCW. It is now represented by its own Association in an increasingly strong way. There is a clear need for CA, CCW and the Association, separately and/or together, to take action to:

- generate interest in protected landscapes as a whole and promoting the relevance and value of AONBs;
- present the needs of AONBs to government and other national interests in terms of policy requirements and resources;
- create a focal point for umbrella funding, from sources such as the European Union, the National Lottery and private sponsorship;
- undertake research and experiments, provide advice, and collect and disseminate good practice;
- organise training programmes;
- form links with other protected landscapes in the UK and abroad.

The role of government
Once the statutory framework and administration and resources have been provided, government has an essential role in creating the right climate at a national level, promoting integrated policies and co-ordinated action, so that AONBs can flourish as living and working landscapes. AONBs should be properly recognised as key multi-purpose elements of the national environmental capital, with a legitimate and valuable role in wider countryside policy, especially for the delivery of biodiversity and sustainability.

All rural policies will need to be sensitive to AONBs and tailored to their requirements, particularly the development of a planning framework which respects their national importance, through the Rural

White Paper, the sustainable development strategy, PPGs and RPGs, Regional Development Agency strategies and structure and local and unitary plans. Policies for agriculture and forestry, minerals, energy, and transport should be equally sensitive. The agricultural departments, for example, should aim to have complete coverage of AONBs by good agri-environment schemes adjusted to the special requirements of the area, and deploy the staff to deliver them. The same should apply to operations by the Forestry Commission, English Nature, the Environment Agency, English Heritage and CADW, and others. It will also be important to encourage the role of private landowners and voluntary organisations in conserving these areas, for example through tax benefits and financial support.

A radical twist to the agenda

The agenda set out above for a more formally recognised and better funded AONB administration, coupled with more active management in all areas, would give them a powerful existence of their own. However, it does not address fully:

- the absence of a mechanism for the designation of areas of wildlife or cultural value;
- the seemingly artificial distinction between AONBs and National Parks.

Areas of national wildlife and cultural value

There remains the lack of a mechanism for the designation of areas (as distinct from sites) of wildlife and or cultural value. While the Agenda proposed applies specifically to AONBs, it could easily be adapted to fill this gap. It would mean that the criteria for designation could include outstanding wildlife and cultural resources as well as scenic quality, singly or in combination. The AONB concept, appropriately retitled, would have a noticeably wider application. This would require simple legislation, though it would be a radical and controversial step.

Given the proposed improved administrative standing and funding priority, the concept could offer much scope for the protection of nationally important groupings of rural resources which do not, at present, qualify for formal administrative recognition. If CA were to maintain the view of CC that there is not much scope for enlarging the existing list of AONBs, areas which have been considered in the past, such as Somerset Levels, Breckland and Yorkshire Wolds, those currently under consideration, such as the Forest of Dean, others recommended by Hobhouse but not designated, and certain estuaries and Heritage Coasts which are not in AONBs, could be given protection by this means. Yet others might be identified as work progresses long term on the environmental capital of Character Areas and Natural Areas.

To adapt the AONB concept in this way is a course of action that should seriously be considered. Its introduction could avoid the very real risk that the present confusing plethora of designations might otherwise continue to grow *ad hoc*. Various suggestions have been made in the past for new titles to replace AONB, but none of them has been considered better than the present one, despite its drawbacks. To embrace the different circumstances outlined here, 'Countryside Heritage Area' or 'Rural Conservation Area', which is close to the title used by Hobhouse, would be worth considering.

AONBs and National Parks

The new agenda does not fully resolve the somewhat artificial distinction between AONBs and National Parks. While it bolsters the position of AONBs very significantly, a danger remains that they would continue to be seen, quite unjustifiably, as second rank behind the National Parks. It could be argued that one way for them to achieve proper status and to be taken seriously is to be given planning powers. This is a vexed question that is worthy of another book! In view of the difficulties it would be likely to cause for local authorities, and in the light of National Park experience, it would be a pity if this were allowed to hold up the implementation of what is now an urgent agenda for AONBs.

Likewise the temptation to rectify the position by suggesting that AONBs should be turned into National Parks, in the way that is currently proposed for the Sussex Downs and the East Hampshire AONBs, would not provide a satisfactory solution. Whilst it is very important for the similarities between the two designations to be recognised, it does not follow that the kind of administration associated with a National Park is appropriate for every AONB, since they vary so much in character, particularly in size and administrative complexity and aspirations.

The only sure way to rectify the situation would require radical thinking, with a thorough review of the system of protected landscapes and its probable replacement with one that accorded the same name and status to all areas identified as being of national landscape, wildlife and/or cultural importance, irrespective of size and management requirements. This would also be a controversial step and, having regard to the history of the National Park movement, does not seem to be a realistic option at present. The sad thing is that there does not seem to be any move towards such an exercise in the longer term.

Meanwhile, there is a danger that *ad hoc* decisions will continue to be taken throughout the UK, as is already happening in England and Scotland. In England, the New Forest is being squeezed into the National Park framework, even though it does not really fit; and the creation of a South Downs National Park is requiring a review of the designation criteria and is likely to perpetuate the two-tier system. Indeed, if the proposal for Conservation Boards for only a few AONBs set out in the Commission's Advice to Government is accepted, it would in effect create a three-tier system in England. In Scotland a two-tier system is being introduced, with a new system of National Parks and the retention of the single purpose NSAs, rather than a radical review of protected landscapes as a whole. There are also areas like the Forest of Dean and the Somerset Levels, where people are searching for, but cannot find, the right way to recognise their national importance.

The Parks for Life initiative offers an opportunity for such radical thinking to take place, but as yet does not have the necessary momentum behind it in the UK. Any review runs the risk, of course, of the very need for protected landscapes being questioned. However, if they are recognised as a special part of the nation's environmental and cultural capital, they will always need special protection and should have no fears. It is hoped that the agenda proposed here might form a contribution to the debate whenever it comes.

A message for the family of protected landscapes

The last 50 years have seen a notable build-up of expertise in the conservation of protected landscapes in the UK. This has developed from two sources: on the one hand, the well-endowed, free-standing National Park system, with its comprehensive role of planning and management; and, on the other, the various more locally-based, but less securely funded and less comprehensive, arrangements applying in AONBs.

The high international reputation of the National Parks and, more recently, the strength of the Association of National Park Authorities, have resulted in information being available world-wide about their role and achievements. This is not so in the case of AONBs, even within the UK. It is hoped, therefore, that the account given in this book of the development of their aims, organisation, funding and management, and of their relationship with planning, will be of more than passing interest to people in various countries concerned with protected areas, whether in administrative, professional or lay capacities, or as residents or visitors. There have been considerable advances, and the adoption of the new framework and agenda for

AONBs proposed in this book would help to consolidate these advances, to secure more effective commitment of official bodies, and to strengthen the financial and administrative base.

There is thus a general message for the family of protected landscapes. At its best, despite many difficulties and a minimal budget, the AONB experience has resulted in considerable management developments that have widened the original single interest in landscape. The stage has been reached, however, beyond which reliance upon outdated legislation and upon persuasion by policy reviews is inadequate for the development of the far wider social, economic and scientific concern that needs to infuse the management of these areas. More firmly based partnerships, adequately financed and working within locally accountable organisations with a strategic outlook, can bring together the skills and financial programmes that few single organisations possess on their own.

The authors suggest, albeit hesitantly, that the AONB concept, improved in this way, has something to offer to members of the family of protected landscapes as a whole, at home or overseas, wherever it is felt that a more comprehensive and participatory approach to management is needed. This new Agenda meets the key requirements identified in Chapter 8 as being essential for protected landscapes to address the challenges of the twenty-first century. The priority given to each of those requirements will of course depend in any one case upon the nature of the area, the problems facing it, the legal, administrative and financial context in national and local terms, and the aspirations of stakeholders, communities and visitors. It is hoped that they provide a starting point for all those concerned with the future of such areas, whether as policy-makers and providers of funds in the national and regional arena, or as administrators, planners, managers, stakeholders, communities and interest groups involved locally.

Postscript   The authors would like to close on a personal note.

This book has been about policy and management for protected landscapes, especially the Areas of Outstanding Natural Beauty, to call them by their rightful, unabbreviated name. Located in England, Wales and Northern Ireland, they, together with the National Parks and the National Scenic Areas of Scotland, are the jewels in the crown of the British countryside. They are, in fact, the most numerous and extensive of such designations, and it has been a great privilege for us to study the very topical question of their future. It has also been a very enjoyable occupation. There have, however, been

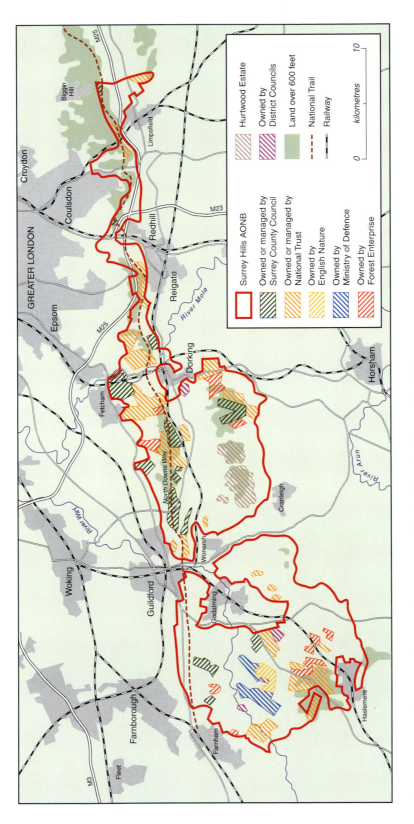

Plate 49 Map of countryside owned or managed by local authorities and public agencies, or privately with major access agreements, in Surrey Hills AONB, 1999.

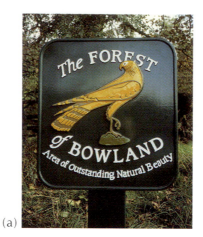

(a)

(b)

Promotion of awareness

Plate 50 Promoting the existence of AONBs is very important to their future. Signs at entry points are a simple way of raising awareness, e.g. in the Forest of Bowland (a), and a centre for the AONB service as in the Mendip Hills, combined here with field studies (b), is another valuable way of raising their profile.

(a)

Land ownership

Plate 51 Ownership of land by organisations such as the National Trust, as in Dorset (a) and the Malvern Hills Conservators (b), can be a huge influence on management in key parts of AONBs.

(b)

(a)

(b)

Land management – agriculture

Plate 52 Schemes to support environmentally friendly farming are crucial to the long-term management of all features in the landscape, e.g. ESAs as in Shropshire Hills (a), and Countryside Stewardship in the Suffolk Coast and Heaths (b).

Plate 53   The retention of grazing is vital to the future management of many commons, as in the Quantock Hills, where the need to fence the commons was disputed for many years.

Land management – commons

(a)

(b)

Land management – woodlands

Plate 54 The management of neglected woodlands is crucial, e.g. in the East Hampshire Hangers (a), and in many instances it is carried out by volunteers, as in East Hampshire (b), who undertake tasks like coppicing.

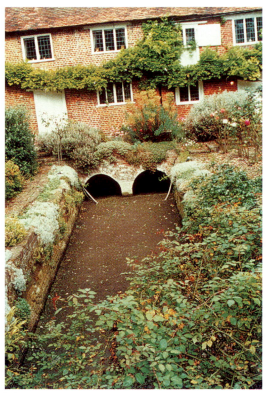

(a)

Links with the wider environment

Plate 55 Links with the wider environment will be increasingly important in dealing with such issues as low flow in rivers, e.g. in the Chilterns where normal flows have been restored to the River Chess (a) before and (b) after.

(b)

(a)

Links with the historic environment

Plate 56 Links with the historic environment will be essential too, ensuring the conservation of features, such as old lime kilns in the Quantock Hills (a) and the rebuilding of stone walls, e.g. in the Forest of Bowland (b).

(b)

(a)

(b)

Links with biodiversity

Plate 57 Links between AONBs and biodiversity planning are crucial, particularly in the wider countryside outside nature reserves, e.g. action to protect hedgerows and hedgerow trees that are so much part of their character, here in Dorset (a). Practical action is vital too, e.g. the conservation of dunes on the Solway Coast (b).

(a)

(b)

Managing recreation and traffic (1)

Plate 58 Information for visitors is a key part of any strategy for managing visitor pressures, e.g. the Symonds Yat visitor centre in the Wye Valley (a) and an information centre in Cornwall, part of the West Cornwall Sign Post Project (b).

(a)

(b)

(c)

Managing recreation and traffic (2)

Plate 59 Alternative forms of transport for visitors to popular areas are used increasingly as a means of avoiding congestion, e.g. the Norden Park and Ride scheme at Corfe Castle in Dorset using a privately owned railway (a) and a bus service for walkers of the South West Coast Path on the South Devon coast (b). Traffic calming, as here in the Surrey Hills, is also an important element of dealing with the increased levels of traffic (c).

(a)

Managing recreation and traffic (3)

Plate 60 Facilities for visitors to enjoy more sensitive areas are important, e.g. the provision of a boardwalk in the Suffolk Coast and Heaths (a). Equally important is the provision for the disabled, e.g. on a farm in Arnside & Silverdale (b).

(b)

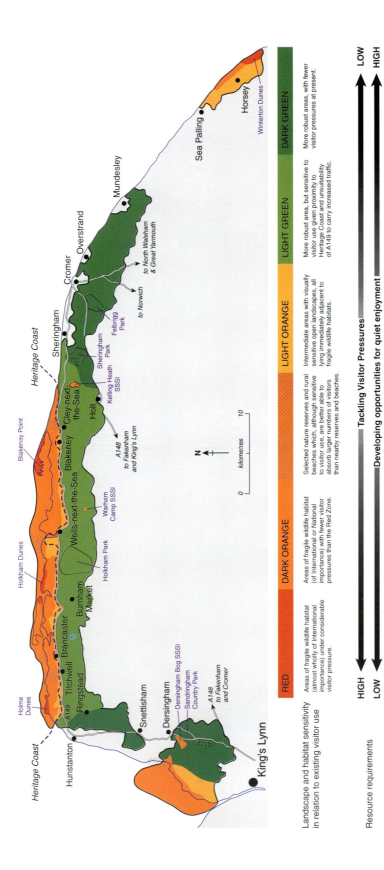

Landscape and habitat sensitivity
in relation to existing visitor use

RED	DARK ORANGE	LIGHT ORANGE	LIGHT GREEN	DARK GREEN
Areas of fragile wildlife habitat (almost wholly of International importance) under considerable visitor pressure.	Areas of fragile wildlife habitat (of International or National importance) with fewer visitor pressures than the Red Zone.	Selected nature reserves and rural beaches which, although sensitive to visitor use, are better able to absorb larger numbers of visitors than nearby reserves and beaches.	Intermediate areas with visually sensitive open landscapes, all lying immediately adjacent to fragile wildlife habitats.	More robust area, but sensitive to visitor use given proximity to Heritage Coast and unsuitability of A149 to carry increased traffic.	More robust areas, with fewer visitor pressures at present.

Resource requirements

HIGH ◄━━━━━━━━► LOW   Tackling Visitor Pressures

LOW ◄━━━━━━━━► HIGH   Developing opportunities for quiet enjoyment

Plate 61 Map of the Visitor Management Strategy for the Norfolk Coast AONB, 1995.

(a)

Fostering the local economy (1)

Plate 62   The future of the local economy in AONBs is crucial. Opportunities exist to make use of redundant buildings for business purposes, e.g. the conversion of a redundant dairy (a) into high-tech industry (b) in the Blackdown Hills.

(b)

(a)

Fostering the local economy (2)

(b)

Plate 63 The management of woodlands, so essential to the character of many AONBs, can provide economic opportunities for local people, e.g. the production of charcoal (a) and the design and manufacture of furniture (b) in the High Weald.

(a)

(b)

(c)

**Fostering the local
economy (3)**

Plate 64   Tourism and recreation can
bring benefits to the local economy,
e.g. through the hire of cycles, as in
Cornwall (a) and the conversion of
redundant buildings for use as camping
barns in the Forest of Bowland (b), or
local shops acting as information points
in the Blackdown Hills (c).

occasions when we wished for more time to sit back and appreciate more fully their qualities, reflect further on problems and possible solutions, and get to know better the many people who are deeply committed to their conservation and to the needs of their communities.

We trust that our assessments of the character, variety and national importance of these precious areas, the pressures on them, the changing policy context, the achievements of management, and the strengths and weaknesses of the system as a whole, are balanced. We hope, too, that our assessments of the current proposals for their future, which we applaud but do not regard as the end of the story, are fair, and that our ideas for their further development are welcome and practicable.

Whether AONBs will continue to be at risk will depend on the efforts of many people: legislators, policy makers and administrators, financial controllers, owners and farmers, managers, rangers and wardens, residents and visitors, and amenity societies. Our book can only be a small contribution to the cause for which they are active. Nevertheless the story that it tells is one that we believe to have relevance at home and overseas. We hope, therefore, that it will be widely read, and that at the very least it will enable more people who care about the quality of protected landscapes and their wonderful heritage to appreciate what is at stake, and what is being done and can be further done to secure their future.

References

[1] Countryside Commission, *Areas of Outstanding Natural Beauty, Policy Statements*, 1983 and (with Countryside Council for Wales), CCP157, CCP 356, Cheltenham, 1991.

[2] Countryside Commission, CCP532, Cheltenham, 1998, and Countryside Council for Wales, CCW Paper 98/74, Bangor, 1998.

[3] Countryside Commission, *Protected Areas Funding Study*, report by Environmental Resources Management, London, 1998.

[4] Countryside Agency and Countryside Council for Wales, *Countryside Training Directory*, CA 5, Cheltenham, 1999.

[5] Kent Downs AONB JAC is working closely with the Parc Régional du Nord – Pas de Calais, with financial support from ERDF.

Appendix 1

Designated Areas of Outstanding Natural Beauty

(1) England and Wales

AONB	Confirmation of order	Area (sq km)
Gower	1956	188
Quantock Hills	1957	99
Lleyn	1957	161
Northumberland Coast	1958	135
Surrey Hills	1958	419
Cannock Chase	1958	68
Shropshire Hills	1959	777
Dorset	1959	1129
Malvern Hills	1959	105
Cornwall	1959 (Extension 1983)	958
North Devon	1960	171
South Devon	1960	332
East Hampshire	1962	383
East Devon	1963	268
Isle of Wight	1963	189
Chichester Harbour	1964	74
Forest of Bowland	1964	802
Solway Coast	1964	115
Chilterns	1965 (Variation 1990)	833
Sussex Downs	1966	983
Cotswolds	1966 (Variation 1990)	2038
Anglesey	1967	221
South Hampshire Coast	1967	77
Norfolk Coast	1968	451
Kent Downs	1968	878

Suffolk Coast and Heaths	1970	403
Dedham Vale	1970 (Extensions 1978,1991)	90
Wye Valley	1971	326
North Wessex Downs	1972	1730
Mendip Hills	1972 (Variation 1989)	198
Arnside and Silverdale	1972	75
Lincolnshire Wolds	1973	568
Isles of Scilly	1976	16
High Weald	1983	1460
Cranborne Chase and West Wiltshire Downs	1983	983
Clwydian Range	1985	157
Howardian Hills	1987	204
North Pennines	1988	1993
Blackdown Hills	1991	370
Nidderdale	1994	603
Tamar Valley	1995	195

Source: Countryside Agency and Countryside Council for Wales, *Directory of Areas of Outstanding Natural Beauty*, 1999, available only on the CA website, www.countryside.gov.uk

(2) Northern Ireland

AONB	Date of designation	Area (sq km)
Lagan Valley	1965	21
North Derry	1966	129
Lecale Coast	1967	31
Sperrin	1968	1010
Strangford Lough	1972	186
Mourne	1986	570
Antrim Coast and Glens	1988	706
Causeway Coast	1989	42
Ring of Gullion	1991	153

Source: Department of the Environment for Northern Ireland, Fact Sheet No.29, 1995.

Appendix 2
Case Studies

Ten AONBs were chosen as detailed case studies to illustrate particular aspects of AONB policy, management and organisation relevant to the book as a whole. Completed in late 1999 and subsequently checked for any significant changes in circumstances, they comprise:

1. **Blackdown Hills**: a quiet pastoral area, with little pressure for change, but a serious lack of local employment. This AONB is of particular interest because of the manner in which management gives priority to community-based initiatives for economic development and to diversification of farming enterprises.

2. **Chilterns**: a large AONB close to London, well known for its chalk escarpment and beech woods, under very great recreational and development pressure. The case study highlights the commendable history of active management and the current achievements of the small AONB team, through partnership with public, private and voluntary agencies.

3. **Cotswolds**: the largest AONB and one of the most distinctive, much affected by pressures from intensive farming and from recreation and tourism. The case study has focused on the reasons why and the way in which the management organisation has recently been restructured.

4. **Forest of Bowland**: of interest as an example of a truly upland area, with considerable importance for wildlife, in which policy has focused on ways of integrating economic development with environmental management, including the promotion of access.

5. **High Weald**: another large and complex AONB, but one with an air of remoteness, although close to London. The case study illustrates the way in which a small management unit acts essentially as a catalyst for economic and environmental initiatives in partnership with others.

6. **Mendip Hills**: an AONB with great landscape variety and persistent problems around its famous 'honey-pots'. It is relevant because of its remarkably integrated countryside management service, its role in environmental education and training and its influence on Countryside Stewardship projects administered by MAFF.

7. **Norfolk Coast**: much of which consists of internationally valuable wildlife areas. This case study demonstrates how the small AONB team concentrates on working closely with major owners, institutional and private, in order to help them develop their management objectives in the strategic interest of the area as a whole.

8. **Purbeck Heritage Area**: an extremely varied part of Dorset AONB, with great pressures for development and recreation. Here the interest is in the work of the Heritage Area Committee and its small team, in conjunction with Purbeck District Council and partner organisations, especially in promoting wildlife conservation, economic development and recreational public transport.

9. **Sussex Downs**: one of the best known AONBs. It has been chosen as a case study on account of its unique Conservation Board and well-resourced management unit, and also because of the recent proposals by government for a South Downs National Park.

10. **Wye Valley**: an exceptionally attractive landscape that has inspired poetry but is under pressure for change from several sources, especially recreation. Wye Valley has a long history of AONB management, integrating the English and Welsh sides of the valley, which has necessarily shifted from project-based work to a focus on strategic issues.

The basic material for these case studies is derived from a wide variety of sources, both written (for example, in landscape assessments, management plans, reports to JACs, fact sheets and newsletters, etc.) and oral (largely from discussions with members of JACs, including partner organisations, and especially with AONB Officers and their colleagues).

1. Blackdown Hills

The Blackdown Hills comprise a little known, truly rural area, 370 sq km in extent, straddling the Devon/Somerset border north of the East Devon AONB. Their landscape, based on an outcrop of upper greensand, is best known for its steep wooded escarpment to the north, overlooking the vale of Taunton. South of this lies a plateau dissected by quiet valleys with attractive cob and thatch villages, and a pattern of traditional, mainly dairy farms with small fields and woodlands, linked by deeply hedged lanes. The AONB is rich in archaeological sites, especially its hill-top Iron Age forts, and has important semi-natural habitats, including 14 SSSIs.

There is a serious lack of local employment opportunities in the area, compounded by the uncertain prospects of many small farms. There are stark contrasts between poverty and wealth. It is these social and economic problems, rather than any significant pressures from development or recreation, which cause concern in the AONB, affecting the viability of community life and the 'health' of the landscape. The area has RDA status. It is also within the Blackdown Hills ESA. This was established in 1994 after designation of the AONB in 1991 had been strongly opposed by local farmers who felt that it would not give them the practical help they needed.

A Joint Advisory Committee, the Blackdown Hills Rural Partnership, was set up in 1995. Led by a local authority chairman, it consists of 20 representatives drawn from the two County and four District Councils, parish councils, four public bodies with responsibilities in the area, and farming, land-owning, wildlife and archaeological interests. With an annual budget of about £60,000 for core and project expenses, mainly from the local authorities and the Countryside Agency, the Partnership employs an AONB Officer and part-time assistant, based in one of the area's villages. They work closely with a Management Team from the main partners.

The thrust of the Partnership's work is towards community-based initiatives, a 'bottom up' approach in which networking and consensus-building play a major role. This is the basis upon which the Management Strategy has been prepared and all bids for resources are made. Village meetings, forums with local interests such as farming, forestry, business, tourism and the environment, as well as an annual Community Conference have been the priority means of getting things done, time-consuming as they are. The Partnership's achievements therefore lie more in 'enabling' a wide range of economic and social projects than in countryside management as such. They include employment generation (such as through an AONB-based Business Directory and Buyers' Guide, farm diversification, specialised green tourism, visitor bus services, bed and breakfast, etc.), village activities (for example, in the arts and local environment), and advice to the local authorities on how planning policies and decisions might facilitate this.

The strengths of the Partnership's approach are obvious. Problems that are constantly present, however, include the uncertainty of short-term funding, the lack of statutory backing, a tendency for partners' priorities to change (especially those with responsibilities outside the area), the lack of resources for monitoring, and the sheer pressure of work in keeping up with participants' expectations. The partnership is currently investigating the merits, especially the possible financial and administrative advantages, of setting up a Blackdown Hills Trust.

Illustrations from the Blackdown Hills AONB can be found in Plates 20, 62 and 64.

2. Chilterns

This case study illustrates the huge task faced by a small AONB team and a somewhat unwieldy Joint Advisory Committee in their praise-worthy efforts to manage where the quality of natural resources and the pressures are arguably as great as in National Parks.

The best known features of the Chilterns AONB, designated in 1965, are its 75 miles of chalk escarpment and open downland, and its beech woods. There are magnificent views from the Ridgeway National Trail and the hilltops north-westwards over the Vales of Aylesbury and Oxford. To the South East the dip slope is extensively farmed, well wooded, and subdivided by valleys, some being impor-tant routeways. The Chilterns landscape contains many archaeologi-cal sites, for example the 17 iron age hill forts on the escarpment, the Icknield Way, Roman roads and settlements, and country houses and parks of the seventeenth to nineteenth centuries. The AONB is also important as a wildlife resource, with three National Nature Reserves and 63 SSSIs clustered along the scarp's remaining chalk downland and semi-natural woodland. The whole area covers 833 sq km, and adjoins the North Wessex Downs AONB to the South West of the Thames. About 100,000 people live in the Chilterns, served by 15 main local authorities.

Being only 30 miles from central London and close to major towns such as Reading and Luton, the Chilterns are as much under pressure as any National Park. Recreation and traffic are among the main impacts on the area's landscape, as is the threat of creeping suburban-isation. Management aims for the AONB therefore include conserva-tion and interpretation of the most popular recreation areas (there are 52 million leisure visits to the Chilterns per annum), and the preservation of local identity, especially in the village environment.

Other problems requiring an equal priority for attention include the ageing of the area's nationally important woodlands, the effect of changes in farming practice especially upon traditional grassland

and heath, and the drying up of watercourses by over-abstraction. Management must therefore promote economic viability for the woodlands, encourage the maintenance of chalk and acid grassland and the restoration of abnormally low river flows, as well as continually keeping residents, councillors and visitors aware of the problems facing the local environment. Without all this effort, in which the well-being of local communities is an important consideration, the characteristic Chilterns landscape, its cultural heritage and valuable wildlife habitats could be seriously at risk.

The responsibility for management has long been one of partnership, for which purpose the Chilterns Conference was established in 1967 as the Joint Advisory Committee for the AONB. The Conference entered a new phase of activity with the completion in 1994 of the second Management Plan and the appointment of an AONB Officer to implement it. The plan is being reviewed in 2000. The Conference's aims, membership and procedures are set out in a formal Partnership Agreement, under which it normally meets twice yearly, guided by more frequent meetings of an Executive Group and a Technical Panel. It draws together representatives of the 15 local authorities and their associated parish councils, eight statutory agencies, and a further eight national and local voluntary bodies: a maximum of 48 individuals. One of the most dedicated members is the Chiltern Society, a registered charity with over 5,000 members, founded in 1965. The Society is among the largest regional volunteer bodies in the country, and its seven specialist groups have an energetic programme of project work and monitoring.

There is a three-year Business Plan for the Conference. Prepared with the assistance of task groups, this is based upon a core budget which was £130,000 for 1997/8 and now stands at £140,000 1999/2000), largely funded by the local authorities and by Countryside Agency grant. The Chiltern Society currently provides £3,200, and some other partners also contribute. It is interesting to compare this budget with the total amount spent in the AONB by the individual members of the partnership, approximately £1.5 million in 1995, with a further £0.5 million likely in hidden costs. This sum included all local authority expenditure on rights of way and on countryside management services, as well as expenditure by the National Trust, the Chiltern Society, English Nature, and Countryside Commission grants. The Conference's activities are of course much more limited. With a core staff of only three, it concentrates mainly on strategic requirements related to Management Plan objectives: design and environmental guidance, advice on major planning applications, support to woodland management, consideration of agri-environment issues, persuading and co-ordinating, and, most importantly, seeking new funds.

The Conference's achievements are remarkable in comparison with its shoestring budget. In addition to the Management Plan and the Woodlands Policy, it has published guidance documents on design and on environmental aims for road management; it has undertaken a Chilterns Visitor Survey, commissioned from the Southern Tourist Board; and has established the Transnational Woodlands Industries Group project (TWIG) with funding of £1,750,000 from the European Commission, of which their share is £312,000 over three years. Other initiatives include the Misbourne and Chess Valleys Project (supporting the restoration of river flows, in conjunction with the Environment Agency, the water companies, local authorities and the Chiltern Society); a Mountain Bike Code of Conduct; 'gateway'signs, a full colour newsletter and many leaflets to increase public awareness of the AONB; conferences and technical workshops; and an annual Woodlands Award. The Conference is also very active in response to consultations, for example putting views to the Countryside Commission on policy for the future of AONBs, and arguing the case for the AONB to have Environmentally Sensitive Area status.

All this is very much to the Conference's credit, but there are nevertheless some difficult issues for the longer term. First amongst these are problems of staffing and finance: the small AONB team members, hard at work as they are, cannot possibly cover all the requirements of the management plan; least of all can they start the important task of monitoring the 'health' of the AONB's landscape. Therefore they depend significantly on help from partners, whose staff availability and financial resources, for example, in countryside management services, are declining. Furthermore, without certainty in funding beyond the year 2000, the very future of the core staff is at risk. Second, there are difficulties of communication due to the size and geography of the area: as the responsibility for local government is shared among four county councils, one unitary and ten district councils, not many elected members or chief officers are in a position to take a 'Chilterns-wide' view of the needs of the AONB. This, understandably, is also a problem with some of the specialist agencies in the partnership. Third, at a time of severe financial constraint, the priority required by statutory local services such as education, makes it difficult for councils to vote money to 'discretionary' activities such as the Conference's budget. Fourth, co-ordination in the interest of the AONB with some of the public agencies in the partnership is difficult, owing to organisational differences and to the priority that they have to give to other aspects of their own national programmes.

The Chilterns Conference has been reviewing its own future in the light of the Countryside Commission's 1998 Advice to Government, and decided in 1999, in principle, to transform itself into a Conservation Board. This would be a 'natural evolution' rather than a radical reconstruction of the Conference, very much to its financial and administrative advantage, with, for example, a larger range of 'enabling' skills in the staff unit. The expectation was that the Government would introduce new legislation to help create such a body, with more resources and with new powers to strengthen its role. There is now a good prospect of legislation being introduced, and the Conference hopes that the proposed Countryside Bill might be amended to include clauses in line with Lord Renton's Bill in the House of Lords (see Chapter 4) for this purpose. The initial aim was for the Chilterns Conservation Board to be up and running by April 2001, but it is now thought that April 2002 would be more likely.

Illustrations from the Chilterns AONB can be found in Plates 16, 22 and 55.

3. Cotswolds

The Cotswolds, covering 2038 sq km, is the largest AONB. This case study shows how operational difficulties encountered in its management were overcome by means of a major reorganisation, a lengthy but ultimately successful process.

The Cotswold AONB was designated in 1966, and comprises a landscape of great harmony derived from a limestone base. The western edge is a 75 mile-long escarpment overlooking the Severn Vale, rising to a height of 330 m, the route of the Cotswolds Way National Trail. Behind this lies rolling countryside: wolds, shallow valleys and wooded crests, with a network of walls, farmsteads, villages and small market towns, built of mellow local stone. The Cotswolds possess an important historic heritage, especially in its Iron Age hill forts ranged along the escarpment, its legacy of Roman roads and small settlements, and its 'wool' churches, great houses and parks. It also has a mosaic of natural habitats, including three NNRs and over 80 SSSIs. 120,000 people live in the AONB, served by five county councils, two unitary and ten district councils.

The age-old beauty and cultural heritage of the Cotswolds is known world-wide, but it is increasingly at risk from the pressures of intensive farming, recreation and tourism, and, to a lesser extent, development. Much permanent grassland has been lost to the plough, stone walls have disappeared, under-grazed old grassland and commons have been invaded by scrub, and ancient woodland has deteriorated through lack of management. Visitor pressure at 'honey-pots', picturesque towns and villages and popular viewpoints has resulted in serious congestion, loss of amenity, and wear and tear, though producing some economic benefit. Modern estate layouts and non-vernacular building materials have conflicted with traditional Cotswolds architecture. Golf courses and radio masts have intruded into the rural scene, as has the occasional wind turbine.

In the face of these pressures, issues such as how best to conserve the farmed landscape and its wildlife, and how to promote sustainable recreation, especially at key sites, have become major concerns. So has the need to keep residents and visitors aware of the long-term nature of the threats and to gain their support for remedial action. Allied to this is the need to gather systematic information on the pressures and their impacts, and on the effectiveness of measures to counter them.

The Cotswolds Joint Advisory Committee was set up in 1967, with Gloucestershire County Council as the lead authority: a 26-strong partnership between local authorities, statutory agencies, farmers, landowners and voluntary groups. The JAC has made valiant efforts to tackle these issues, setting up an enthusiastic team of 250 voluntary wardens, undertaking environmental projects, establishing in 1992 an AONB Officer and Management Unit, and producing, in 1996, a well thought-out Management Plan. By this time the JAC's annual budget, with Countryside Commission support, was running at around £300,000. A major extension to all this activity was the designation by MAFF in 1996 of the Cotswold Hills and Upper Thames Tributaries ESAs; these cover about half of the area, and soon began to show results, particularly in dry-stone walling. Other recent initiatives by individual partners include strategies for tourism and economic development and for environmental improvement projects in the market towns.

Over the last few years, however, the partnership unfortunately ran into more than its fair share of operational difficulties. These tended to be generated by problems of communication that can arise in any large, loose-knit organisation, but they caused the implementation of the Plan to lose momentum, and there was some loss of staff. Understandably, relations amongst the partners, particularly on questions of finance, grew strained. This became such a problem that in 1998 the main partners decided to make a courageous attempt to find a new way forward. They succeeded, and a reconstituted JAC with a primarily strategic role (the Cotswolds AONB Partnership, consisting of 14 local authorities, 5 statutory agencies and 6 voluntary bodies, a President and a Chairman) now meets twice a year, holds an annual forum, and is served by working groups. The financial arrangements have been renegotiated, and the draft budget for 1999/2000 is over £230,000, contributed half by the local authorities and half by the Countryside Agency. A reorganised AONB Unit, consisting of a Partnership Director and five core staff came into being during 1999. Cotswolds District Council, whose area covers the core of the AONB and which has been very active in environmental matters, became the lead authority, but the team has a free-standing location near the centre of the AONB.

The outlook for Cotswolds AONB is once again good, but it has taken several years and much personal effort to get there.

Illustrations from the Cotswolds AONB can be found in Plates 14 and 27.

4. Forest of Bowland

The Forest of Bowland is one of the truly upland AONBs characterised by its grandeur and isolation. A part of the Pennine Chain, largely in Lancashire, it is dominated by the deeply incised gritstone fells with summits above 450 m and vast tracts of heather-covered peat moorland. As an AONB it is of particular interest for the steps being taken not only to conserve the landscape and to enable people to enjoy it but also to secure a viable rural economy for its population of 15,000. It is also illustrative of the importance of a management plan and partnerships as a basis for successful funding bids.

The area, 802 sq km in total, is particularly important for its wildlife, with some 13 per cent being designated SSSI. Furthermore, its international importance as a major breeding ground for upland birds (red grouse, hen harrier, merlin and golden plover) is recognised through designation as a Special Protection Area under the European Birds directive. As a result, English Nature and RSPB are active partners in the AONB, working closely with farming and landowning interests on the high moor.

Management activity in the AONB started in the early 1970s, with a Lancashire County ranger service running Beacon Fell Country Park, which continues to provide an important focus for visitors to the AONB. In 1986 Lancashire County Council led the formation of a JAC, and a countryside management service was started to give practical advice and assistance to farmers and landowners. By the early 1990s the service covered the whole AONB with four staff dedicated to the area, including the AONB Officer and an Access Officer. Currently, however, the only person dedicated full time to the area is the AONB Officer, though he has part of the time of three countryside management staff and a country park ranger. This seeming decline in the scale of the service in the AONB, at a time when the issues involved with its management are increasing, is illustrative of the problems being experienced countrywide by AONBs: local authorities are having to find savings in their budgets year on year and may have other priorities, and there is no certainty of funding. The current annual budget of the JAC is £184,000.

Notwithstanding these constraints, the AONB is very much a focus of activity benefiting from strong underpinning by Lancashire County Council with Countryside Agency grant. The publication of a management plan in 1995 provided a basis for the submission of successful bids for Objective 5b and LEADER II funding from the EU, thus enabling progress to be made towards a viable rural economy while ensuring that environmental issues are not forgotten. These efforts have been boosted further with the choice of Bowland by MAFF to be one of two areas in England where the means of integrating rural economic activity with positive environmental management would be tested, as a precursor to the introduction of the new rural development measures under the revised CAP (see Box 7.1 in Chapter 7).

The provision and management of public access has been a feature of the AONB service. Beacon Fell Country Park was one of the first to be established in England and still continues as a place where visitors can learn about the area. Equally important has been the negotiation of access agreements with private owners over some 3,260 acres (1,320 ha) of open moorland, one of the few areas in either AONBs or National Parks where this has been achieved. The experience of that work, particularly the integration of access with nature conservation and shooting interests, will be of great value when the right to roam over open country is enshrined in legislation. In this context the work of North West Water, one of the privatised water companies, which owns some 27,000 acres (10,935 ha) in Bowland is very interesting. The company is pursuing a policy of integrated management embracing farming, conservation, access and water supply.

Associated with the physical access to the area have been the provision of public transport links with Preston and the towns of north-east Lancashire and the organisation of a guided walks programme. Bowland was also an area chosen by the Youth Hostels Association to establish one of the first chains of five camping and bunkhouse barns. Basic accommodation is provided with good access to the network of paths in the area. Owned and operated by farmers on working farms and making use of redundant buildings, the barns not only provide for recreational needs but also help the local economy.

The wide range of activities for which the AONB is the focus, particularly through the work of the AONB Officer, is indicative of what can be achieved when there is a clear view of what needs to be done, as expressed through the management plan and when there are others prepared to work in partnership. However, even in such an active AONB, the long-term sustainability of its activities is a major issue. As with so many AONBs the level of service is dependent on the priorities of the local authorities at any one time, and is having to compete with other activities that are required by statute. Long-term stability of resources, particularly for staff dedicated to the area, will be crucial if the benefits of an integrated approach are to be fully realised.

Illustrations from the Forest of Bowland AONB can be found in Plates 28, 32, 50, 56 and 64.

5. High Weald

The High Weald is one of the largest AONBs in England (1460 sq km) and perhaps one of the least known. It is notable for the extent of woodland cover (23 per cent), much of which is ancient woodland (continuous as woodland since 1600); also for its rolling ridges and valleys dominated by small fields and thick hedgerows amongst the woodland, significant areas of lowland heath, particularly in Ashdown Forest and its distinctive brick, tile and weatherboard houses. It has an air of remoteness and intimacy that is surprising in busy and crowded south-east England. As an AONB it is of particular interest for the way in which management has been approached and for the focus on linking conservation of the area with the local economy.

Agriculture is central to the rural economy and forestry remains a traditional Wealden activity. However, farming is marginal in economic terms and is on the brink of collapse. It displays many of the characteristics of an upland rural economy while being only 40 miles from London. The AONB has very high land values associated with its proximity to London and suffers from land fragmentation and the use of land for quasi or non-agricultural purposes. There are similar concerns about the future of woodlands, many of which are unmanaged. The proximity of major economic growth areas is the cause of considerable pressure for development, and a change in population structure, with retired or commuter residents, is affecting the nature of village life. Ironically for such a seemingly prosperous area one-third of the AONB is designated as a Rural Development Area, signifying that there are serious problems in terms of the local economy. Not surprisingly, given its proximity to such a large population, there is increasing pressure for recreation too.

The AONB is complex in administrative terms, with fifteen local authorities. The High Weald Forum was established in 1989 with representatives of the local authorities, national and regional bodies and amenity groups. A Joint Advisory Committee meets as a sub-group of the Forum with representatives from the local authorities and the key areas of interest, nature conservation, farming, woodland and local communities. The role of the Forum is to consider the needs of the High Weald as a whole and to encourage partners to adopt policies and practices that help the conservation of the AONB. It achieves its aims primarily through the AONB Unit, which was established in 1992, and through the activities of the members of the partnership.

The Unit itself is very modest for such a large area, with just two posts on limited-term contracts, and an annual budget of £66,000, which includes a small projects budget of some £9,000. While additional staff have been taken on following the provision of extra funding for AONBs in 1998/9 and for specific initiatives, again on short-term 2 or 3-year contracts, there continues to be a reliance on the partners in the Forum to deliver the management plan. This is a particular issue in relation to countryside management services, where only half the AONB is covered by services provided by three of the partner authorities (West Sussex County Council, Kent County Council and Tunbridge Wells Borough Council) and the Unit does not have the capacity to fill the gap.

Notwithstanding the issue of scale, the Unit has demonstrated the value of looking at issues in AONB-wide terms. Its aim has been to influence the management of the AONB, through the provision of information, advice and guidance to partners of the Forum. The core function of the Unit is seen to be helping, informing and co-ordinating those involved in the management of the AONB, and raising levels of appreciation and understanding of AONB issues. Overseeing the implementation of the Management Plan that was prepared by the Unit in 1995 has been one of its main tasks.

The gathering of information about the AONB has been a vital task as a basis for better decision-making amongst the partners and to identify and anticipate future policy trends and how they might affect the area. Typical of the kind of research has been the development of a detailed database on products derived from land management in the Weald and their implications for the landscape; establishing the status of organic farming in the area; and an assessment of trends in development in the area.

The development of pilot projects to test ideas has been a hallmark of the Unit's work. In particular, it has focused on the link between the management of the landscape and the rural economy and how the two can be mutually supportive. The High Weald Design Project has been typical of this approach, with the development of a commercial furniture enterprise to support the woodland industry in the AONB. The pilot demonstrated how local craftsmen could use timber from sustainably managed woodlands to produce attractive furniture and sell it on a commercial basis. The project has now moved from the pilot phase to the establishment of a company to take it forward on a commercial basis. In a similar vein the Wealden Meadows Initiative has developed a saleable product – wildflower mixes direct from meadows in the Weald – which are being used to help re-establish flower-rich meadows in the area. The development of the High Weald Landscape Trail, co-ordinated by the Unit, is planned to give a boost to the local economy, through a well-marketed green tourism initiative.

A further example of the catalytic approach adopted by the Unit has led to the establishment of the High Weald Land Management Initiative, as part of a national programme being developed by the Countryside Agency. Research into the state of farming and a major conference in 1997, initiated by the Unit, highlighted the concern for the future of farming and the rural economy in the area. The plan is to develop and test a framework and mechanisms for the delivery of effective integrated rural support, to maintain and enhance the environmental, economic and social fabric of the High Weald. During the three years of the project the Countryside Agency will make some £800,000 available for practical support as well as two staff to run it.

Raising awareness of the AONB and the provision of information about it has been central to the work of the Unit. The establishment of its own office in the area, the design of a logo, regular newsletters, a leaflet about the AONB and the establishment of its own website have all contributed to the establishment of an identity for the AONB and indeed to the Unit. At a more practical level the provision of training courses on various aspects of the landscape and leaflets about habitats have all contributed to the understanding of the importance of the area and what needs to be done to look after it.

The significant progress made by the Unit on behalf of the AONB acting as a catalyst for activity by others and drawing in other resources, for example £500,000 from the Heritage Lottery Fund for heathland management, demonstrates what can be done using very limited resources, effectively two people. This is very similar to the approach in places like the Chilterns. However, this is in stark contrast to the scale of core resources available to some AONBs, such as Dorset, the Sussex Downs and the Cotswolds. This raises the issue of what is the most effective way of securing the long-term conservation of a large AONB. While the answer is by no means clear, it is vital that whatever approach is adopted, there is long-term security for the core service.

Illustrations from the High Weald AONB can be found in Plates 37 and 63.

6. Mendip Hills

Mendip Hills AONB has a small but unusually diversified management organisation, some notable achievements, and, in the Cheddar Gorge, a unique problem.

Designated in 1972 and covering 198 sq km, the AONB is the most scenic part of the wider Mendips area of Somerset. It rises steeply from north and south to a height of 325 m, and is a distinct ridge with a fascinating landscape of crags, gorges and caves, springs, dry valleys, wooded slopes, and two large lakes. Central to it is a sparsely populated plateau with regular field patterns and dry-stone walls, to the west of which are individual hills. With its limestone base, the AONB is part of a huge aquifer (a Groundwater Protection Area), and contains a valuable range of habitats and geological sites, including two NNRs and 25 SSSIs. Historically, with over 200 SAMs, it has one of the country's greatest concentrations of archaeological remains from palaeolithic to modern times: caves, barrows, burial mounds, hill forts, Roman sites, important relics of sixteenth and seventeenth century lead mining and of later industrial activity.

Changes in traditional farming practice and an increase in pig farming are perhaps the most acute pressures on the AONB's landscape. There are new farm buildings but walls, hedges, swallet-holes and unimproved grassland have been lost. Development pressures include quarrying (which is restricted) and the heavy industrial traffic that goes with it; radio masts and the possibility of wind turbines. Adverse impacts also come from visitor pressure at 'hot spots'. Parking and road congestion detract from the enjoyment of the landscape at Cheddar Gorge (visited by 1 million people per annum). There is also congestion at the large man-made lakes (Bristol Water reservoirs), and some villages. Uncontrolled off-road driving and scrambling on private land is a problem in terms of noise and landscape damage at a few sites.

Key events in efforts to tackle these pressures were the introduction of a warden service, including volunteer rangers, in 1985, the establishment of a JAC in 1987, the preparation of a Mendips Local Plan in 1989 (now gradually being replaced by District Local Plans), the selection of the AONB as a target area for Countryside Stewardship in 1991, the appointment of an AONB officer in 1995, the completion of a Management Plan and Business Plan in 1998, and a Landscape Assessment in 1999. The JAC, which has recently been restructured to enable it to implement the Management Plan more effectively, consists of 44 members including representatives of the funding partners (the five local authorities and the Countryside Agency). The current annual budget of about £140,000 includes £25,000 for project work. There is particularly close liaison with major landowners such as the National Trust, the Somerset Wildlife Trust, Forest Enterprise, and the area's several large estates, as well as with the 800-strong Mendip Society. The Society is about to inaugurate its own grant-aiding system for projects within the AONB.

The JAC's management task benefits greatly from the location of its staff, the AONB Officer, two Wardens and an Administrative Assistant in the Charterhouse Centre, a residential field study and activities centre in the heart of the area which is funded from the County Council's environment budget and its own income generation. Working closely together, this team and the centre staff have a unique opportunity for raising awareness of the AONB as a whole, its purpose, and value of its many resources. The key role of the AONB Officer is to ensure the successful implementation of the Management Plan. The Wardens, helped by volunteer rangers, carry out a wide variety of countryside management and training projects, in regular touch with local communities, schools, visitors to the

AONB, and people attending courses at the Centre. Their work also goes well beyond normal countryside management; together with the centre staff, they can be called upon to play a key role in rescue emergencies, and they help to prevent crime by taking part in the Hillwatch Scheme. The team as a whole has been particularly successful in its efforts, in partnership with FWAG and others, to pave the way for Countryside Stewardship projects administered by MAFF. By 1999 there were 45 agreements under the scheme covering about 15 per cent of the AONB, including 1,250 ha of unimproved grassland and heathland (about 15 per cent of the AONB), and addressing some of the key issues identified in the management plan.

Despite these and other achievements, the Mendips JAC faces difficult unresolved issues. Like all AONBs the most critical of these is the lack of assured core funding after the year 2001. Another has been the lack of public transport, but a consultant's study and various initiatives by the JAC has resulted in an action plan to improve services, especially for recreational bus routes from Bristol, supported by the JAC local authorities and Bristol City Council. These are linked to guided walks and events. Development control has also been a problem. Although the JAC has produced a set of guidelines for consultation on planning applications, there are still questions of interpretation and consistency to be overcome.

Most AONBs have their own sagas of long-standing problems on the ground, but few of these can be as stubborn and complex as the transport, economic and environmental needs of the Cheddar Gorge, the most important limestone gorge in Britain. The National Trust and the Longleat Estate, as majority owners, have undertaken several initiatives to improve visitor movement, with limited resources, but there is a need for a long-term comprehensive plan covering all interests: landscape, wildlife, archaeological, recreational and commercial, with necessary funding allocated to it. Studies for this are proceeding, but a solution has yet to emerge. Consensus, so vital to AONB management in general, can be a painful and time-consuming process.

Illustrations from the Mendip Hills AONB can be found in Plates 38, 45 and 50.

7. Norfolk Coast

A long coastal strip backed by gently rolling chalkland and glacial moraine, the AONB was designated in 1968 and incorporates the remotest and wildest of Norfolk's renowned marsh coastland. It is of particular interest for the niche that the AONB's project unit is carving for itself in an area that is dominated by the presence of numerous conservation organisations as landowners and managers.

The unique scientific and ecological value of the area, containing some of Europe's most important salt marsh, intertidal flats, dunes, shingle and grazing marsh, is recognised through many national and international designations – SSSI, NNR, SPA, potential SAC and Ramsar – which cover some 25 per cent of the AONB. These very sensitive areas are managed by organisations such as the RSPB, English Nature, National Trust and the Norfolk Wildlife Trust. These organisations have worked with the AONB Project to produce *A Vision for Nature Conservation in the Norfolk Coast AONB 1997 – 2022*, which is recognised within the management strategy (see Box 6.12).

The area is under significant physical threat from rising sea levels and coastal erosion. It is also suffering from the effects of its increasing popularity with day and weekend visitors and holiday-makers, notably traffic along the narrow roads and in the 'honey-pot' villages as well as damage to sensitive habitats. As a result its distinctive character is being eroded. Changes are also taking place in the local communities with many more people retiring to the area and the increase in the number of holiday homes, making it difficult for local people to stay in the area. It is within this context that the Norfolk Coast Project was set up in 1991 with the purpose of co-ordinating action amongst the existing organisations which were already active in the area, thus achieving things which no single organisation would have been able to.

The Project is run by a small team, comprising the Project officer at management level with policy and planning responsibilities, an assistant and a part-time administrator, all of whom are on short-term contracts. It is guided by an officer working group, which reports to a Joint Advisory panel from the funding bodies – Norfolk County Council, North Norfolk District Council, Kings Lynn and West Norfolk Borough Councils and the Countryside Agency. Its annual budget is £60,000 (1997/8). Unlike many AONBs, the Project has no direct countryside management capacity. This reflects the fact that there are a number of other organisations fulfilling this role: the conservation organisations owning and managing key sites, a number of large estates similarly managing visitor pressures on their land and the highway authorities managing rights of way and implementing traffic management.

Sustainable use of the area has been and remains at the heart of the Project's work. Its aim is to secure the economic value of tourism for local people while ensuring that visitors do not erode the very qualities they come to enjoy. In 1995 a visitor management strategy was completed, the basis of which is the zoning of the area according to the ability of particular areas to withstand pressures. All the project partners have now adopted this as part of their work. It has now been incorporated into the overall management plan for the AONB that was completed in 1998, together with a strategy for transport. A wide range of initiatives aiming to spread the pressures and to increase awareness amongst visitors of the sensitivity of the area and the impact they can have on it, have followed the development of these strategies, including:

- a visitor management handbook for AONB site managers;
- a good visitor code;
- publication of the *Norfolk Coast Guardian* each year to provide information for visitors about what they can do and the activities and services provided for them, including the promotion of local products that visitors can buy;
- the development of public transport for visitors and local people – a special 'Coastliner' service now runs throughout the year;
- the promotion of cycle routes and quiet lanes and the calming of traffic in the villages;
- access opportunities for the disabled.

The development of a relationship with local people is a very important part of the way in which the Project operates. This is particularly important because the future well-being of the local economy is intimately tied up with the management of the AONB, not least because visitors bring a much-needed boost to incomes. Thus the involvement of local people in the preparation of the various strategies for the AONB has been crucial. This continues through the publication of a regular newsletter and an annual forum at which particular issues are discussed.

The AONB project has clearly carved a niche for itself in developing the strategic approach to the AONB and bringing all the partners together. However, the long-term sustainability of this approach with such a small unit and without an associated countryside management capability will be a challenge, since it is always much harder to demonstrate the success of strategies as opposed to practical work on the ground. As with the majority of AONBs the question of funding remains a major issue for the Project. The issues that have to be tackled, such as visitor and traffic management and the planning of the coast in the face of rising sea levels, are all long term and yet the commitment locally and nationally remains short term.

Illustrations from the Norfolk Coast AONB can be found in Plates 22, 28, 31, 42, 43 and 61 (map).

8. Purbeck Heritage Area (in Dorset AONB)

Dorset AONB covers about half the county, but the greatest pressures on its landscape are concentrated on the Isle of Purbeck, especially its section of Heritage Coast. Here, research into visitor numbers, coupled with the need to strengthen the local economy, prompted the establishment in 1993 of the Purbeck Heritage Committee to 'Keep

Purbeck Special' and reverse the process of gradual decline and deterioration. This case study shows how the challenge is being tackled. Formed jointly by Purbeck District Council and Dorset County Council, and funded by them and the Countryside Agency, the Committee brings together conservation, landowning and tourism interests to build partnerships and raise money for managing the area's resources. It meets three times a year under an independent Chairman appointed by the Countryside Agency, and holds a wider annual Forum. Its budget for 1999/2000, including core funding of the AONB Officer and minor project work, was about £45,000. The Heritage Area covers more of Purbeck than just the AONB: additional land of comparable scenic value, including ecologically important heaths and extensive woodlands. The total area is 350 sq km.

The landscape is immensely varied. To the south are attractive limestone, clay and chalk cliffs, such as at Durlston and St Alban's Heads and Lulworth Cove; inland from this lies the sweeping chalk ridge of the Purbeck Hills; further to the north, valley pastures, forest and open heath, the latter being a colourful setting for much of Poole Harbour. The South West Coast Path follows the whole coastline. There is a range of valuable habitats in the area, six NNRs, 41 SSSIs (including most of the coast) and the Durlston and Kimmeridge Voluntary Marine Nature Reserves. Elsewhere, traditional stone villages and the ancient market town of Wareham, 168 SAMs such as the spectacular ruins of Corfe Castle, hill forts, barrows, and Celtic field patterns all give Purbeck, part of Hardy's Wessex, a strong sense of history and local identity.

There have been some worrying problems in the area. Heathlands of international value have been eroded by development or lack of management for years, although protection has now been considerably strengthened. Mineral workings impinge on the valley landscapes. Adverse trends in the local economy are affecting life in Purbeck as a whole: with many small farms suffering decline there is less maintenance of traditional features, and, as tourist preferences change, holiday facilities in the small resort of Swanage have become unfashionable. Yet the pressure of visitors to the Heritage Area (4.5 million per annum, greater than in some National Parks), is causing erosion, disturbance to wildlife, recreational conflicts, road and parking congestion at 'hot spots' on the coast and inland, even at Durlston Country Park.

The strategy, prepared by the Committee in 1995, aims to conserve Purbeck's environmental quality, to diversify the local economy (helped by being in a RDA), and to co-ordinate action for this. Priority is given to an 'awareness' campaign, to attracting funds for conservation, to promoting sustainable tourism (attracting staying rather than day visitors, developing under-used facilities and improving the environment of 'hot spots'), and to integrating traffic management (reducing traffic flows to environmental capacity, and creating more park-and-ride facilities). In all this, the Committee sees its role as that of an 'enabler', rather than being directly involved in implementation of a multitude of projects. As a result it uses its limited funds and its outward-looking public relations to encourage others to contribute to a wide variety of initiatives.

One example of particular interest is the Biodiversity Action Plan, co-ordinated by RSPB through a Project Officer funded by DETR and the Committee. This, with a focus on key habitats and species, is strongly linked to important CS targeting by MAFF, to heathland projects by English Nature, Forest Enterprise and the National Trust, and to the conservation efforts of landowners, several of whom manage large estates, and of farmers. It has already resulted in noticeable improvements in the quality of heathland.

Another noteworthy achievement is the very active financial support the Committee has won for housing and economic development initiatives, jointly with partners such as the RDC, £1.26 million, over three years, from the Government's Capital Challenge Fund.

The Committee's efforts to promote public transport is yet another highlight: the 'Linkrider' coastal path bus service, and the £600,000 financial support given by the local authorities, English Partnerships, the former RDC and Countryside Commission, and industrial sponsors to the Norden Park and Ride scheme. This, operating in conjunction with Swanage Railway, was given an England for Excellence Award by the English Tourist Council in 1999.

Working entirely within a single District, but in partnership also with the County Council which has long been active in Heritage Coast and Country Park management, the Committee's output derives great benefit from staff integration, including the Purbeck Heritage Officer, within the District Council's Community Services and Planning Department. This enables the departmental time of landscape architects, arboriculturalists, planning and conservation officers, tourism marketing staff, and administrators to be devoted as necessary to management of the Heritage Area. It also helps AONB issues to be seen in a wider geographic context, which is particularly important on account of proximity to the Bournemouth/Poole conurbation.

In common with all AONBs, the Committee has been very anxious about future funding, being uncertain at present what core support it will be getting after the next year or two. It has nevertheless resolved to continue in existence for at least five years, and the Purbeck Heritage Officer has been established as a permanent appointment, now supported by a Tourist and Countryside Officer. Even assuming that the Countryside Agency will be able to make this more secure, it also sees the need for a 'Friends of Purbeck' society in the partnership, contributing local knowledge, expertise and voluntary project work, and possibly acting as a fund-raising Trust.

Illustrations from the Purbeck heritage Area can be found in Plates 14 and 59.

9. Sussex Downs

No book on AONBs can afford to overlook the national significance of the Sussex Downs and the imaginative formation of the Conservation Board.

Sussex Downs AONB, designated in 1966 after lengthy negotiations between the former National Parks Commission, landowners and interest groups, is one of the best-known landscapes in Britain. Its rolling chalk scenery stretches from the East Hampshire AONB boundary to the Sussex Heritage Coast at the Seven Sisters and Beachy Head. The magnificent north-facing escarpment is 80 miles long and rises to 280 m, broken at four points by major river valleys. Along it runs the South Downs Way National Trail, giving fine views over the woods, heaths and farmland of the wealden part of the AONB. The chalk uplands and their many small dry valleys, dipping towards the south, are within the South Downs ESA. The whole area is rich in history, especially its barrows, hill forts, Celtic fields and strip lynchets, and it contains an important range of natural habitats, including four NNRs and 55 SSSIs.

The AONB covers 983 sq km. Its population of 47,000 is served by twelve local authorities: East and West Sussex County Councils, Brighton and Hove Unitary Council, and nine Borough and District Councils. Immediately adjacent to it, around one million people live in the Sussex coastal belt.

Pressures on the downland landscape have caused concern for many years. Even as early as the 1920s, steps were being taken to preserve it. Hobhouse proposed that the South Downs in Hampshire and Sussex should be a National Park, but this was later rejected by the National Parks Commission because post-war ploughing up had been so intensive that it no longer met the designation criteria set out in the 1949 Act. National Park status (see below), however, has long been seen by some conservation groups as the best way of securing protection. The pressures are continually increasing: the larger coastal towns are running short of land for development outside the AONB, village environments are at risk from incremental change, intensive agriculture has resulted in a massive loss of traditional downland and its bodiversity, and recreational activity, with 32 million leisure visits a year, is higher than in any National Park.

In the years following designation the individual local authorities continued to be active in protecting their own parts of the Downs, but in 1986, in line with Countryside Commission policy at the time, the two County Councils prepared a Statement of Intent for conserving the AONB as a whole. Under this they set up the Sussex Downs Forum as a consultative body, and meet annually. At the end of the decade, however, renewed interest in National Park status, the Commission's 1990 review of AONBs which advocated better co-ordination of management in them, and the designation of the ESA, all caused the local authorities to propose that the Forum should be replaced by a statutory joint committee, the Sussex Downs Conservation Board.

The Board was formally set up in 1992 with strong support from the Commission, which saw it as a national experiment in AONB management, with a degree of independence from local government. Its objectives are to conserve and enhance the beauty of the Downs, to promote quiet enjoyment consistent with this, and to encourage sustainable economic and social development. The Board consists of 24 representatives from the local authorities, 12 people nominated by the Commission, and an independent chairman. There is an executive committee, meeting quarterly, and a planning committee, meeting monthly. The Board's Countryside Management Service has also established a number of area liaison groups, but these are not formal committees. Initially the Board was to be funded, half by the Commission and half by the main local authorities, for a trial period until 1998. This has been extended to 2001 to give time for more permanent arrangements to be made. The amount of 'core funding' by the Commission was a radical departure from their normal grant-aid policies. The annual budget was £1.3 million by 1997/8, but public sector economies have since caused this to drop to just over £1 million, with the Commission's contribution reduced to one-third. The remaining two-thirds are met largely by the two County Councils and Brighton and Hove Unitary Authority, with all District Councils contributing as well.

The Board employs a multi-disciplinary staff of 30, headed by the Sussex Downs Officer. This team prepares and implements the Management Strategy, promoting a range of strategic projects for landscape and nature conservation, archaeology, information and interpretation, for community needs, and bidding for various funds. It also gives advice to the local planning authorities on development plans and planning applications affecting the AONB, backed by a 'right to be heard' at their meetings if the Board objects strongly to a proposal that the planning authority may be minded to approve. The team's countryside management service, to which the responsibilities of the main local authorities have been transferred, plays a central role in implementation. This includes area management, site management, habitat creation, advice on farming and forestry practice, and maintenance of 2000 km of rights of way in addition to the South Downs Way itself. Working from four area offices and assisted by 200 volunteer rangers, the service has a regular presence throughout the AONB, in close touch with local authorities, other public bodies, landowners, the National Trust, and also being in regular contact with local communities and visitors.

In 1995 the Board's achievements, some of which have won prestigious awards, were reviewed by consultants on behalf of the Commission. They reported that the Board had successfully met the two main purposes for which it was set up: establishing an AONB-wide countryside management service, and engaging in planning. This was an important step forward in the search for a suitable permanent organisation. It also had implications for future administration in AONBs generally, on which the Commission was about to consult widely. In 1997, the Government called for, and the Commission launched, a specific consultation about the needs of the South Downs as a whole, comprising the Sussex Downs AONB and the adjacent East Hampshire AONB (where a Joint Advisory Committee had been set up in 1991, had prepared a management plan and was implementing this in the normal way). The response favoured a body with stronger status and more secure funding than the existing Board, with a remit that covered both AONBs, a total area of 1374 sq km.

Bringing together the results of this and the wider consultations, the Commission's 1998 Advice to Government paper recommended that local authorities responsible for management of AONBs should be enabled, if they wish, to establish Conservation Boards tailored to local circumstances but backed by a new legislative framework (see Chapter 4). In doing so, they had clearly been influenced by the achievements of the Sussex Downs experiment and the manner in which the formation of the Board had given the local authorities a stake in management, and the Board a formal consultative role in planning. In a separate section of the paper the Commission put forward four options for the Downs, one of which was National Park status. They concluded that a National Park could not be justified against the criteria of the 1949 Act, and that other important considerations also militated against it. Stating unequivocally that National Parks and AONBs give equal protection, the Commission recommended that the most appropriate arrangement for managing the South Downs should be a statutory Conservation Board in the form that they were proposing to be available for AONBs generally.

This recommendation, backed by the intention to provide secure core funding, was well received in principle by the local authorities, although some interest groups still maintained that the Downs could only be properly safeguarded, and recreational needs provided for, by becoming a National Park. Some differences of approach between the existing Board and the Hampshire authorities needed to be resolved, however. One of these was the structure of the new Board, how this could be kept to workable proportions and yet still act widely as a partnership. Another important question requiring to be resolved in detail was the role of the Board and its countryside management service as the means of linking strategy and local implementation (including grant-aid mechanisms, etc.) with the key agencies operating in the whole Downs area, and with the views of the people living there. The form of delivery of services might well vary in certain parts of the area, within the overall co-ordination of the management plan. Meanwhile the Board and the East Hampshire Joint Advisory Committee have been working together closely to prepare the basis for a strategic management plan for the whole South Downs area.

A new situation was created, however, by the announcement by John Prescott, Deputy Prime Minister, on 29 September 1999, that he had asked the Countryside Agency to consider, in consultation with local authorities, a National Park for the South Downs. The accompanying press statement by DETR explained that the Agency was being asked to look again at the way the National Park designation criteria, which emphasised open country with a degree of ruggedness or wilderness, are operated, with a view to recommending how a National Park could best operate in the Downs. Michael Meacher, Environment Minister, added that the Government intended to do more to conserve and enhance AONBs, which are equal in terms of landscape significance to National Parks, and that details of new measures would shortly be provided. Both statements were warmly welcomed by the Agency, and the Board expressed its hope that there would be a smooth transition to a National Park Authority. The reactions of East and West Sussex and Hampshire County Councils were rather more cautious.

The Agency has now resolved to investigate the concept of a National Park for the South Downs, and is carrying out consultations before deciding to make the necessary Designation Order. The procedures, with the possible need for a public inquiry, will take time. The establishment of the Board, however, has enabled very useful experience to be obtained for the benefit of those AONBs where there is a need to replace informal co-operative arrangements with an organisation which has statutory backing and more secure funding. It clearly influenced the package of proposals in the Advice Paper as a whole, and has highlighted the kind of issues that need to be considered when change is contemplated.

Illustrations from the Sussex Downs AONB can be found in Plates 13, 34, 39 and 43.

10. Wye Valley

Wye Valley AONB has a long history of partnership from which much has been learned and applied. The AONB extends for 28 miles from north to south along the route of the River Wye, from a few miles south of Hereford downstream to the edge of Chepstow in Monmouthshire. The river winds peacefully through the Herefordshire lowlands and the Wye floodplain. It then runs between the spectacular wooded cliffs of the limestone Wye Gorge, which occasionally open out around broader stretches of farmland. Seven miles across at its greatest width, the AONB spans from plateau ridge to plateau ridge on the English and Welsh sides of the gorge, the Wye itself being a distinctive and unifying influence throughout. About 30,000 people live in the AONB, served by one Unitary Council on the Welsh side and, on the English side, one County, one Unitary, and one District Council.

Designated in 1971, Wye Valley covers 326 sq km and adjoins the Forest of Dean National Forest Park, with which it overlaps marginally. Among its three NNRs and 45 SSSIs there are habitats of international importance. These include three candidate SACs, covering the whole river, most of the Gorge woodlands, and a series of bat roost sites. There are also large tracts of ancient broadleaved woodland, mostly owned by Forest Enterprise. Among the famous historic sites in the AONB are Goodrich and Chepstow Castles of Norman origin, and Tintern Abbey dating from the twelfth century. The Offa's Dyke National Trail passes through the area, as does the Wye Valley Walk that runs from the source of the River Wye to its mouth.

The Wye Valley landscape has inspired well-known British poets and writers, but it is now under pressure for change from several sources. Intensive farming is reducing the amount of riverside meadows of high scenic and wildlife value, and other characteristic features, such as orchards, are also being lost. Large limestone quarries have a serious impact in parts of the area, and there is the possibility of extension. Recreation and tourism (around two million visits per annum, higher than in some National Parks) are causing congestion, erosion and disturbance at attractions such as Symonds Yat from which there are dramatic views of the gorge and its wildlife, and at Tintern Abbey. The use of the Wye itself for canoeing, rafting and for fishing has become a serious source of conflict. Pressure for road improvements, due to the growth of through and recreational traffic in the AONB, is also viewed with concern.

The Wye Valley JAC, consisting of leading members of the four local authorities, six statutory agencies and five voluntary bodies, was established in 1972. Much can be learned from its record of achievements, especially how it has gained an understanding of the planning and management process. This is impressive in its own right, and the more so because of the administrative complexity of an AONB divided by a national boundary.

In 1981, after a pilot study, the JAC published a Management Plan. This was one of the first management plans for an AONB, a model of its kind. It was strong on positive action, with an ambitious list of projects for conservation and enhancement on the ground, and it also proposed systematic monitoring of the landscape. A Wye Valley Countryside Service of three wardens was instituted at the time. Like many other multi-agency projects, however, the assumptions made in the plan about funding, staffing and co-ordination turned out to be over-optimistic, and it became clear towards the end of the decade that a major review was necessary. The central issue to be tackled was the inadequacy of resources in the face of growing pressures for change, a problem that required the JAC to raise the status of the AONB in the minds of the public and the bodies concerned with its administration. For this purpose a draft report was published in 1990. It foreshadowed a more streamlined organisation, an AONB Officer in a pivotal role, a clearer allocation of priorities, an enhanced warden service with more volunteers, and a drive to seek specific resources for projects.

The ground having been prepared in this way, a revised Management Plan was published in 1992 by the JAC and its working party of technical officers. This differed from previous efforts in its strategic analysis of the AONB's management requirements, its broad policy objectives and its clearer assessment of responsibilities for implementation. On the strength of it, an AONB Officer was appointed later that year, in a co-ordinating role. There has been a great deal of progress on the plan's more important projects and it is about to be reviewed. Among its achievements are the production of supplementary strategy documents including guidelines on woodland management and on sustainable tourism (partly funded by EU), a Nature Conservation strategy for the whole AONB, management studies for Symonds Yat, Tintern Abbey, the Wye Valley Cycleway, and a variety of 'awareness' information leaflets for visitors and residents. One disappointment has been the need for a public inquiry to resolve a dispute over the legitimate navigation authority. However, this has consolidated support for maintaining a largely natural river and allowing enjoyment of the countryside against a business consortium wishing to develop the river for motorised craft. At the time of going to print a decision is still awaited. Another disappointment has been the lack of staff time to find suitable indicators of landscape change as a basis for monitoring. This problem, which exists widely in AONBs, even in National Parks, only just is beginning to be addressed.

The successes of management in the Wye Valley (on a more or less static budget of £74,000) are due to the enthusiasm of the JAC (indeed there is almost a competitive relationship between the English and Welsh sides), and the support given to the AONB Officer by the local authority technical officers' group. This partnership greatly increases the expertise and services available to the AONB's hard-working core staff of three, and can add value to the JAC's slender funds by 'tailoring' AONB projects and local authority programmes to the same end. Furthermore, the lessons learned by the organisation as a whole from past experience on management planning and implementation have been put to good use. Even the controversial demise of the Countryside Management Service, when local authority rangers were reorganised a few years ago, is now seen by some to be an advantage, on balance, as it has enabled the AONB Officer to focus more widely on strategic aspects of the partnership's work, including sustainable social and economic initiatives. For all its administrative complexity, Wye Valley may still be coherent enough to be managed as an informal partnership, employing a small strategic team with good communication skills, rather than as a statutory board with a directly employed countryside management service.

Illustrations from the Wye Valley AONB can be found in Plates 9, 23 and 58.

Appendix 3

IUCN Categories of Protected Areas and Guidelines for Protected Area Management – Category V Protected Landscapes[1]

Categories of Protected Areas

I. Strict Reserve/Wilderness Area
Protected Area managed mainly for science or wilderness protection.

Ia. Strict Nature Reserve: Area of land and/or sea possessing some outstanding or representative ecosystems, geological or physiological features and/or species, protected primarily for scientific research and/or environmental monitoring.

Ib. Wilderness Area: Large area of unmodified or slightly modified land and/or sea, retaining its natural character and influence, without permanent or significant habitation, that is protected and managed so as to preserve its natural condition.

II. National Park
Protected area managed mainly for ecosystem protection and recreation. Natural area of land and/or sea, designated to:

(a) protect the ecological integrity of one or more ecosystems for present and future generations;

(b) exclude exploitation or occupation inimical to the purposes of designation of the area;

[1] IUCN, *Guidelines for Protected Area Management Categories*, Gland, Switzerland, 1994.

(c) provide a foundation for spiritual, scientific, educational, recreational and visitor opportunities, all of which must be environmentally and culturally compatible.

III. Natural Monument

Protected area managed mainly for conservation of specific natural features. Area containing one, or more, specific natural or natural/cultural features of outstanding or unique value because of its inherent rarity, representative or aesthetic qualities, or cultural significance.

IV. Habitat/Species Management Area

Protected area managed mainly for conservation through management intervention. Area of land and/or sea subject to active intervention for management purposes to ensure the maintenance of habitats and/or to meet the requirements of specific species.

V. Protected Landscapes/Seascapes

Protected area managed mainly for landscape or seascape conservation and recreation. Area of land, with coast and sea as appropriate, where the interaction of people and nature over time has produced an area of distinct character with significant aesthetic, ecological and/or cultural value, and often with high biological diversity. Safeguarding the integrity of this traditional interaction is vital to the protection, maintenance and evolution of such an area.

VI. Managed Resource Protected Area

Protected Area managed mainly for the sustainable use of natural ecosystems. Area containing predominantly unmodified natural systems, managed to ensure long-term protection and maintenance of biological diversity, while providing a sustainable flow of natural products and services to meet community needs.

Guidelines for Protected Area Management – Category V Protected landscapes

Protected Landscape or Seascape: protected area managed mainly for landscape or seascape conservation and recreation.

Definition
Area of land, with coast and sea as appropriate, where the interaction of people and nature over time has produced an area of distinct character with significant aesthetic, ecological and/or cultural value, and often with high biological diversity. Safeguarding the integrity of this traditional interaction is vital to the protection, maintenance and evolution of such an area.

Objectives of Management

- To maintain the harmonious interaction of nature and culture through the protection of landscape or seascape and the continuation of traditional land uses, building practices and social and cultural manifestations;
- to support lifestyles and economic activities which are in harmony with nature and the preservation of the social and cultural fabric of the communities concerned;
- to maintain the diversity of landscape and habitat, and of associated species and ecosystems;
- to eliminate where necessary, and thereafter prevent, land uses and activities which are inappropriate in scale and/or character;
- to provide opportunities for public enjoyment through recreation and tourism appropriate in type and scale to the essential qualities of the areas;
- to encourage scientific and educational activities which will contribute to the long-term well-being of resident populations and to the development of public support for the environmental protection of such areas; and
- to bring benefits to, and to contribute to the welfare of, the local community through the provision of natural products (such as forest and fisheries products) and services (such as clean water or income derived form sustainable forms of tourism).

Guidance for Selection

- The area should possess a landscape or coastal and island seascape of high scenic quality, with diverse associated habitats, flora and fauna along with manifestations of unique or traditional land-use patterns and social organisations as evidenced in human settlements and local customs, livelihoods, and beliefs.
- The area should provide opportunities for public enjoyment through recreation and tourism within its normal lifestyle and economic activities.

Organisational Responsibility

The area may be owned by a public authority, but is more likely to comprise a mosaic of private and public ownerships operating a variety of management regimes. These regimes should be subject to a degree of planning or other control and supported, where appropriate, by public funding and other incentives, to ensure that the quality of the landscape or seascape and the relevant local customs and beliefs are maintained in the long term.

Appendix 4

Some notes on further reading

A great many written sources have been used for this book: government publications, including Acts of Parliament, reports by government committees, White Papers, planning and other policy guidance documents; Directives from the European Union; international Conventions; Advice Papers, annual reports, policy statements, policy and research studies from public agencies; Development Plans from local authorities; Management Plans, Landscape Assessments and reports of many kinds from individual AONBs; academic and professional books, articles and conference reports; publications by major voluntary bodies

These are fully recorded in the references for each chapter and it is thought that a single detailed bibliography, derived from the lists, would be of little value to most readers. Instead, this Appendix highlights some of the key documents relevant to the text as a whole that may be of interest for general reading. Only the titles of the publications are given; full particulars need to be obtained from the chapter reference lists.

For those who wish to follow up the historical introduction to the family of protected landscapes in Chapter 1, selective reading is recommended from the *Dower, Hobhouse and Huxley Reports* themselves, from John Blunden and Nigel Curry's perceptive commentary in *A People's Charter*, from the full account of the passage of the 1949 Act through Parliament in Gordon Cherry's *Environmental Planning Series, Volume 2*, and from the more specific AONB story described in Margaret Anderson's paper in the *Town Planning Review*. The *Report of the Sandford Committee* and *Fit for the Future* (the Edwards Report) both add a useful perspective on changes in National Park policies that have a bearing on ideas for the future of protected areas generally.

The geography of AONBs in Chapter 2, and the account of changes and pressures in Chapter 3 have both made extensive use of the Landscape Assessments produced by the Countryside Commission for each AONB, and of other data sources including the Commission's consultation paper, *Providing for the Future*, and the subsequent *Advice to Government*. A choice of reading from the landscape assessments will convey graphically the quality and variety of landscape types in AONBs, and the important association with poetry, art and music arising from the history and scenery of these areas. The consultation and advice papers and the *Protected Areas Funding Study* (see below) are essential reading for those interested in pressures, on which there is little information elsewhere.

Chapter 4 contains a stage by stage analysis of policy development at national level. For more detailed study, perusal of the Himsworth and Smart & Anderson Reports, the subsequent *Policy Statements* by the Commission and Welsh Countryside Council, the *Consultation and Advice Papers* already mentioned and that of CCW, will reveal more fully the notable growth of policy aspirations from the early 1980s and through the 1990s, towards a major (and as yet unfulfilled) proposal for legislation. To do so will also show up the difficulties encountered in making a detailed case for additional long-term finance for AONBs, due to lack of data and to a natural reluctance to think the unthinkable because of the pressures of financial constraint on AONB budgets. Hence the need arose for the *Protected Areas Funding Study*. Although this consultants' report has not been formally published, the reader will find that it has assembled, as far as possible in the time available, a fascinating glimpse of the characteristics of individual AONBs, the management tasks to be tackled, and their financial requirements. Together with the *Directory of Areas of Outstanding Natural Beauty* and the many AONB Management Plans and Annual Reports now in existence, this is useful background for those who wish to follow up Chapter 5's account of the development of administration, organisation and staffing, management and business planning in AONBs, and of the importance of partnership.

It is difficult to pick out from the sources used in Chapters 6 and 7 those that are widely relevant to land management, rural development and planning issues in AONBs, other than the ones already mentioned and individual AONB Management Plans. The long-expected White Paper on the countryside, due to be published in 2000, should provide a useful overview within which relationships between the roles and policies of agencies such as MAFF, FC, EA, EN and CA may become more clearly established. It will be essential reading. Meanwhile the reader may find that the government statements in December 1999 on *New Directions for Agriculture* under the EU Rural Development Regulation, and the additional *Cash Commitment to Countryside Conservation and Regeneration*, are useful pointers towards the greater integration of rural policies that has long been advocated. A look at the more advanced AONB Management Plans, the UK Biodiversity Strategy, and the regional volumes of the Countryside

Commission's 'Countryside Character' programme can give a good indication of some of the benefits that can flow from such integration.

Chapters 8 and 9 draw conclusions from the earlier parts of the book, and do not therefore introduce significant new sources. Within the context of general principles for protected landscapes they consider the shortcomings of the present AONB system, and they set out an agenda for the action that has wider implications of the place of AONBs in the family. The agenda is explained and justified in the text; it stands on its own rather than drawing extensively on ideas expressed elsewhere. In the circumstances, the reader may benefit more from studying the development of ideas on the future needs of protected landscapes in general rather than the specific texts referred to in these chapters. Three promising expositions are to be found in *National Parks for Scotland* (Scottish Natural Heritage), *Advice to the Welsh Office on Protected Landscapes in Wales* (Countryside Council for Wales), both of which are in earlier chapter references, and in the UK Parks for Life Task Force's *Action for Protected Areas in the UK (Report of the Bath Workshop)*.

Index

access, public 11, 12, 35, 45, 121, 137, 138, 141, 215
Addison, Sir Christopher 11
Agriculture Act, 1947 151
    1986 21, 116
agriculture/farming 27, 30, 48, 53, 54, 57, 58-9, 66, 67, 68, 69, 106, 115-20, 150-1, 155, 167, 216, 219, 225, 229, **Plates** 14, 20, 33, 34, 35, 36, 48(a), 52
    attitudes to 11, 12, 17, 52, 150
    diversification 151, 155
    environmental schemes 21, 34-5, 54, 60, 71, 74, 116, 117, 118, 119, 120, 153-4, 155, 181, 183, 215
    whole farm plans 100
Amenity and Lands (*Northern Ireland*) *Act*, 1965 20
Amenity Areas 12
Anderson, Margaret 67, 109
Anglesey AONB 26, 31, 32, 33, 44, 204
archaeology & history 40-1, 44, 208, 209, 208, 209, 212, 218-9, 223, 225, 229, **Plates** 24 (map), 25, 26, 56
architectural interest 44, 216, **Plate** 27
Areas of Outstanding Beauty AONBs)
    attitudes to 22-3, 25, 39, 41, 106, 157, 181-2
    change, monitoring 47, 60-1
    Charter 86
    designated areas, lists of 204-5, **Plates** 5, 15, 17 (maps)
    differences v. National Parks 2, 16, 17, 23, 38, 42, 79, 182, 200-1, 227
    Directory of 33, 67, 107
    environmental enhancement 155
    expenditure 104, 142, 210
    functions, core, in relation to 73, 75
    geography & importance of 25-37
    human influences in 2,
    improvements to 189-203
    land management 115-47
    landscape quality 39, 51, 159, 185
    monitoring & research 171, 185, 196-7, 217, 230
    policy towards, national 65-88, 158
    recreation & tourism 38, 55, 65, 74, 136-42, 209, 229, **Plates** 58-61
    review of 183-5
    size 31, 32,
    socio-economic functions 76, 77, 141, 157, 162, 167, 169, 185, 208, 222
    staffing 69, 93-5, 193, 197
    Staff Forum 86, 109
    statutory framework 74, 183, 187, 190-2

Arnside & Silverdale AONB 26, 28, 29, 30, 32, 33, 36, 37, 42, 43, 44, 105, 120, 205, **Plates** 23(c), 45(a), 60(b)
assessments, landscape 13, 39, 40, 47-9, 69, 155, 161, 170, 219
Association for AONBs 86, 109, 183, 193, 198
Association of National Parks 109, 111, 121
    Accord with Environment Agency 126

biodiversity 4, 48, 69, 76, 121, 125, 124, 126, 127-35, 177, **Plate** 57
Biodiversity Action Plan, UK (BAP) 125, 126, 128, 130, 131, 177
Birds Directive, EC 4, 133, 135, 177
Blackdown Hills AONB 26, 28, 29, 32, 33, 35, 37, 43, 47, 48, 109, 118, 120, 142, 169, 205, 206, **case study** 208-9, **Plates** 20, 62, 64(c)
    Business Association 142, 160
    management strategy 102, 208
    Rural Partnership, JAC 96, 160, 208-9
    website 109
Bodmin Moor, Cornwall 154, 168
Breckland, Norfolk & Suffolk 13, 35
broad-leaved trees 121, 122
business plans 104, 210, 219

CADW 44, 195
Cannock Chase AONB 26, 28, 29, 30, 32, 33, 36, 37, 43, 45, 55, 56, 107, 204, **Plate** 37(a)
Capital Challenge Fund 105, 224
Cardigan Coast 13
Character Areas 5, 18-27, 28, 127, 200, **Plate** 15 (map), 16
chalk & limestone areas 26, 27, 30, 36, 48, 117, 209, 218, 220, 223, 225, 229, **Plates** 22, 23(c), 33, 34, 35
Channel Tunnel rail link 168
Charnwood Forest 13
Chichester Harbour AONB 13, 26, 28, 29, 31, 32, 33, 37, 42, 43, 44, 45, 93, 204, **Plate** 44(b)
    Conservancy 91, 92, 96, 105, 135, 166, 167
Chiltern Society 107, 110, 210
Chilterns AONB 26, 27, 28, 29, 30, 32, 33, 34, 37, 43, 45, 48, 49, 54, 55, 56, 89, 107, 110, 120, 121, 122, 129, 138, 144, 152, 159, 204, 206, **case study** 209-11, **Plates** 16, 22, 55
    Conference, JAC 90, 96, 105, 106, 110, 209, 210, 211-2
    Visitor Survey 139
    Misbourne & Chess Valleys Project 129, 210
    Woodlands Project 122, 210
climatic change 6, 57, 125

Clipsham 13
Clwydian Range AONB 26, 32, 33, 44, 110, 165, 205, **Plate** 6
coasts 13, 16, 26, 30, 31, 54, 117, **Plates** 11, 12, 22(c), 46(b), 47
Committees
    Countryside Review 17
    Land Utilisation in Rural Areas 11
    National Park 11
    National Parks (England & Wales) (Hobhouse C'tee) 12, 38
    National Parks Review Panel (Edwards C'tee)) 17, 42
    Scottish National Parks Survey (Ramsay C'tee) 18
    Standing C'tee on National Parks 12
    Wildlife Conservation Special (Huxley C'tee) 12, 180
Common Agricultural Policy (CAP) 3, 116, 152, 153, 178, 195, 215
    Agenda 2000 155
    Rural Development Regulation 153
common land 35-6, 37, 134-5, **Plate** 53
communities, rural 50-2, 61, 69, 77, 155
Congress of Local and Regional Authorities of Europe (CLRAE) 83
conifers 49, 120
conservation 124-5, 169, 178, 183, 191, 209, 221, **Plates** 56, 57
    economic value of 152, 158, 160
Conservation Areas 12, 14, 38, **Plate** 1
    Boards 70, 75, 76, 77, 78, 186, 211, 225-6, 227
Convention on Biological Diversity 4, 87, 128, 131, 177
Cornwall AONB 26, 28, 29, 30, 31, 32, 33, 35, 37, 43, 44, 45, 50, 55, 107, 118, 204, **Plates** 18, 26 (b & c), 40(a), 44(a), 58(b), 64(a)
Cotswolds Way, national trail 137, 212
Cotswolds AONB 12, 26, 27, 28, 29, 31, 32, 33, 34, 35, 36, 37, 43, 44, 45, 48, 50, 54, 89, 107, 118, 120, 140, 141, 168, 204, 206, **case study** 212-4, **Plates** 14, 27(b)
    Partnership, JAC 95, 212, 213
Council for Europe 4, 83, 153
Council for the Protection of Rural England (CPRE) 49
counter urbanisation 151
countryside
    character & natural areas 5, 28, 162
    communities in 50-2
    holistic/integrated approach to 5, 6, 86, 178, 215
    recreation & tourism 16, 55-6, 136
    stewardship 116, 117, 118, 119, 154, 155, 219, 220, **Plate** 52(b)
    tranquil areas 49-50
Countryside Act, 1968 17, 67

Countryside Agency (CA) 5, 18, 109, 151, 195, 198, 223, 228
  access, public 138
  Advice to Government 77, 228
  grant support 104, 137, 140, 213, 214, 226
  land management initiatives 217
  website 32,
Countryside & Rights of Way Bill, 1999 78, 111
Countryside Commission (CC) 5, 13, 17, 109, 187-8
  Advice to Government 72, 74, 75, 97, 98, 185, 227
  advisory role 14
  Character of England map 18, 127
  Countryside Stewardship 116, 117, 118, 119, 154, 155, 219, 220
  critical environmental capital 162, 170
  Directory of AONBs 33, 67, 107
  Guide for Members of JACs, staffing 90, 93, 94
  Heritage Coasts 21
  landscape assessments 170
  management of protected countryside, plans 72, 97, 98-104
  planning advice, guidance 161-2
  policy reviews of AONBs 18, 65-78, 85, 89-90
  powers 14
  pressures on AONBs, study 53-6
  recreation & tourism 136, 137
  rural traffic initiatives (STAR) 143, 144
  village design statements 162
Countryside Commission for Scotland 18
Countryside Council for Wales (CCW) 18, 44, 48, 68, 71, 75, 98, 109, 136, 137, 138, 187-8, 195, 198
  Advice to Government 76, 154
  Rural Regulation 154
Countryside in 1970 conferences 17
Countryside Information System (CIS) 27-8
  Countryside Management Services (CMS) 91, 94, 96, 107, 120, 197, 214, 217, 219, 226, 227, 228, 230, 231
Cranborne Chase & West Wiltshire Downs AONB 26, 28, 29, 32, 33, 35, 37, 43, 44, 50, 107, 118, 205, **Plate** 29
critical environmental capital 162, 170
cultural associations, values 2, 39, 41, 45, 74, 77, 142, 199
cycles, cycleways 145, 222, **Plates** 43(b), 64(a)

Dedham Vale AONB 13, 26, 28, 29, 32, 33, 35, 37, 43, 45, 48, 118, 120, 205, **Plate** 36(a)
Delamere Forest 13
Denbigh Moors 13

Department of the Environment (DoE) 21, 153
Department of the Environment, Transport & the Regions (DETR) 27, 36, 224
designation criteria for AONBs 13, 14-5, 16, 38, 39, 68, 79, 156, 180-1, 183-5, 189-90, 191
development, controls 2, 48, 49, 53, 54, 56, 57, 66, 75, 133, 164-9, 220
  rural, policies 150-6, 156-8, 159, 161-2
disabled, facilities for **Plate** 60(b)
diversification, farm 151, 155
Dorset AONB 26, 27, 28, 29, 30, 31, 32, 33, 34, 35, 37, 40, 41, 43, 44, 45, 48, 50, 54, 107, 118, 120, 131, 145, 204, **Plates** 14, 26(a), 51(a), 57(a), 59(a) *and see* Purbeck, Isle of (**case study** 222-5)
Dower, John 11, 12, 38, 39
downland 36, 48
dry-stone walls 48, 119, 120, 213
Dungeness 13

Earth Summit, Rio de Janeiro 4, 128
East Devon AONB 26, 28, 29, 30, 31, 32, 33, 36, 37, 43, 45, 204, **Plate** 42(b)
East Hampshire AONB 26, 28, 29, 32, 33, 35, 37, 43, 48, 49, 56, 75, 99, 118, 120, 146, 169, 186, 204, 227, **Plate** 54
  JAC 166, 167, 228
economics/commerce 31, 45, 136, 139, 152, 160, 161
education & interpretation 129, 141
Edwards, Professor Ron 17, 42
English Heritage 44, 74, 142, 161, 195
English Nature (EN) 5, 18, 106, 109, 127, 134, 135, 142, 161, 195, 214, 221, 224
English Partnerships 224
English Tourist Board 137
  Council 224
Enterprise Neptune 16, 20
Environment Act, 1995 15, 17, 42, 126
Environment Agency 106, 109, 124-7, 128-9, 195
  Accord with Association of National Parks 126
  Action Plan for Conservation 124
  Local Environment Agency Plan (LEAP) 125
environmental
  capital 167, 169
  groups, lobby 16
  impact, care 142
Environmentally Sensitive Areas (ESAs) 13, 21, 34-5, 116-8, 170, 208, 213, **Plates** 19 (map), 20, 52(a)
estuaries 26, 31, 48, **Plate** 10
European Action Plan, Parks for Life 83

European Community (EC), European Union (EU) 4, 21, 34, 105
  Birds Directive 4, 125, 131, 133, 135, 177
  Common Agricultural Policy (CAP) 3, 116, 152, 178, 195
  Agenda 2000 155
  Rural Development Plan for England 153-4
  Rural Development Regulation 153
  Habitats Directive 4, 83, 125, 131, 133, 135, 177
  LEADER II & + 156, 214
  Natura 2000 133, 154
  Objective 5b areas, structural funds 34, 51, 105, 152, 155, 214
  RECITE II programme 123
European
  Environment Agency 83
  Landscape Convention 4, 83-4, 89, 177
  Regional Development Fund (ERDF) 140

Farm Woodland Premium Scheme 154
Farming & Wildlife Advisory Group (FWAG) 220
finance *see* funding
fisheries 125
Flamborough Coast 13
footpaths, long-distance *see* trails, national
Forest Enterprise 106, 219, 224, 229
Forest of Bowland AONB 26, 28, 29, 30, 32, 33, 34, 37, 43, 44, 48, 49, 50, 97, 105, 106, 110, 119, 123, 146, 154, 204, 206, **case study** 214-5, **Plates** 28(b), 32, 50(a), 56(b), 64(b)
  Bowland Initiative 155
  Lancashire Woodlands Initiative 123
Forest of Dean 13, 42
  National Forest Park 229
forestry, afforestation 48, 49, 57, 74, 117, 120-4, 154, **Plate** 48(b)
Forestry Authority 71
Forestry Commission 109, 121, 195
Forestry Strategy for England 121
friends organisations 107, 195, 225
funding 68, 70, 71, 74, 76, 78, 104-5, 195, 211, 224
  budgets of AONBs 210, 213, 214, 216, 218, 219, 221, 226, 230
  study 30, 54, 71, 97, 104, 119
fund-raising 105, 142

genetically modified crops 59
Glamorgan Coast 13
global warming 57
government priorities, responses 4, 5, 11, 16, 17, 57, 78-9, 198
Gower AONB 16, 30, 31, 32, 33, 34, 35,

Gower AONB (cont)
44, 93, 96, 107, 110, 165, 204
Commons Initiative 134-5
Countryside Forum 96, 134-5
Heathland Group 135
Management Plan 163
grassland, pastures 26, 49, 117, 119
limestone 36, 119
lowland 48
managed 28
grazing 48
green belt 22
Groundwater Protection Area 218

habitat(s)
action plans 132
loss 47-9
management area, IUCN category 233
protection 22
Habitats Directive, EC 4, 133, 135, 177
heathland, heaths 26, 30, 36, 48, 57, 117,
119, 127, 134, 135, 160, 223, 224,
Plates 7, 23
hedgerows 48, 54, 117, 119, 120,
Plate 57(a)
Heritage
Coasts 13, 17, 20-1, 30, 93, 118, 137,
145, 222, **Plate** 5 (map)
Lottery Fund 103, 135, 218
Heseltine MP, Michael 66, 68
High Weald AONB 26, 28, 29, 30, 32,
33, 36, 37, 43, 49, 120, 122, 123, 138,
161, 205, 206, **case study** 216-8,
Plates 37(b), 63
Design Project 123, 217, **Plate** 63(b)
Forum 123, 216
Land Management Initiative 217
Landscape Trail 217
Wealden Meadows Initiative 217
website 109
Hill Farm Allowance Scheme 154
Hill Livestock Compensatory Allowance
154
Himsworth, Kenneth 65
historic features, landscapes 44, 208,
209, 212, **Plates** 24 (map), 25, 26, 56
Hobhouse, Sir Arthur 12, 13, 14, 15, 38,
199, 225, **Plate** 1 (map)
holiday
homes 221
villages 169
honey-pot sites 55, 138, 221
housing 54, 56, 58, **Plate** 37(a)
Howardian Hills AONB 26, 28, 29, 30,
32, 33, 37, 43, 119, 122, 168, 205,
Plate 8
Huxley, Sir Julian 12, 180
proposed scientific areas, 1947
Plate 1 (map)
inquiries, public

North Pennines 38-9, 156-7
international commitments &
influences 3, 4, 6, 22, 69, 81-4, 133,
152, 177, 181
International Union for Conservation of
Nature and Natural Resources
(IUCN) 1, 4
categories of protected areas 232-3
guidelines for protected area
management 233-4
Parks for Life 4, 81, 82, 177
UK Committee 83
interpretation see education &
interpretation
Isle of Wight AONB 26, 28, 29, 31, 32,
33, 37, 43, 44, 55, 140, 204,
Plates 10, 39(a), 48(a)
Island 2000 Trust 96, 105
Isles of Scilly AONB 26, 27, 28, 29, 31,
32, 33, 37, 43, 205, **Plate** 16
Environment Trust 92

job creation 152, 158-9, 160
Joint Advisory Committees (JACs) 66,
67, 68, 69, 75, 89-112, 165, 170, 184,
208, 209, 210, 213, 216, 219, 220,
221, 229-31

Kent Downs AONB 26, 28, 29, 30, 32,
33, 37, 43, 48, 49, 120, 121, 168, 169,
204, **Plates** 8, 27(a)
management strategy 102
Kimmeridge Voluntary Marine Nature
Reserve, Dorset 223

land cover 27-30
Cover Map 27, 29, 36
management **Plates** 52-4
landfill tax 96
landscape(s)
assessments 13, 39, 40, 47-9, 60, 69,
150, 155, 161, 170, 219
historic 44
living & working 2, 3, 31, 51, 68
protection 11, 22, 72-3
quality 39, 51, 159
land-use change 6, 58-9, 60
LEADER II, LEADER + 156, 214
'Leisure in the Countryside' 16
Less Favoured Areas 35
life-style, changes 6, 57-8
Lincolnshire Wolds AONB 13, 26, 28, 29,
30, 32, 33, 37, 43, 205, **Plate** 13(b)
Lleyn AONB 26, 31, 32, 33, 44, 48, 168,
204, **Plate** 11
Local Agenda 21 195
Local Biodiversity Action Plan (LBAP)
130, 131, 132
Local Environment Agency Plan (LEAP)
125

Local Government Management Board
(LGMB) 129, 130, 131
Local Plans 162
Local Transport Plan (LTP) 145
logos, signs 109, 218
'lowland agricultural England' 25, 27

Malvern Hills AONB 26, 28, 29, 30, 32,
33, 35, 37, 43, 55, 146, 204
Conservators 92, 105, 141, **Plate** 51(b)
management/managers 31
of protected countryside, principles 72
functions 97-104
plans 48, 65-6, 69, 77, 97, 98-104, 131,
138-42, 146, 147, 164, 170, 179,
193-5, 197, 210, 213, 217, 219, 220,
221, 230
staffing & training 69, 93-5, 193, 197
management agreements, conservation
116, 117
Market Towns Initiative, Cotswolds 141
Meacher MP, Michael 78, 228
meadows, hay 48, 117
Mendip Hills AONB 26, 28, 29, 32, 33,
37, 43, 44, 48, 55, 56, 110, 118, 119,
120, 146, 168, 205, 207, **case study**
218-22, **Plates** 35(a), 38(b), 45(b),
50(b)
Heritage Fund 108
Hillwatch Scheme 220
JAC 96, 105, 106, 118, 119, 219
Mendip Society 107, 108, 110, 219
Mendips Local Plan 219
mining, minerals 44, 50, 167, 168, 169,
223, **Plate** 26(c)
Ministry of Agriculture, Fisheries &
Food (MAFF) 21, 66, 71, 106, 117, 155,
215, 220, 224
Ministry of Works & Planning 11
Misbourne & Chess Valleys Project
129, 210, **Plate** 55
moorland, moors 26, 30, 48, 214,
Plates 6, 23(b)
motorways 50, 169
Mourne AONB 20, 205, **Plate** 4

National Nature Reserves (NNRs) 22, 43,
44, 209, 218, 221, 223, 225, 229
National Park Committee 11
National Parks 2, 11, **Plates** 1, 3, 4
Accords 126
agriculture in 67
aims 12
Association for 109
designation criteria 13-16, 32, 181-2,
227
differences v. AONBs 25, 181-2, 182,
200-1, 227
early proposals for 12

National Parks (cont)
  environmental capital 170
  expenditure 104, 142
  forestry in 121
  funding 70, 71
  IUCN categories 232-3
  landscape change 49
  management plans 98, 99
  planning controls 159
  Review of National Park Policies
    (Sandford Committee), 1974 17
  Review Panel (Edwards Committee),
    1991 17, 42, 109
  Scotland 18-9, 80-1, 86, **Plate** 4
  sustainable development 170-1
  upland character 25
  visitor numbers 54, 55
*National Parks and Access to the
  Countryside Act,* 1949 3, 13-16, 22, 38
National Parks Commission 12, 14, 17,
  21, 38-9, 42, 225
National Scenic Areas (NSAs), Scotland
  19, 80, 81, 131, **Plate** 4
National Trails *see* trails
National Trust 16, 20, 45, 76, 106, 107,
  134, 141, 142, 159, 160, 219, 220,
  221, 224, **Plate** 51(a)
Natura 2000 133, 154
Natural Areas (NA) 127, 131, 134
natural beauty, conservation of 38, 39,
  41, 42, 167
Nature Conservancy Council (NCC) 42
nature conservation 12, 17, 22, 38, 116,
  122, 124, 128, 130, 134-5, 221, 230
  management agreements 116
*Nature Conservation and Amenity Lands
  (Northern Ireland) Order,* 1985 20
New Forest 25, 55, 75, 78, 79
    Nidderdale AONB 26, 27, 28, 29,
    30, 32, 33, 36, 37, 43, 44, 47, 105,
    146, 152, 170, 205, **Plates** 3, 25(b),
    27(c)
  management plan 161
Nitrate Sensitive Areas 181
noise 50
Norfolk Coast AONB 26, 28, 29, 31, 32,
  33, 35, 37, 42, 43, 44, 49, 55, 106,
  107, 120, 140, 146, 168, 204, 207,
  case study 220-2, **Plates** 22(c), 28(a),
  31, 42(a), 43(b), 61 (map)
  Conservation Plan 134
  Cycling Initiative 144, 222
  JAC, Panel 96, 221
  Project 221
  Visitor Management Strategy 140, 144,
    221, 222, **Plate** 61 (map)
  Transport Strategy 144, 222
North Devon AONB 26, 28, 29, 31, 32,
  33, 34, 35, 37, 43, 44, 45, 50, 204,
  Plate 11

North Downs Way, national trail 137
North Pennines AONB 26, 27, 28, 29, 30,
  32, 33, 35, 36, 37, 38-9, 43, 44, 50,
  55, 105, 118, 156-7, 168, 169, 205,
  Plates 6, 18
  management plan 101
  Tourism Partnership 140, 157
North Wessex Downs AONB 26, 28, 29,
  32, 33, 37, 43, 44, 47, 50, 205,
  Plates 33, 36
Northern Ireland 19-20, 205, Plate 4
Northumberland Coast AONB 26, 28, 29,
  31, 32, 33, 34, 37, 42, 43, 44, 105,
  139, 141, 204, **Plates** 12, 25(a)

Objective 5b areas 34, 51, 105, 152, 155,
  214
off-road driving, scrambling 219
Offa's Dyke national trail 229
open land/space 36-7, 182, **Plates** 31, 32
orchards 54, 117, 229

park and ride schemes 105, 145, 224,
  Plate 59(a)
parking, car 138, 141, 143, 145,
  Plate 41(b)
Parks for Life 4, 81, 82, 177
  European Action Plan 83, 86
  and see IUCN
partnership agreements 90-1, 103, 210
Pennine Way, national trail 45
Pennines 13, 49
  and see North Pennines AONB
Phillips, Adrian 156-7
planning 129, 171
  applications 56
  bargaining 166
  consultation procedures 165, 226, 227
  controls 12, 15, 66, 74, 80, 133, 150,
    152, 158, 164-9
  guidance, guidelines, PPGs 159, 161-2,
    164, 165, 169, 194
Plans, Structure & Local 159, 162-4, 219
  Supplementary Planning Guidance
    164, 194
pollution 124, 143
  noise 49, 50
population centres, proximity to 32, 34,
  209
Prentice MP, Gordon 78
Prescott MP, John 78, 228
pressures upon AONBs 50, 52-6, 60-1, 167
Protected Areas 1, 81-4
  categories, IUCN 232-3
  Europe 82
  isolationist view of 4, 82
  management guidelines, IUCN 233-4
  nature conservation 12
Protected Areas Funding Study 30, 54, 71,
  97, 104, 119

protected landscapes 1-8, 20-3, 72-3,
  177-182, **Plates** 2, 19, 21, 24 (maps)
  IUCN categories & management
    guidelines 232-4
public relations 107-11, 120, 141, 196,
  211, 218, 219, 222, 223, 230, **Plate** 50
Purbeck, Isle of 40, 41, 54, 165, 168, 170,
  222-5, **Plates** 14, 59
  Heritage Area 97, 106, 107, 132, 145,
    164, 207, 223, 224
  Heritage Committee 105, 107, 110,
    131, 140, **case study** 222-5
  Biodiversity Action Plan 224
  and see Dorset AONB

Quantock Hills AONB 26, 28, 29, 30, 32,
  33, 36, 37, 43, 204, **Plates** 53, 56(a)
quarrying 219, 229, **Plate** 38(b)

radio & telecommunication masts 168,
  219
railways 50
Ramsar Convention 4, 133
Ramsar designated sites 41, 43, 44, 135,
  221
Ramsay, Lord 18
rangers, countryside *see* Countryside
  Management Services
RECITE II programme, EU 123
recreation 12, 16, 31, 32, 53, 54, 55, 58,
  65, 74, 79, 122, 128, 136-42, 181,
  182, 209, 225, **Plates** 41-5, 58-61, 64
renewable energy 57
Renton, Lord, Bill in House of Lords 72,
  76-8, 158, 186
reserves, national & regional 11
  IUCN categories 232
resources
  managed, IUCN category 233
  natural 7, 22, 61, 142
  water 125
Review of National Park Policies
  (Sandford Committee) 17
reviews of policies towards AONBs
  see Countryside Commission
Ridgeway, national trail 137, 209
rights of way *see* access
rivers, catchment areas 26, 57, 125, 129,
  Plate 55
Royal Society for the Protection of Birds
  (RSPB) 48, 106, 131, 134, 142, 159,
  160, 214, 221, 224
rural
  communities, economy 2, 50-2, 53,
    152, 158-9, 216, **Plates** 17, 18
    (maps), 62-4
  development policies 150-6, 156-8
Rural
  Development Areas (RDAs) 34, 51,

Rural
  Development Areas (RDAs) (cont)
    151, 161, 208, 216, 223, **Plates** 17, 18
    (maps)
  Development Commission 18, 51, 137,
    151, 157, 158, 163, 223
  Development Plan 153-4
  Development Regulation 153
  Enterprise Scheme 154
  White Papers 5, 16, 152, 159

Sandford, Lord 17
satellite imagery 103
Scheduled Ancient Monuments (SAMs)
  218, 223, **Plate** 24 (map)
  and see archaeology & history
Scientific Areas, Huxley Committee 12,
  180, **Plate** 1 (map)
Scotland 18-19, 79-81, 86
Scott, Lord Justice 11, 12, 56, 150, 152
Scottish Natural Heritage (SNH) 19, 80,
sea level, rise 57, 221
services, rural 51, 52, **Plate** 59(b)
Shropshire Hills AONB 26, 27, 28, 29, 30,
  32, 33, 34, 35, 37, 43, 45, 107, 118,
  205, **Plates** 35(b), 40(b), 48(b), 52(a)
signposting 110, 120, 167, 211, **Plates**
  50(a), 58(b)
Sites of Special Scientific Interest
  (SSSIs) 22, 42, 43, 44, 116, 180, 181,
  208, 209, 218, 221, 223, 225, 229,
  Plate 21
Smart, Professor Gerald 67, 109
Solway Coast AONB 13, 26, 27, 28, 29,
  31, 32, 33, 36, 37, 42, 43, 44, 56, 120,
  204, **Plates** 22(b), 57(b)
Solway Rural Initiative 92, 96, 140, 161
Somerset Levels & Moors 27, 35, 42
South Devon AONB 26, 27, 28, 29, 31,
  32, 33, 34, 37, 43, 45, 55, 56, 91, 107,
  146, 152, 204, **Plates** 10, 59(b)
  JAC 91, 97
  Visitor Survey 139
South Downs 12, 75, 227, **Plate** 13
  National Park, proposed 13, 78, 80,
    186, 225, 227, 228
  Way, national trail 45, 137, 225
South Hampshire Coast AONB 26,
  28, 29, 31, 32, 33, 37, 42, 43, 44, 75,
  79, 204, **Plates** 12, 47
South West Coast Path, national trail
  45, 137, 146, 159, 160, 223, **Plates**
  44(a), 59(b)
Special Area of Conservation (SAC) 43,
  44, 133, 221, 229
Special Protection Areas (SPAs) 41, 43,
  133, 214, 221
stakeholders, AONB management 73, 89,
  170, 194-5, 197
Statements of Intent, AONBs 66

Strategic Traffic Action in Rural Areas
  (STAR) 144
Strategy for Sustainable Development,
  UK, 1999 169, 171, 178
suburbanisation 58
Suffolk Coast & Heaths AONB 26, 27, 28,
  29, 30, 31, 32, 33, 34, 35, 37, 43, 45,
  44, 45, 48, 55, 105, 111, 118, 120,
  140, 168, 205, **Plates** 38(a), 41,
  46(b), 52(b), 60(a)
Supplementary Planning Guidance 164,
  194
Surrey Hills AONB 26, 27, 28, 29, 30, 32,
  33, 36, 37, 43, 44, 45, 54, 107, 138,
  138, 141, 144, 146, 204, **Plates** 7, 49
  (map), 59(c)
Sussex Downs AONB 26, 27, 28, 29, 30,
  32, 33, 34, 35, 37, 43, 48, 49, 50, 52,
  55, 56, 75, 93, 107, 118, 120, 128,
  146, 161, 163, 186, 204, 207, **case
  study** 225-8, **Plates** 13, 34, 39(b), 43(a)
  Conservation Board 70, 72, 76, 92, 95,
    104, 128, 166, 167, 225, 226
  Forum 226
  Management Strategy 101, 144, 226
  Ouse Valley Project 128
Sussex
  Downsmen, Society of 107
  Heritage Coast 225
sustainability 5, 6, 51, 69, 76, 81, 84, 103,
  121, 128, 152, 153, 159, 162, 167,
  169-71, 178, 179, 184, 221

Tamar Valley AONB 13, 26, 29, 30, 31,
  32, 33, 37, 43, 47, 109, 128, 146, 152,
  205, **Plates** 8, 26(b)
  Countryside Service 128
  Discovery Trail 128
telecommunication, radio masts 168,
  219, **Plate** 40
tilled land 30,
timber, commercial 122, 123
Tir Cymen 116
Tir Gofal 21, 35, 116, 117
tourism 45, 53, 54, 55, 74, 136-42, 160,
  229, **Plates** 41-5, 64
  accommodation 142
Tourism Partnership, North Pennines 140
Town and Country Planning Act, 1947 151
Town & Country Planning (Scotland) Act,
  1972 19
traffic 49, 50, 51, 54, 58, 143, 144, 146,
  209, 219, 221, 224, 229, **Plates** 42(a),
  59(c)
  Road Traffic Reduction Act, 1997 143
  roads 50, 69, 74, 168, 169
  rural box, traffic management 145
trails, national 45, 137, 138, 146, 159,
  160, 212, **Plates** 5 (map), 44(a)
training *see* management/managers

tranquil areas, tranquillity loss 49-50,
  Plates 6, 30 (map), 31, 37, 38, 39, 40
Trans-national Woodland Industries
  Group (TWIG) project 123, 210
transport 51, 52, 74, 143, 145-6, 220, 221,
  222, 224, **Plate** 59
Transport Policy & Programme (TPP) 144
  White Paper 143

United Nations Conference of
  Environment & Development,
  Rio de Janeiro, 1992 4, 81
upland
  areas 25, 26, 27, 36, 216, **Plate** 6
  communities 154

village design statements 162
visitor(s) 45, 53, 54, 55, 160, 209, 210,
  212, 219, 221, 223, 229, **Plates** 41-5,
  58-61
  surveys 139, 210
voluntary sector 107, 120, 131, 133,
  Plate 54

Wales 30, 31, 35, 44, 48, 49, 71, 76, 86,
  110, 117, **Plates** 6, 11
walls, dry-stone 48, 54, 119, 120, 213,
  Plate 56
wardens *see* Countryside Management
  Services
Water Protection Zones 181
water resources 125, 129
Welsh Assembly 110
West Wiltshire Downs *see* Cranborne
  Chase etc. AONB
White Papers, government 5, 16,
whole farm plans 100
wild country/wilderness 12, 30, 79
  category, IUCN 232
Wildlife and Countryside Act, 1981 22, 116
wildlife
  value of 199, 214
  conservation 6, 12, 22, 41, 42-4, 116,
    127-135, 167, 180, 221, 229
Wildlife Trusts 106, 142
wind farms, power 50, 57, 169, 219,
  Plate 46(a)
Woodland Grant Scheme 121, 154
woodlands 26, 29, 30, 41, 48, 53, 57, 74,
  117, 120-4, 216, **Plates** 8, 23(a), 54,
  63
World Congress on National Parks &
  Protected Areas, Caracas, 1992 4, 81
Wye Valley AONB 26, 28, 29, 30, 32, 33,
  37, 43, 44, 45, 55, 121, 122, 138, 140,
  141, 146, 205, 207, **case study** 229-31,
  Plates 9, 23(a), 58(a)
  Cycleway 230
  JAC 97, 106, 122, 229-30
  Walk 229